ME AND MY
BIG
MOUTH

WHEN
CLOUGHIE
SOUNDED
OFF IN
TVTIMES

Graham Denton

First published by Pitch Publishing, 2019

Pitch Publishing
A2 Yeoman Gate
Yeoman Way
Worthing
Sussex
BN13 3QZ
www.pitchpublishing.co.uk
info@pitchpublishing.co.uk

A CIP catalogue record is available for this book
from the British Library.

ISBN 978 1 78531 531 2

Typesetting and origination by Pitch Publishing
Printed and bound in India by Replika Press Pvt. Ltd.

Contents

For Atticus Thomas Neville Bayman,
a little look at what football was like
when your grandad was just a boy

STICK WITH BADMINTON, GIRLS... LEAVE FOOTBALL TO THE MEN

This week in World of Sport *you can see the All-England Badminton Championships from Wembley Pool, London, in which the cream of the world's players will be competing for the most prestigious title in the game. Brian Clough looks at our prospects. Badminton? He can sound off about that as well*

Margaret Beck, centre, and Gillian Gilks at last year's championships

Two Yugoslavian geese stand between Miss Margaret Beck and her second successive All-England Badminton singles title.

Incredible? Well, you and I might play with everlasting, poorly flighted plastic shuttlecocks in our local badminton courts, but the shuttles used in such big championships as Saturday's are far from pre-pressed imitations. Feathers for each shuttlecock come from the wings of two Yugoslavian geese. The Yugoslavs have fanned up quite a trade in goose feathers since the Chinese, who used to be the main suppliers, decided to take up badminton in earnest and kept all their feathers.

I have enjoyed badminton for many years, and though I don't claim to be

Rudi Hartono, the great Indonesian master, tensed for a winning smash

any sort of expert, I consider it to be the basic game of all games. It strikes at the root of what all sport is about: co-ordination between eye and muscle, agility, fitness and guile.

Watch one of the top players on Saturday. See him serve, leaning into the net, his face creased in concentration. Is it going to be a soft shot, just dropping over the net, or a flick to the back of the court? The great player never shows his hand. His arms, his whole body, will make the same movements whether it's going to be a slow shot or a fierce one.

The light-footed Indonesians, Japanese and Chinese have cornered the market in good, men players like Rudi Hartono, the Indonesian master, who will be defending his title for

the fifth time this week. In Jakarta, he and his fellow internationals join intensive training camps before a big event like this one, playing, breathing and living badminton every day.

There, it is the country's national sport, enjoying the status that football does in Britain.

But where we score in badminton is with the ladies. We have a world champion in Margaret Beck, a 23-year-old Cumberland girl who now shares a flat in Surrey and works in Fred Perry's sports shop in London's West End. A close contender for her title is Sussex girl Gillian Gilks.

Margaret approaches her sport like a true champion, and plays badminton for two hours three times a week, and does a daily round of gruelling exercises to keep her at peak fitness.

"The most valuable exercise is doing 10 yard sprints backwards and forwards, turning each time," she says. "I do 10 spurts of 10 yards, rest for one minute, then do another 10. In all I go through this routine eight times. That's like sprinting half a mile.

"It sharpens my reflexes, helps my speed off the mark, and my stamina. Anyway, if I know I have been thorough in my gym work, I feel psychologically right. If I miss a day, I feel as if I have cheated myself and it affects my game."

Margaret started playing badminton when she was 13. "In Cumberland, there was nothing else to do. I was hanging around trying to think of something to fill in my time, so in the end I joined my brother in a game. It was just one of those incredible things, but I can honestly say that I felt in my element playing badminton.

Right from the start I saw the shuttlecock well. I could co-ordinate easily, I could hit it hard and soft at will. My career just snowballed from there."

When you see Margaret on Saturday you'll be watching a perfectionist at work. She seldom eats before a big tournament, and if she does it's only a bar of energy-giving chocolate half an hour before she goes on court.

To me, it's a pleasure to see a girl like Margaret Beck playing a graceful sport like badminton, which is more than I can say for lady footballers, cricketers and the like. I may be old fashioned but I think women look ungainly playing football, or throwing a lump of lead on the athletics field. On the other hand, they can look beautiful on the track, on the tennis court, or the golf course.

I think the secret is that if they can retain their charm and femininity, if they can keep that special something which sets women apart, and still participate in a sweating, energy-consuming, strength-sapping sport, then I'm all for it. But if they don't, they are doing themselves and their sex an injustice.

I think the dividing line between what looks good or bad in any sport is when it ceases to be pleasing to the eye. Two boxers knocking the life out of each other, but with ringcraft and skill, can be good to witness. A hammer thrower spinning on his axis like a gyroscope can be a joy to watch. The same applies to women. If it looks good, it's O.K. by me. And badminton, a ballet of power and deft skills, is one of those games I could watch all day.

Acknowledgements

For their help and guidance in making this book possible, my heartfelt thanks go to the following: Graeme Wood (whose Twitter posts sparked the idea), David Abbott (TI Media Limited), Paul Camillin, Jane Camillin, Duncan Olner and Michelle Grainger, as well as my wife, Dianna, and children, Catherine and Frankie, for their love and support throughout. The encouragement of both author David Snowdon and my old poetry chum James Carter was also very much appreciated. Cheers!

Introduction

'LOUD mouth. Big head. A proper Charlie. Genius. These are just a few of the names Brian Clough has collected in his days as a football manager and television commentator. Which is true? The simple answer would be to say that Clough is all of these, for he is a bewildering maze of inconsistencies.'

So began a feature titled 'That Mister Clough' in the 22–28 September 1973 issue of *TVTimes*. It was written by way of an introduction to the man – 'the frankest voice in football' – who, the following week, was joining the popular TV listings magazine 'with a regular, hard-hitting column … which will be devoted to all football enthusiasts throughout the country.' Launched 18 years earlier, the periodical known for its access to actors, with a large circulation and readership, was now giving a stage to someone who loved nothing better than a chance to play to an audience.

A maze of inconsistencies he may have been, but that Mister Clough needed little introduction. What he indubitably *was* was the most media-savvy manager English football had ever known. No other figure in the game before had had a flair for publicity quite like him. And if football, as one of the many clichés about it goes, is a game of opinions, around that time no one played it more passionately or with greater enthusiasm than this son of the north east. Among the UK population of over 56 million, it had made him a household name.

Clough got the nation talking about football. Love him or hate him – and he certainly divided the crowd – the man who, in 1975, *Radio Times* would label 'soccer's most outspoken luminary' was almost impossible to avoid. Even in the days when coverage of the sport was infinitely more limited compared with what it would eventually become, Clough was virtually omnipresent. Popular with the press, he provided perfect copy with his forthright outlook on the game, his inflammatory comments about those running it and often bitter and savage attacks on his managerial peers, his words seized upon whenever he opened his mouth.

Whether it be on the back or front pages of the tabloids, on TV chat shows, during appearances on ITV's *On the Ball* or *The Big Match*, performing as a pundit on World Cup panels, giving pre- and post-match interviews on the radio, making after-dinner speeches, featuring in the football magazines of the day like *Goal* and *Shoot!*, or penning pieces for the papers, Clough was there, airing his views and sharing his thoughts on every subject under the sun, little caring whether or not anyone wanted to know them. So familiar was his face, his voice ('Now then, young man …'), his mannerisms, TV impressionists could do even a poor take-off and no one was in any doubt who the impersonation represented.

Depending on how the mood (or someone) took him, Clough could be charming or rude, polite or abusive, his language coated with honey or laced with poison. But one unchanging aspect of his personality was a total, sometimes brutal, honesty. Ever since his playing days when, as a livewire striker with first Middlesbrough then Sunderland, he set a Football League record of 251 goals in 274 matches, Clough had established a reputation as a blunt and straight-to-the-point individual, whose habit of expressing himself without inhibition had garnered him as many enemies as friends. Such an attitude often led to tense relations with both management and teammates.

At Ayresome Park, where Clough considered the club far too easy-going at times, he was quite prepared to ruffle feathers in his burning desire to make his team the best in the business, as evidenced by one example from his early days there. On Monday mornings on the training field, when the club's coach asked about any mistakes that had been made during the weekend away game – bizarrely, he often didn't go with the team – it was Clough who boldly marched up to the manager, Bob Dennison, to point out how ridiculous a situation it was. From then on, the coach travelled to every single away game. Clough wasn't necessarily popular, but he, and the club, knew he was right.

His influence soon grew. Too big for some. As adept at finding the back of the net as he was, Clough, with his cutting words, could incur the wrath of colleagues just as easily. Certain players suspected him of talking behind their backs. When he openly attacked the side's defensive deficiencies, then also publicly accused some of his teammates of betting against the team and deliberately letting in goals, for one friendly game against Hibs they actually hatched a plan to freeze him out and not supply him with any of the passes he liked to feed on. On another occasion, a round robin was sent to the manager staunchly expressing how they didn't want Clough as their captain.

As a player, arguably he had every right to mouth off. 'No centre-forward in soccer history can boast a record comparable to the trail which ace marksman Brian Clough blazed through six full seasons of league football,' enthused Argus (of the *Sunderland Echo*) in the programme notes of Clough's testimonial match in 1965. 'Dixie Dean, Hughie Gallacher and Arthur Rowley scored more with time on their side, but none of them matched the pace at which Brian made goals his business'.

Only needing half a chance and the ball was in the net, Clough had a phenomenal strike rate. In successive campaigns, in 1957/58 and the following year, he finished as the Football League's top scorer with 40 goals and 43 respectively. For three years on the trot he led the Second Division list and by 1960 had become probably the most lethal forward playing in British football, Clough's scoring feats so prolific and regular that, as sportswriter Basil Easterbrook put it, 'His stature would be denied only by fools or men of malice.'

If such deeds didn't necessarily win him universal admiration, to supporters at the two clubs on Teesside and Wearside he was an idol who looked likely to surpass the net-finding milestones of all of his legendary predecessors. There's little doubt that but for a fateful Boxing Day in 1962 when, playing on a rock-hard Roker Park pitch against Bury, a collision with the Lancashire club's goalkeeper resulted in badly torn ligaments and, as Easterbrook wrote, 'Injury transformed him from headliner to has-been,' the 'ace marksman' would have continued hitting the target with unswerving accuracy.

In those testimonial programme notes – for the match, Sunderland versus a Newcastle United Select XI, played on 27 October 1965 before an impressive 31,898 crowd – Clough was labelled a 'lively leader indeed, and a loveable character', with the author requesting: 'Let's wish him [Clough] good fortune in the future on whatever sphere he chooses to follow.' Having already enjoyed a brief spell coaching Sunderland's youth team, the sphere Clough chose to follow was management.

Just half an hour after the end of the game, in which the retired frontman netted both goals for the home club in a 6-2 defeat, Clough revealed he had accepted his first managerial position.

Two days later, having signed a two-year contract, the 30-year-old became the country's youngest manager, taking over at Fourth Division Hartlepools United – in 1968 the 's' and the 'United' were dropped from the name when the boroughs were united – and bringing in as his assistant his friend and former Boro teammate Peter Taylor (then in charge at non-league Burton Albion). 'If you want to see some good stuff from Saturday onwards, get yourself down to a little place called Hartlepools,' Clough had told guests at his testimonial dinner. 'It won't be a little place for very long.'

Recommended to the Hartlepools chairman, Ernie Ord, by the former Sunderland and England forward Len Shackleton, author of a well-respected column for the *Sunday People*, Clough was true to his word. The north-east club won that Saturday game, Clough's first in charge, 3-1 against Bradford – though it was actually away from home – plus the two after that and, despite United finishing the 1965/66 season in 18th, there were definite signs of progress. Hartlepools, after languishing in the bottom two of the Fourth Division, had had to seek re-election to the Football League four times in the previous five seasons.

Clough threw himself lock, stock, and barrel into the job, helping to paint the run-down stadium, making fundraising appearances at social clubs to tackle the club's financial plight, even driving the team's bus in an emergency and working without wages for a couple of months. More importantly, on the field, along with the ex-goalkeeper Taylor, he injected greater confidence into the players, introducing new training methods as well as a fresh scouting system. And it paid off. In 1966/67, Clough's first full season as a manager, he guided the perennial strugglers to an eighth-place finish, an achievement that didn't go unnoticed. In June 1967, after Tim Ward quit following several boardroom disputes, Clough, again on a recommendation from Shackleton (to chairman Sam Longson), was taking over at Derby County, Taylor moving with him.

Within five years at the Baseball Ground, the duo had guided the East Midlands club from the muddy depths of the Second Division to the silvery peak of the First, and by the end of 1971/72 Derby were crowned champions for the first time in their 88-year history when both their nearest challengers, Leeds United and Liverpool, cracked at the death on the season's nail-biting final night of football. Clough described the triumph as 'a small miracle', but it was one he'd been predicting. 'He has been talking of what his team were going to do ever since they [Derby] clinched the Second Division championship [in 1968/69],' noted *Football League Review* editor Bob Baldwin after the Rams' title success.

It was a success that was tough for some to stomach. Throughout his days at Derby – a club that was among the 12 founder members of the Football League back in 1888 – Clough's achievements as a football manager went hand in hand with his burgeoning life in the public spotlight. Yet while those achievements spoke for themselves, Clough was rarely content to let them do so. Given that spotlight, Clough had very often rubbed people up the wrong way with his swaggering approach. It had resulted, Baldwin wrote, in 'thousands of armchair and taproom critics' – 'the Brian Clough haters' to whom you only had to 'show them his photograph or turn up the television volume, and they become incensed'.

Broadcaster Bryon Butler once referred to Clough as a 'tilter at windmills'. Sometimes it seemed as though he randomly cast stones into a pond to see just how many ripples he could make, or he actively whipped up a storm of controversy simply to enjoy sitting at its centre. For the faithful that congregated at the Baseball Ground, Clough pronounced like a high priest and had them believing his every word; he'd given the club's supporters a team to identify with again after too long. But 'Outside Derby,' wrote Baldwin, 'Clough is the epitome of the anti-hero. People don't like the way he says things about their own particular sacred cows. They found him abrasive, a cocky upstart who spoke without any First Division championship or FA Cup success to back up his words.'

Always aware how much those words could offend, and the comeback they could have, Clough nevertheless refused to ration them. Why should he? What was the point in being, as he later expressed it in his 2002 autobiography, *Cloughie: Walking on Water*, 'expected to offer an honest opinion, and then saying next to nothing or being cautious and particularly careful just to avoid upsetting somebody'. When he spoke, he sincerely believed he was voicing 'what the ordinary turnstile-clicking football fan' was thinking. Brian Moore, Clough's friend with whom he regularly worked on ITV, marvelled at his 'almost unerring ability to tell the public what they wanted to hear – or, just as important, what they wanted to argue about'.

Yet as cocksure and confident as he came across, Clough wasn't without self-misgivings. 'I constantly doubt my ability to manage,' he told *TVTimes* in the September 1973 feature. 'If Hitler had sat down and thought for a minute that he was wrong, we wouldn't be here today. He'd have sorted himself out and made the right moves.' No period would test those doubts quite like the following few months.

By the time Clough stopped writing for *TVTimes* towards the close of 1974, he had undergone probably the most tumultuous experiences of his entire time in football – making an abrupt departure from a top First Division outfit, then taking over a struggling Third Division side, before becoming boss of another club he appeared to loathe intensely and had done his level best to deride. And finally, after his failure there, he was left completely out in the football wilderness.

The columns, contributed almost weekly under the title 'Clough Sounds Off', reflect these dramatic personal changes, but as a rule cover wider footballing matters – from Clough's concerns about the country's lack of goalscoring talent and the failings of the national team to his views on the British Championship, the World Cup and schoolboys football. Some pieces throw up genuine surprises. Others include extremely prescient statements about what the future holds for the game. Here and there are lines and phrases that, over time, may well have become oft-repeated, classic Cloughisms had they been more familiar to the public. All of them offer a unique insight into the mind of a most remarkable manager who, in truth, was anything but the ordinary turnstile-clicking football fan.

Given added significance, too, because the last of them just pre-dates the time Clough joined Nottingham Forest, where (the reader knows) the rebuilding of his managerial reputation really began, and where his greatest achievements were realised, in this book the columns are ordered sequentially by the date they appeared in *TVTimes*. Where there are gaps means that either the columns were missing due to industrial action resulting in no magazine being printed, no column featured because of emergency or General Election issues, or, as was the case following the World Cup finals in the summer of 1974, there was a long break before the columns commenced again at the start of the next Football League season.

As the editor, I've also omitted some because I considered the subject matter – skiing, badminton and horse riding – wasn't relevant enough to what is essentially a 'football' themed book. There are one or two that I was simply unable to access as well. Even though, physically, the columns were squeezed into far narrower spaces within each issue of *TVTimes* than they are in the pages of this book, the paragraphs in each have been arranged as they originally appeared, for authenticity's sake. That said, various typographical errors have been corrected. Whilst, to comply with the publisher's style guidelines, certain grammatical amendments have been made. But, essentially, the content of each column remains exactly as it was.

The story of Clough's career has been thoroughly documented on film and in print, his maverick methods examined in minute detail. While I've tried not to repeat a lot of the well-known tales that are so familiar to many, inevitably, to give context to some of the columns, it's been impossible to avoid. Mostly, though, I've attempted to expand, where I thought it necessary or interesting, on at least one of the topics touched upon in a column. In some cases more so than others. Whilst a number of columns are published without any further comment at all.

Reading all of them it's clear that they are of a time, and obvious that things were 'different' back then. It was a time when the highest echelon of English football was the First Division (these days effectively the third tier); an era when footballers played 'soccer' (more than football) and it was a game watched, apparently, only by men – and working-class men at that. If the past is another country, then football now, performed in multi-purpose stadia, on immaculate pitches, by perfectly honed athletes earning astronomical sums of money, is a nation a million miles away from the place it used to occupy.

The one constant, of course, is that football was and still is the preserve of human beings. And it's Clough's humanity that I hope comes through in his writing. Even after all these years, Clough's 'voice', authoritative, powerful, direct and brimming with self-conviction, possesses a resonance. Like a page-turning novel, it commands your attention, compels you to want more.

In September 1973, *TV Times* had observed that endeavouring to find out what made Clough tick was 'like trying to dismantle a computer with a toothpick'. Ultimately, maybe it's wiser not to even attempt to do so, but to simply enjoy the fact that he always had something to say for himself. That Mister Clough wasn't always right – often, far from it – but whatever he said was usually worth taking notice of.

29 September–5 October 1973

Every week in *On the Ball* you can see the controversial and outspoken Derby County manager Brian Clough talking football, and now he joins *TVTimes* as a regular columnist. He doesn't promise to please everybody, but he will make you sit up and listen. To kick off, he takes a hard look at his own reputation as the biggest mouth in soccer ...

ME AND MY BIG MOUTH

WHEN I appear on television I know I invite trouble. I know I'm not everybody's cup of tea, I know I upset people. It's got to the point now when even if I'm paying a player a compliment, people take it the wrong way. If I say John Smith is the greatest goalkeeper in the world, 91 other goalkeepers think I'm telling them they are a load of rubbish.

I have one rule when I appear: to tell the truth. And I hope that apart from being entertaining, this column will, above all, be truthful. I love giving my opinion because I can't bear saying nothing.

The drive from Derby to London to appear on television is a pretty long one in my terms – I'd be a lot better off playing with the kids. And when I get to the TV studios I can't stand all that messing about with make-up and endless rehearsals. So by the time it's my turn to go on and say something, I'm not going to waste all that time and come all that way and not deliver.

I believe a hell of a lot of people can ramble on for an hour and still say nothing. Politicians are first-class examples and football pundits are no exception. But when I go on, I want to give people something that's close to my heart. The way I see it, if England turn in a hopeless performance somebody's got to say it. There's no use toning it down and saying, 'Oh, they'll be better when they play at Wembley.' Somebody has got to lay it on the line. It's usually me.

There is too much woolly minded pap around in the newspapers and on television today. People are afraid to get down to business. They talk round a subject, as if it were a bad germ; they never get into it and say exactly what they feel. Expressing my honest opinion keeps me going, makes me feel alive. I'm often dead sure it's going to crucify me in the end, but that's a chance I'm going to take. I've been around for a long time now – 14 years, on and off, as a television talker, and eight years as a manager – and I'm still in a job.

Of course, I'm always saying things I regret. When I come home after being on the television, my wife says, 'Why on earth did you have to go and say that? Why don't you think just for a second before you say something? Why don't you just say nothing?'

I also find myself getting into trouble. I said in a Sunday newspaper article that Leeds United shouldn't have been fined the ridiculously low sum of £3,000 and warned for what the Football Association said was, 'allowing players to bring the game into disrepute'. I said they should be made to start the season in the Second Division. The FA wanted me to explain exactly what I meant, and I got a ticking off from my own chairman.

And yet when I leave the ground, the reaction from ordinary people I meet is entirely different. I don't mean television people and journalists. I mean the soccer fans, the people who push through the turnstiles and keep me in a job. They are in complete agreement with me.

I'm always sorry afterwards that I've caused a row and caused so much criticism and ill-feeling. But in retrospect, I think I was wrong in my article about Leeds. They should have started the season in the Third Division. However, I think all the publicity about my remarks may have helped to bring about the brilliant, clean start Leeds have made to this season.

A few years ago the chairman of Middlesbrough, where I was a player, said I shouldn't go around voicing my socialist views so much. He said, 'Be careful, Brian. One day, you might have to go to a Tory for a job.' Well, I told him that if anybody was so biased and bigoted that they couldn't accept someone of opposing political beliefs, then I wouldn't work for them anyway and they knew what they could do with their job.

That's just the way I feel about appearing on television. They take me for what I am – not some puppet of their organisation, but a football manager giving his views about football, for richer or poorer.

I am 37 now, and well aware that I'm approaching middle age. And to tell you the truth, I've reached the age where I don't give a damn what people think or say about me. I'm reasonably respected in the game because I've had good results, and I think the rank and file believe I speak with a straight tongue. And they are the people I'm talking to.

I often wonder what people think of these so-called experts who mouth away their thoughts on the box. I'm sure they don't watch me because they're waiting for an outburst. I think they watch me because I try to voice what they are thinking, I try to be a mouthpiece for the ordinary football fan, the bloke who spends five days or five nights a week in the factory and the high point of his week is standing up on a terrace shouting his head off at a football match.

I want to identify with him, and when I say on television that I think a game wasn't worth paying good money to see, it would be nice to think that there were ten million people sitting at home saying, 'He's right, you know.' That's the man I'm after, the hardcore football supporter.

I do get things wrong, though. You can't win them all. The biggest clanger I dropped was in June, when England played Poland in that terrible World Cup qualifying match. Even when they were losing 1-0 at half-time I was still saying they'd win it in the second half. Everybody knows what happened. Alf Ramsey made no substitutions and we lost 2-0. I had to admit I was wrong – but I can't make a habit of it.

There are 92 managers in the Football League, give or take the odd vacant position and a few unemployed bosses, and only two or three are asked regularly to speak their minds on television. You can't be right all the time, but unless you're right most of the time they'll soon push you off and get somebody else.

On the subject of that Poland match, this is a good opportunity to talk about the crucial game against the Poles at Wembley on 17 October. I think we will qualify. I passionately believe that, and I know that if we don't, it will be the biggest blow to football this country has ever known.

It will also be the death knell for Sir Alf Ramsey, and rightly so. Ramsey is paid to get us to Munich, an event that represents the pinnacle of football, a showpiece for our own footballing strength. Football is essential for the nation because it gives more people more pleasure than anything else I can think of, and it'll be a blow to the nation if we don't make it.

That's why Alf has got to do it this time. There's just about a month to go before what I think will be the most decisive day ever in our national game.

* * * *

Just over two weeks after he sounded off in his first column for *TVTimes*, Brian Clough was opening his big mouth as Derby County manager for the very last time. On Tuesday, 16 October 1973, 24 hours before 'the most decisive day ever in our national game,' Clough, along with his assistant Peter Taylor, after six and a half dramatic, often traumatic, years, were on their way out of the Baseball Ground, having tendered their resignation letters on the Monday and then had them accepted at a board meeting the next day.

As the papers had it, their decision followed further disputes – and 'an orgy of allegations' the *Daily Telegraph* reported – between Derby's self-made millionaire chairman Sam Longson and Clough over the manager's controversial statements and outspoken comments on TV and in print. The last straw, according to *The Telegraph*, came when, in his ghosted newspaper column, Clough accused some of his England players of 'cheating' by not giving 100 per cent because of their preoccupation with the forthcoming

World Cup match with the Poles. The truth, however, was far more complex.

Ever since arriving in the East Midlands from Hartlepools as a young up-and-coming manager in 1967, Clough, in tandem with Taylor, had transformed Derby beyond recognition, reviving the club spirit and fashioning them from an ailing, average Second Division side into champions of England for the very first time and then European Cup semi-finalists. At the same time he had also created for himself a presence in the media spotlight like no other football manager in the game's history.

Initially encouraged by Longson, Clough's ever-expanding public profile became a source of escalating embarrassment and no little annoyance for the Derby chairman. The chief bone of contention was not so much the volume of Clough's output – though Longson saw it as a drain on the time and attention he should be devoting to the needs of the club – as what he said, the manager's fiery outbursts frequently making headlines for all the wrong reasons. The often acid attacks on fellow bosses, the sniping potshots at rival clubs, the biting observations about those at the FA were, Longson believed, a poor reflection on his club and, increasingly fed up with putting out the fires that Clough's inflammatory proclamations had sparked, the man from Chapel-en-le-Frith went from occasionally telling Clough to 'calm down' when the manager's name hit the papers to openly expressing his total opposition.

He wasn't the only one who took issue with Clough; from the moment the manager began to receive payment for his opinions, some public sympathy was lost, and unforgiving critics charged him with being deliberately provocative. 'Controversial' was almost a prefix whenever Clough's name came into a conversation.

He'd even had a go at the Derby crowd. On 3 September 1972, the day after Clough had watched his defending champions defeat Liverpool 2-1 at the Baseball Ground, his strong verbal attack on the home side's supporters – 'They started chanting only near the end when we were a goal in front. I want to hear them when we are losing. They are a disgraceful lot,' he ranted – forced Longson to disassociate himself and the board from his manager's remarks and apologise to the fans. An open confrontation between Clough and his employers seemed imminent.

Later that month, in another Sunday newspaper article, Clough suggested that the FA Cup, the most famous cup competition in the world, should be suspended for a year to give England the best possible chance in the World Cup. A month earlier, at a sportswriters' lunch, he'd already stated quite firmly that, given the present league set-up, England had no prospects whatsoever at the finals. Clough believed that 'the top club managers have the power to change the game in England, but they don't trust each other'. It wasn't what the Football League hierarchy wanted to hear. Derby were warned they faced disciplinary action if they could not persuade Clough to modify his criticism of the establishment.

A major opponent of Sir Alf Ramsey – the following January, the Derby boss openly declared he was 'willing to swap jobs' with the England supremo – Clough had also made caustic remarks about the two-year international ban placed on the Rams defender Colin Todd for refusing to go on an England under-23s tour that summer. Todd was 'suspended for being honest,' Clough told the sportswriters' gathering. Prior to Derby's European Cup first-round second-leg tie away to Yugoslavian champions Željezničar on 27 September 1972 (a 2-1 win to seal a 4-1 aggregate), Longson was summoned and told that Clough was not to make any further comments about matters not concerning the East Midlands club.

To Clough, it was simply a matter of standing by what he considered his right to free speech. The *Daily Telegraph* sympathised. 'He is totally involved in football, and perfectly entitled to speak about it, even if he does ruffle a few feathers,' one journalist ventured. 'Clough's abrasive personality might irritate a lot of people, but the other side of the coin was demonstrated after the Željezničar game, when he insisted his players meet the tiny knot of County fans who had travelled to the match.' 'These people have come 2,000 miles to see you,' Clough told his players, referring to the Derby fans staying in the same hotel. 'Go and shake their hands and thank them.'

Clough, though, had very few sympathisers following the night of Sunday, 28 January 1973 when he was guest speaker at an awards ceremony in which Peter Lorimer was honoured as Sports Personality of the Year at the Yorksport dinner under the auspices of Yorkshire Television at the Queens Hotel in Leeds. It was a prestigious prize, voted for by Yorkshire Television viewers, that had previously been won by the Formula One racing driver Jackie Stewart, and one that important figures were invited to present. On this particular occasion, it was the Prime Minister of the day, Harold Wilson.

Kevin Keegan, then in the early stages of his Liverpool career, was also present. On what was 'meant to be a nice evening,' Keegan recalled in the *Shoot!* annual of 1982, 'Clough stood up. Instead of proposing the toast, he announced, "I'm off to the lavatory" – and he didn't return for nearly a quarter of an hour. It still amazes me how patiently everyone waited.' Clough was actually away for 11 minutes. After listening to several speeches praising Leeds United, he was then called out to respond to a toast, but instead informed the 500 or so guests: 'I have been sitting here for two and a half hours and I am not replying to anything or anybody until I have had a wee. And I'm being very serious – you get on your bloody feet and go to the toilet, you get a beer, and then if you've not got to get up early in the morning, get back and listen.'

When he did return, having – according to his autobiography – been waylaid by someone who wanted to talk to him about Edward Heath's love of sailing, Clough launched into a full-blown lambasting of Leeds's Scottish international, Lorimer (he'd won the award 'despite the fact that he falls when he hasn't been kicked, and despite the fact that he protests when he has nothing to protest about'), the West Yorkshire club (who 'should be deducted ten points and relegated for their cynicism') and their players (Billy Bremner was 'a little cheat'; Eddie Gray had had so many injuries 'if he'd been a racehorse he would have been shot' – a line Clough would famously repeat).

Lorimer, luckily for him, wasn't there to hear it, having collected his trophy then been whisked away in a waiting taxi to join his teammates at a Birmingham hotel (Leeds faced an FA Cup replay with Norwich at Villa Park the following night). But those who were, a largely local and partisan audience for whom the Leeds players were their idols, were left absolutely gobsmacked and greatly offended by the outburst. Boos rang out. People were on their feet, shouting 'get off' and 'sit down', to which Clough merely responded by saying, 'I was not particularly glad with the idea of speaking to you lot. I have to stand up here, but you are sitting in the crowd, which hides you.' He then described one complaining member of the audience as a 'mumbler', adding, 'we are becoming a nation of mumblers. Stand on your feet if you have anything to say. Come up here and make the speech if you think you could do better than me.'

When he finally realised he'd gone too far, some apologies were made, but by this time many guests had already had enough and left the room. Clough was unrepentant in the following days. He told the *Daily Mirror*: 'They didn't tell me beforehand it was being filmed. They didn't brief me on what I could and could not say. And if in future they want a puppet to get up and say something to please everybody in the room, I suggest they invite Basil Brush, instead of asking a football manager to give up his only day off of the week.' Whether or not the astonishing tirade was a classic example of Clough's honesty – or outrageousness – or just downright rudeness, Keegan regarded it as 'an all-time low' for English football in the 1970s.

Still Clough balked at being gagged. In a BBC TV interview the following month, he stated in all seriousness that he would like to be the 'supreme football dictator' in England. Already wanting a suspension of the FA Cup, he publicly avowed that he would also stop league football from March 1974, thus giving the national team three months' free preparation for the World Cup finals. Then, in April, came another episode to have Longson pulling out whatever hair he had left.

In their European debut, having disposed of Željezničar and swept aside Benfica (their 3-0 aggregate success meaning Derby became only the second club, after Ajax, to keep a clean sheet against the Portuguese over two legs), the Rams then defeated Czechoslovakia's Spartak Trnava 2–1 to set up a cup semi-final meeting with Italian giants Juventus. In the first leg in Turin, Derby were beaten 3-1, and Clough's initial European adventure looked to be all but done, especially as two key men, Archie Gemmill and Roy McFarland – the two players already on bookings from previous rounds – received first-half cautions that ruled them out of the return. But even though Clough would admit that the Italians were superior on the day, he was convinced that some skulduggery was afoot and that Juventus had had the German referee Gerhard Schulenburg on their side, too.

Throughout the 90 minutes, Schulenburg made many calls that were questionable. Whereas much of the home side's persistent and violent fouling went unpunished, the German came down harshly on all the Derby players' tackling and the cautions for Gemmill (tripping Furino in retaliation after the Italian's elbow had smashed into his face) and McFarland (clashing heads with Cuccureddu in a fair aerial challenge) seemed most unjust and more than a little suspicious. It looked 'like a put-up job,' Gerald Mortimer of the *Derby Telegraph* observed post-match. Peter Taylor's witnessing of Juve's German midfielder Helmut Haller entering the officials' quarters at half-time only added to Clough's sense that Schulenburg was corrupt.

Francisco Marques Lobo, the Portuguese official for the second leg, would later reveal to journalist Brian Glanville that he'd thwarted an attempt to bribe him to bend the return match in Juve's favour – a set of car keys were dangled and £5,000 in cash put in front of him – by a notorious match-fixer, a Hungarian named Dezso Salti, allegedly enlisted by the Italian champions. Lobo wouldn't take the bait (and despite reporting the incident to UEFA, it was conveniently covered up), but Clough was certain some Machiavellian malpractice had taken place in the first leg and the manager made it very well known immediately after the game in Turin, emerging from the dressing room to tell the expectant Italian reporters, 'No cheating bastards do I talk to. I will not talk to any cheating bastards.'

As vindicated as Clough clearly felt, his disparaging remarks to the assembled journalists at the press conference about the Italian national character and their conduct during the war was one more black mark against him in Longson's books. Two weeks later, as Alan Hinton missed a second-half penalty and Roger Davies was sent off, Derby could only finish goalless in the return game and exited the competition. A seventh-place league finish, 14 points behind champions Liverpool, was also a disappointing end to the club's title defence.

Three weeks before the next campaign commenced and the County boss once again made himself a magnet for trouble. On 5 August 1973, echoing what he'd said in his diatribe at the Queens Hotel, Clough, using a *Sunday Express* article, savagely attacked the FA's decision to fine Leeds £3,000 for their 'above average misconduct' but suspend the punishment, calling for Leeds's demotion – Revie's team should have been 'instantly relegated,' he wrote – for their poor disciplinary record and persistent violation of the game's laws. 'No wonder Don Revie was smiling broadly as he left the disciplinary commission's hearing in London,' Clough noted. 'I looked at his happy face smiling at me out of my newspaper in Spain. It just about spoiled my holiday to read that the £3,000 fine has been suspended until the end of the coming season.'

Revie had always done his best not to rise to any bait, though five months earlier, frustrated at Clough's continual sniping at both his club as well as rival managers – Ramsey, Sir Matt Busby and Malcolm Allison just three who'd been on the receiving end of Clough's verbal lashings – the Leeds manager had responded in his Saturday column in the *Yorkshire Evening Post*. 'I think it is wrong to criticise your colleagues as Clough does,' Revie wrote on 10 March, 'because the job is difficult enough without any of us slitting each other's throats.' Revie went on to say that it must be abundantly clear to football followers that he and the Derby manager weren't 'exactly the best of friends,' and, as their relationship stood at that moment, 'he is the last person with whom I would wish to be stranded on a desert island, and no doubt he feels the same way about me'.

Relations between Clough and Longson were at this point more overtly fractious, too. The previous autumn, on the subject of trying to reach an amicable agreement on his new contract, Clough reckoned that he and the Derby board were still 'a million miles apart'. Now, on the issue of what Longson perceived as Clough's non-curriculum activities, the gulf appeared to be even wider. 'I believe the most important thing of all is the relationship between the manager and the board,' Clough had written in *The Sun Soccer Annual 1972*. 'By that, I mean the link between manager and chairman. I would even go so far as to say that unless a manager has the right kind of understanding with his chairman, he has no chance at all. He might as well pack it in.' Longson and Clough now had anything but 'the right kind of understanding'. Longson was nearing his limit.

Following Clough's panning of their handling of the Leeds case, the FA formed an emergency committee to decide whether to accuse the manager of bringing the game into disrepute. Clough, on a number of occasions, had been told that his club was embarrassed by his frankness. Now, fearing actual expulsion from the league, Longson became more and more convinced that, before Clough landed himself and Derby in even deeper waters, a moratorium on all Clough's media appearances was the only solution.

Clough, of course, was heading in a completely opposite direction. In 1967, shortly after joining Derby, he'd been lined up to take over from Jimmy Hill as Coventry City manager. Now, two days after *The Express* article appeared, he joined London Weekend Television on a part-time basis, agreeing to be a pundit on both the *On the Ball* and *The Big Match* programmes, having been approached to take the place of Hill who would be working for the BBC from the new season on. 'I merely switched channels,' Clough said. 'This is no different to the amount of TV work I have been doing in the last three or four years.' Longson, naturally, saw it differently. To him, it was one more soapbox for Clough to climb upon and possibly cause further damage to Derby's reputation.

Without the distraction of European football, hopes were high among the club's supporters that the East Midlanders would enter the 1973/74 season as genuine title contenders. They made a decent start. A 1-0 win at Old Trafford on 13 October, secured by an early Kevin Hector goal, left them third in the table. But behind the scenes the ructions had been ongoing. In the week before the victory over United, in a letter signed by Longson, the Derby board issued an ultimatum to Clough: 'Stop engaging in literary work by writing articles in the press and stop entering into commitment with radio and television,' it read. Longson, in a rather desperate attempt to prompt Clough into quitting, had also had the grille pulled down on the club bar to stop both Clough and Taylor drinking. It didn't work. On 11 October, a call by Longson at a board meeting for both the pair's sackings had also failed due to lack of support. The long-simmering feud between chairman and manager, however, was soon to boil over.

At Old Trafford, Clough was alleged to have made a 'Harvey Smith gesture' (a V-sign) towards Sir Matt Busby and United's chairman Louis Edwards (following Clough's annoyance that there was no seating for his players' wives at the ground), and, although Clough vehemently denied it, Longson said that Busby 'was under no illusion as to what took place'. He demanded that Clough say sorry. Clough refused to do so. He, too, was reaching his snapping point.

The break wasn't long in coming. Derby director Jack Kirkland, whose brother, Bob, had been on the club's board before resigning after an ongoing power struggle with Longson, was another of the anti-Clough faction in the boardroom. He was said to have a particular dislike for Peter Taylor. When Kirkland weighed in, demanding to know exactly what Taylor's role within the club was – Kirkland instructing Taylor to meet him at the ground two days later to explain the precise nature of his duties – both Taylor and Clough had had enough. Taylor kept his appointment with Kirkland on the Monday but, feeling undermined – 'He [Taylor] had been humiliated by a man who was not entitled to question anything unless he'd been asking Peter for the time of day,' Clough wrote later – he told his partner that that was it, he was finished. The pair wrote out and submitted their letters of resignation that evening.

Several times before, they'd had at least one foot through the exit door. Most recently, in early April 1972 when, with Derby in the thick of their title hunt, although Liverpool and Manchester City were the favourites, Clough and Taylor met up with Coventry City chairman Derrick Robins and director Mick French on Easter Monday and agreed to accept the vacant job at Highfield Road, as replacement for the sacked Noel Cantwell. When Clough then asked for more time to come to a final decision, Coventry, angry at having essentially been given the runaround, withdrew their offer in a letter to the Derby manager.

The story was that Longson had no idea what was going on, and was told by Clough on a late-night visit to the chairman's house that he and Taylor were leaving unless Derby matched the wage the Sky Blues were offering – said to be three times the salary they were on at the Baseball Ground – even though the opportunity to go to Coventry was now gone. If it was basically a bluff to get a pay rise out of the Derby chairman, it worked. Somehow they got Longson to 'persuade' them to stay and give them more money. This time, with their offer to quit, if Clough and Taylor hoped to rally support from their few backers on the board and somehow force out the Longson regime, it was doomed to fail. On the morning of 16 October Longson announced to the press that he and the directors had accepted the resignations and, despite saying that they'd done so 'with a certain amount of sadness', Longson wasn't shedding any tears. One paper put it that 'he [Clough] and Taylor's departure will be a great loss' to Derby, but the chairman had got just what he wanted.

Demands for the duo's reinstatement would be made. There was a threat of strike action from the players; the formation of a group by furious supporters, the Derby County Protest Movement, which director Mike Keeling joined after resigning from the club; moves initiated by playwright Don Shaw, Bill Holmes, an ex-footballer, and respected local MP Phillip Whitehead. Public meetings were held, showdowns sought, there was even a march on the Derby streets – but Longson wasn't backing down. 'We will go into the Second Division with our heads in the air,' he stated defiantly, 'rather than winning the First Division wondering whether the club will be expelled from the Football League.'

The storm wouldn't die down for a few weeks, despite the almost immediate appointment of Dave Mackay on 23 October as Clough's replacement – the ex-Derby captain was approached only after Ipswich Town boss Bobby Robson had turned down the job. When the unsettled Derby players issued a signed statement in support of their former management team, Longson replied with a letter detailing his criticisms of Clough. 'Nobody regrets the current situation more than I do. I brought him here, I have glorified in his success and I leave it to the supporters of Derby County to judge me and my board,' it concluded. 'Hysteria is prevalent at present with some supporters. All in all, I say enough is enough. In conclusion, I must stress the point that Derby County will always survive and that no individual is bigger than the club.'

Peter Taylor had warned Clough about his 'false relationship' with Longson for years. The Derby chairman, Taylor felt, whilst initially revelling in the exposure that Clough had brought to his club – Clough later claimed that Longson had even loaned him his car to make journeys for TV appearances – had grown jealous of the rise in the manager's popularity and, according to Clough, 'started to go around insisting in that gravelly voice of his, "I'm the one who runs Derby County – not Brian Clough."' Longson in fact was the one, Clough wrote in his autobiography, 'who put his own interests, image and reputation before those of the club'. The chairman's complaints about Clough's media work, the worries about him landing Derby in 'very serious trouble' and getting their wrists severely slapped by the football authorities were, in both Taylor's and Clough's view, just a smokescreen, a convenient excuse to try to banish from the family someone Longson had once referred to as his 'adopted son'.

Clough would also later claim that it was Taylor who instigated the double resignation – he was set on the path and wouldn't change his mind and because they were a partnership Clough went along with it, too. Whether or not the resignations were made in the belief that the strength of feeling among supporters et al. would lead to their reinstatement – Clough would admit that in his heart he thought they would be invited back – they were very mistaken. It was, as Clough rated it in his autobiography, 'the worst move of our lives'. The worst it may well have been – but far more unexpected ones were still to come.

13–19 October 1973

In one of the most crucial games in their history, England play Poland in a World Cup qualifying match at Wembley on Wednesday. You can see all the excitement of the game on ITV. The famous ITV soccer panel – Derek Dougan, Malcolm Allison, Brian Clough and Jackie Charlton – will join Brian Moore. Here, Brian Clough gives advice to England's selectors ...

SIR ALF PLEASE NOTE: WEDNESDAY'S NO NIGHT FOR VIRGINS

WHETHER or not England book a ticket to the World Cup finals in Munich next June depends on one thing – Sir Alf Ramsey's team selection for Wednesday's vital game against Poland at Wembley. Nothing but bad choice of players was the reason England lost 2-0 in Katowice earlier this year and now the heat is on.

But that magnificent 7-0 win over Austria three weeks ago, and the attacking spirit the team displayed, was the perfect tonic for the fans and the players. In that match they showed what they could do if they were allowed to go forward, unlike that agonising game in Poland. Then, Alf played straight into the Poles' hands. He picked a side with seven defenders, a side which screamed out to anyone who could read the programme: 'We have come here not to lose. A draw will do.' The Poles, with 100,000 fans howling for them, were after the biggest scalp in soccer; they had the carrot of Munich dangling in front of them, and we handed them the initiative on a plate. In picking the English side, Alf did their coach the biggest favour of his life.

Even when they were 2-0 down with 40 minutes to go, with players like Channon and Macdonald waiting on the substitutes bench, Alf persisted with his defensive tactics. I'm not much of a manager for putting on substitutes, and I concede that it is debatable whether, at that stage, it would have made any difference, but surely here was a case where extra power in attack would have given England a chance?

To me, Alf's crime after that game was when he deluded himself in saying that England put up a magnificent performance, and that he was proud of the way his team played. Players always take a lead from the manager and no doubt the England team also thought they had played magnificently.

You wouldn't catch me saying that at Derby. We lost 5-0 at Leeds last season. It was a diabolical performance, and I was the first to say so to the players. I got them in the dressing room and I said to them, 'Don't take your boots off, I've got something to say. I can't bottle it up, so you're going to get the lot.' I got it all off my chest – I had a go at them for an hour and a half. Every one of those lads knew how I felt. It sunk in. But what does Alf say when we're thrashed by a bunch of part-timers from Poland? 'It was a magnificent performance!'

But Wednesday is another day and Alf must pick a side to win. With two important exceptions it doesn't matter who he picks. We have such a wealth of good players in England, it doesn't matter if the back four reads: Smith, Jones, Brown and Green. The names mean nothing, provided he picks a balanced side with the accent on attack, and tells them that he wants goals.

For a match like this, when everything depends on the result, he must go for experience. Two names pick themselves. One is Peter Shilton, who is untouchable as the first-choice goalkeeper. The second is Bobby Moore. England did well without Moore against Austria, but Wednesday's match will be a vastly different affair.

Much as I have praised the talents of Colin Todd in the past, I would write the name of Moore on my team sheet before anybody else because he has been around and because he knows how to play and keep his head when the stakes are high. Wednesday night is not a night for virgins.

England made the Poles look good in Katowice simply because they were not prepared to take them on. Most of the spectators praised the skills of Lubański, who scored that second goal which finished England. In fact, Bobby Moore, in one of his rare moments, offered him the goal like a birthday present.

Granted, Lubański placed it well, but none of the Polish players has played in anything like the company we enjoy watching every week – the English First Division. They wouldn't last five minutes at Elland Road or Anfield.

I talk as a football manager – I am never concerned about individual players on the opposing side.

I wouldn't be concerned if Poland were playing Pelé at his peak. What matters is the overall strength of the side. If there were 11 Pelés, we'd have reason to be worried. But, man for man, any England team with the emphasis on attack ought to be all over the Poles on Wednesday.

I believe this match is so important to us that, provided Alf picks the right team, there is no way England can fail to qualify. No matter how many goals they would have needed to win through to the last 16 at Munich, I would still put my 50p on England.

If they don't, I'm afraid it will be the end of the road for Alf. I don't see how he could continue to manage an England team which failed to find a place in soccer's number-one pageant, the World Cup.

* * * *

Slated for selecting far more destroyers than creators – while other continental national teams had developed hard men, powerful in the tackle, who could also play creatively, England had taken a wrong turn with intimidators like Stiles and Storey – Sir Alf Ramsey acquiesced. In April 1972, bowing to pressure from all sides – the FA, English club managers, the press and TV – the England manager had selected a side for the European Championship quarter-final first leg at home to West Germany with six attacking players – Ball, Bell and Peters, Hurst, Chivers and Lee – occupying the middle and front three spots. But on the night, with Borussia Mönchengladbach's fleet-footed midfield ace Günter Netzer inspirational, the visitors outplayed and out-thought their opponents and ran out crushing 3-1 winners. It was one time when the side had cried out for a defensive midfielder, to negate the attacking German. Ramsey, in retrospect, was bitterly resentful of his own weak-mindedness. He soon reverted to type.

Subsequent to that Wembley defeat, by the time England faced Poland in Katowice on 6 June 1973, they'd lost just one of 12 internationals, again at the Empire Stadium, a surprise 1-0 Home Internationals setback to Northern Ireland (which, together with the beating by the Germans, meant a first-ever occasion England had lost two matches in a row at Wembley). But their football, largely expedient and functional, and devoid of genuine inventiveness, won few admirers. Rather than possessing any artistic flourishes, Ramsey's sides painted by numbers.

Amongst those 12 games were two World Cup qualifiers against Wales, the first a scrappy 1-0 win at Ninian Park, Colin Bell's 35th-minute strike decisive in what was Ramsey's 100th match in charge, the second a wretchedly physical encounter at Wembley when a largely scratch Welsh side reserved a real shock for England, drawing 1-1. On a cold January evening, 62,273 had turned out to watch the two teams fight out, often quite literally, a stalemate, and probably wished they hadn't bothered.

It was a disastrous result for England, all the more so for the fact that, less than four months later, they convincingly beat the same opponents 3-0 in the Home Internationals, recording a first victory on home territory for two years. 'It should be easy for England,' predicted Wales manager Dave Bowen ahead of the World Cup clash in June. With second-half goals from Leighton James and Trevor Hockey, Bowen's side had beaten the Poles 2-0 in Cardiff that March and, he said, 'Poland never looked in England's class. We should have won 4-0.'

Despite Bowen's insistence that Ramsey's men faced a simple task, few were fooled. Poland on the night had been caught cold after coming back from a three-month winter break in their domestic season, made mistakes they were unlikely to repeat and underrated a Welsh XI who, in the event, gave one of their most inspired displays for years.

Against England, Poland were much warmer – and far too hot for their opponents. In the ninth minute when Gadocha swung in a free kick from the left, his shot found its way into the net off the foot of Moore and the arm of Shilton. Then, early in the second half, Moore, making an uncharacteristic hash of a tackle, was dispossessed by Lubański, who raced clear to make it 2-0. To compound the visitors' misery on a grey night in one of the country's vast coal mining areas, 14 minutes from time, Alan Ball became the second England player to be sent off (another Alan – Mullery – being the first, almost exactly five years earlier) after grabbing Ćmikiewicz by the throat and kneeing him in the groin following a scuffle. With the game in the bag, Poland chose to close up shop and hang on to their lead, and the group had been thrown wide open.

Ramsey, despite England's first-ever World Cup qualifying defeat, was 'impressed' by his side's performance. Clough, adding comment and analysis for the BBC, wasn't. He wasn't the only one. Ramsey's deployment of 'seven defenders' might have been an exaggeration on Clough's part, but the England manager's extra-cautious approach, the lack of adventure, playing five across the middle with only Chivers up front, was roundly condemned. Even at two goals down, Ramsey had refused to alter his sterile philosophy and introduce any attacking substitutes.

Poland hadn't qualified for a World Cup since 1938, but their gold medal at the 1972 Olympics – secured by a brace from their captain Kazimierz Deyna in a 2-1 final win over Hungary – had served notice of their promise. Far from being a bunch of part-timers, they had a well-organised team of undoubted ability, from the schemer Deyna, with his fine touch and awareness, to the dangerous Lato down the right flank. In midfield, players like Maszczyk worked tirelessly for the side. While at the back, the 6ft 4in blond giant, Jerzy Gorgoń, was so imposing in the all-red strip that he'd earned the nickname 'The Telephone Booth'. Though Clough would describe him as 'a boxer in football boots', the Górnik Zabrze player was a sound and trustworthy defender.

In their next qualifying match, on 26 September in the same Slaski Stadium where they'd seen off England, the Poles beat Wales 3-0, but it was a quite brutal encounter which saw Trevor Hockey sent off in the first half (on what proved to be the hirsute midfielder's final international appearance) and left Dave Bowen describing it as a 'war without guns'. According to the reports several players of both sides deserved the same fate as the dismissed Aston Villa man. Of 59 fouls in the game, 37 were committed by Kazimierz Górski's side.

Nevertheless, that victory meant that, when they came to London for their first-ever appearance at Wembley, Poland needed only a draw to give England's World Cup dream the severest reality check. Yet despite arriving in fine fettle – seven days prior to lining up to be introduced to FIFA president Sir Stanley Rous on that Wednesday night in the English capital, the Poles had had the better of a 1-1 friendly draw with Holland in Rotterdam – they were still regarded as little more than a last stepping stone on England's path to Munich. Even their own press wrote them off as no-hopers.

On that mild autumn evening in October, two days after resigning at Derby, Brian Clough took his place on the panel in his new role as ITV's chief pundit and was optimism personified. Opening in slightly idiosyncratic fashion – 'I've got a nail here in my hand and I want it to go in the Polish coffin – or perhaps it could go in Sir Alf's,' he said provocatively, brandishing a small object before the camera's lens – he went on to allay the nation's fears: the massive TV audience tuning in should settle down, put their feet up, make a cup of tea; England were certain to win, he said, and easily. The unorthodox Polish number one Jan Tomaszewski (making his 13th appearance for his country) Clough branded 'a circus clown in gloves'. 'What manager would have him in his team?' he asked.

Few could argue with Ramsey's selection. He went with the same XI that had put seven without reply past the Austrians –

England's highest score against a foreign side since 1961 – in a highly encouraging warm-up game just three weeks earlier. Aside from Sheffield United's Tony Currie, who was winning only his fifth full cap, experience ran throughout the team – every player was into double figures in the appearances column. Bobby Moore, the one-time Captain Colossus now looking decidedly lightweight and clearly no longer the utterly unflappable performer he once was, had been left out for that Austria game. Unlike Clough, Ramsey evidently believed England could do just fine without him again.

Even at half-time when, despite nursing a broken finger after a third-minute 50-50 challenge with Allan Clarke, Tomaszewski and his circus act had somehow stopped England making a breakthrough and the sides went in level, Clough saw no cause for concern. 'Don't worry. Relax. It will be all right in the second half,' he reassured the viewers. 'It was exactly what everyone wanted to hear – a brilliant angle,' reflected Brian Moore in his 1976 book, *Big Match*. Yet the tension nagged and gnawed away. Nerves remained extremely frayed. The England players still had a lot of business left to do.

If it had been a boxing match, the referee might have called a halt after those first 45 minutes. England inflicted damage from the off and by the break Poland looked exhausted, desperate, clinging on. But the wounds were only superficial. Spirited and resilient, the visitors hung in there. Over the whole 90 minutes, England had 35 shots to Poland's two, but, of those two, they made one crucial one count. Domarski's 55th-minute strike – firing a pacy, low first-time drive under the diving Shilton after Lato had robbed a hesitant Hunter on the touchline before feeding the unmarked striker the ball – was a sucker punch from which England never fully recovered.

Although Clarke restored parity eight minutes later with a softish penalty after Peters was pushed over, for all England relentlessly pummelled away in the final 27 minutes, they couldn't land the all-important blow. With a mix of unbelievably good fortune and inspired, sometimes incredible, keeping, man of the match Tomaszewski continually repulsed the frantic assaults on his goal. When substitute Kevin Hector, thrown on with just two minutes to go, narrowly missed with his first touch in international football, the game was up. Seconds later, as Hunter launched the ball into the box, 'Have England got time now?' ITV's Hugh Johns asked. 'No they have not!' was his answer. 'It's over. It's all over.' The whistle blew and England's hopes were punctured irreparably; the pain of failure to make the World Cup finals for the first time since initially entering the competition in 1950 was felt in an instant by millions.

In his post-match analysis Clough still refused to accept that Tomaszewski was anything other than an eccentric who'd just got exceptionally lucky. 'You keep calling him a clown,' snapped a finger-wagging Brian Moore, 'but in fact that fellow has made some fantastic saves.' Fellow pundit Derek Dougan was siding with the ITV host, calling it an adverse comment on Clough's part, but the newly unemployed manager would have none of it. If the last line of the Polish defence had made him eat his words he was still refusing to swallow.

Moore confessed a little while later that most of the professionals actually agreed with Clough's estimation of Tomaszewski, 'even if they were a little less flamboyant in their criticism of the Pole's technique'. The clamour of protests immediately afterwards about Clough's remarks – even an MP and a member of the House of Lords felt strongly enough to write and complain – suggested that some were looking to make Clough the scapegoat for England's exit. But Clough, as he always did, was only saying what he believed. He wasn't the one who should be held to account.

The majority of accusatory fingers, of course, were pointed in Ramsey's direction. It was sportswriter David Miller's assessment that the England manager 'had reaped the whirlwind of the unchecked thuggery of the last ten years which had stifled the development of players of the class of Jimmy Greaves, Johnny Byrne and Joe Baker'. Maybe so. Yet on the night – 'the most disappointing' of his life, Ramsey called it – England were unsuccessful for one reason only: their end product in front of goal. That was largely down to one individual. Tomaszewski might not have been a name as easy to remember as Banks or Shilton or Clemence, but it was one that was now deeply etched into the psyche of English football. No one was going to forget it in a hurry.

CLOUGH SOUNDS OFF

In one of the most crucial games in their history, England play Poland in a World Cup qualifying match at Wembley on Wednesday. You can see all the excitements of the game on ITV. The famous ITV soccer panel—Derek Dougan, Malcolm Allison, Brian Clough and Jackie Charlton—will join Brian Moore. Here Brian Clough gives advice to England's selector

Sir Alf please note: WEDNESDAY'S NO NIGHT FOR VIRGINS

Catastrophe at Katowice: Poland's Banas (on the ground) scores the first vital goal, to the amazement of England's Bobby Moore (left)

WHETHER or not England book a ticket to the World Cup Finals in Munich next June depends on one thing—Sir Alf Ramsey's team selection for Wednesday's vital game against Poland at Wembley.

Nothing but bad choice of players was the reason England lost 2-0 in Katowice earlier this year and now the heat is on.

But that magnificent 7-0 win over Austria three weeks ago, and the attacking spirit the team displayed, was the perfect tonic for the fans and the players. In that match they showed what they could do if they were allowed to go forward, unlike that agonising game in Poland. Then, Alf played straight into the Poles' hands. He picked a side with seven defenders, a side which screamed out to anyone who could read the programme: "We have come here not to lose. A draw will do." The Poles, with 100,000 fans howling for them, were after the biggest scalp in soccer; they had the carrot of Munich dangling in front of them, and we handed them the initiative on a plate. In picking the English side, Alf did their coach the biggest favour of his life.

Even when they were 2-0 down with 40 minutes to go, with players like Channon and McDonald waiting on the substitutes' bench, Alf persisted with his defensive tactics. I'm not much of a manager for putting on substitutes, and I concede that it is debatable whether, at that stage, it would have made any difference, but surely here was a case where extra power in attack would have given England a chance?

To me, Alf's biggest crime after that game was when he deluded himself in saying that England put up a magnificent performance, and that he was proud of the way his team played. Players always take a lead from the manager and no doubt the England team also thought they had played magnificently.

You wouldn't catch me saying that at Derby. We lost 5-0 at Leeds last season. It was a diabolical performance, and I was the first to say so to the players. I got them in the dressing-room and I said to them: "Don't take your boots off, I've got something to say. I can't bottle it up, so you're going to get the lot." I got it all off my chest—I had a go at them for an hour and a half. Every one of those lads knew how I felt. It sunk in. But what does Alf say when we're thrashed by a bunch of part-timers from Poland? "It was a magnificent performance!"

But Wednesday is another day and Alf must pick a side to win. With two important exceptions it doesn't matter who he picks. We have such a wealth of good players in England, it doesn't matter if the back four read: Smith, Jones, Brown and Green. The names mean nothing, provided he picks a balanced side with the accent firmly on attack, and tells them that he wants goals.

For a match like this, when everything depends on the result, he must go for experience. Two names pick themselves. One is Peter Shilton, who is untouchable as the first choice goalkeeper. The second is Bobby Moore. England did well without Moore against Austria, but Wednesday's match will be a vastly different affair.

Much as I have praised the talents of Colin Todd in the past, I would write the name of Moore on my team sheet before anybody else because he has been around and because he knows how to play and keep his head when the stakes are high. Wednesday night is not a night for virgins.

England made the Poles look good in Katowice simply because they were not prepared to take them on. Most of the spectators praised the skills of Lubanski, who scored that second goal which finished England. In fact, Bobby Moore, in one of his rare moments, offered him the goal like a birthday present.

Granted, Lubanski placed it well, but none of the Polish players has played in anything like the company we enjoy watching every week—the English First Division. They wouldn't last five minutes at Elland Road or Anfield.

I talk as a football manager—I am never concerned about individual players on the opposing side.

I wouldn't be concerned if Poland were playing Pele at his peak. What matters is the overall strength of the side. If there were 11 Peles, we'd have reason to be worried. But, man for man, any England team with the emphasis on attack ought to be all over the Poles on Wednesday.

I believe this match is so important to us that, provided Alf picks the right team, there is no way England can fail to qualify. No matter how many goals they would have needed to win through to the last 16 at Munich, I would still put my 50p on England.

If they don't, I'm afraid it will be the end of the road for Alf. I don't see how he could continue to manage an England team which failed to find a place in soccer's number one pageant, the World Cup.

19

20–26 October 1973

Muhammad Ali, formerly Cassius Clay, steps back into the boxing ring this week against the Dutch heavyweight Rudi Lubbers, a fight you can see live on *World of Sport* on Saturday via satellite from Jakarta in Indonesia. Brian Clough, never at a loss with advice, assesses the former world champion, and sends him this message …

CARRY ON FIGHTING, ALI … WE CAN'T DO WITHOUT YOU

I know, as a football manager, how success brings no relief from pressures and problems; and when you're at the top there's only one way you can go – down.

Nothing else pleases the knockers more than to see the big boy dumped on his backside. And that's the way it is with Muhammad Ali.

He has had 25 fights since he won the heavyweight championship in 1963 – that is an average of one fight every four months, if you don't count the three years when he was forbidden to enter the ring because he refused to join the US Army. And as those dancing legs start to pedal a fraction slower than they used to, people are saying he is finished, over the hill, ought to pack it in and get himself a chat show on television.

I couldn't disagree more. Boxing is at such a low ebb at the moment that in my opinion the sport can't do without Ali. My message to him is, 'Keep on fighting. Carry on until you can't give us one ounce more pleasure.'

Anybody who plays sport at any level shouldn't pack it in until they've exhausted their capabilities, because I think it is essential to play as many times, to box as many times, to try as many times as you possibly can.

When you retire, you're retired an awful long time. The average retiring age for a sportsman, depending on what sport he is in, is around 33. That is half a man's lifetime and he has still a long way to go.

Why people want to retire I will never know, because the alternative to playing is what I'm doing, and that isn't an alternative … it's purgatory.

There is a dividing line, of course. There is also something pathetic about a champ or great performer in any field having fallen past his peak and being on the verge of ridicule. This is much more likely to happen in an individual sport, like boxing or tennis, than in a team game like soccer.

Muhammad Ali wins or loses on his own, with nobody around him to cover for him. When he does decide to call it a day, it is going to be the hardest decision he'll ever make in his life.

I think Ali will carry on until he has had one more crack at Joe Frazier, and one more crack for the world title. Then I don't think he'll go near a gymnasium again. He'll never want to go and see fights again.

I believe he has done a lot of his fighting purely for the money; he has gone into the ring when he didn't really have to fight at all, and I'd put this week's fight against Rudi Lubbers in that bracket. Joe Bugner lumbered to a points win over Lubbers in January and the Dutchman just isn't in the same class as Ali.

You've got to admire a bloke like Ali, who isn't one of these boxers who sit on their last purse and only get up to fight when the time limit for retaining their titles is running out. He has taken on anybody who'd fight him; he hasn't ducked anything, and that takes courage.

It is the same sort of courage he showed when he made a stand about not going into the forces. I think that was remarkable. He could have gone into the army quietly and never seen the butt of a rifle, let alone Vietnam. He would have been given some gentle job back home and the whole business would have been forgotten.

But he stuck to his principles to the point where he was prepared to go to jail rather than into the army. I think his motives were good – and if more people had done the same thing, the Vietnam War would have been over a lot quicker.

Any war is bad. I don't think anything throughout history has been solved by people dropping bombs on each other. All war brings only misery, death, poverty and famine, and it takes people like Muhammad Ali to fight that small bunch of politicians and generals who cause all this bloodshed.

It is a contradiction, really, that a man who makes money knocking the hell out of somebody should be prepared to go to jail in the cause of peace. But I don't see boxing as a vicious, cruel sport, and Muhammad Ali has shown many times that he is not interested in the killer punch. Two years ago he deliberately spared Buster Mathis, who staggered through a last round like a lump of jelly; one punch would have flattened him.

Boxing, of course, can be dangerous, but I don't believe it is any more so than other sports. In soccer, you'd be surprised how many players of 30 and 35 end up with their knees and ankles swollen by crippling arthritis.

And what sport can demand more courage of a man than motor racing, where it is not your fists against somebody else's, it is *you* against a machine? I don't know how a racing driver can climb into a car before a race. He is the one who's punch-drunk, not the boxer.

Ali has made as many fans with his mouth as he has with his fists. I think he is a very underestimated man in this respect, and this applies to everybody who talks a lot. People tend to say, 'Oh, can't he talk!' But they never listen to *what* he says. Through all his boasting and drum-banging, he has come up with some beautiful lines on politics, on violence and on the state of the world.

But, above all, he has brought art to a sport lacking in finesse. Boxing, without Muhammad Ali, is like a cake without the icing.

❋ ❋ ❋ ❋

'I'm Muhammad Ali, the world know[s] who I am; they know I'm confident; they know I talk. But there's some fella in London,

England, named some Brian [Ali scratches his head as he acts out a struggle to recollect the name] – erm, Brian Clough. Some soccer player or something. Anyway, I heard all the way in America, I heard all the way in Indonesia that this fella talks too much. They say he's another Muhammad Ali – there's just one Muhammad Ali. And I want you [to know], whoever you are … you're not a fighter, and you don't take my job. I'm the talker. Now Clough, I've had enough. Stop it!'

On Sunday, 21 October 1973, when Clough joined his fellow Brian, Moore, on ITV's football highlights show, *The Big Match*, fully expecting to pass comment on the action from one of the previous day's games, his host had a little surprise in store for him: a jovial Moore introduced a recorded video message from a 'special guest' who had 'something to say to all *Big Match* viewers, and to one contributor in particular'. The 'guest' was Muhammad Ali; the 'contributor', Brian Clough.

The former world heavyweight boxing champion and the now ex-Derby County manager had much in common and, in many ways, as highly charismatic, candid and controversial figures who created extremes of opinion with no in-betweens, the two were kindred spirits. As with Clough, many of the epithets attached to Ali over the years had less to do with his sporting prowess than his linguistic athleticism, and were seldom complimentary; the Louisville Lip, Blabbermouth, Ali the Arrogant just three of the numerous labels.

Stripped of his world title in 1967 and subsequently denied a boxing licence due to his refusal to be drafted to army service, Ali returned to the ring three and a half years later but, after beating Jerry Quarry in Atlanta and Oscar Bonavena in New York, suffered a first-ever professional defeat, knocked down by Joe Frazier in the 15th and final round of what was nicknamed 'The Fight of the Century' at Madison Square Garden on 8 March 1971 and losing a punishing bout on a unanimous decision. It marked the end of Ali's 31-fight unbeaten record.

The following year, though informing the world that boxing 'is no longer an important part of my life' and he fought only to secure his children's future, after six fights and six wins (including one against Britain's Joe Bugner), Ali was once again the number-one contender for the world crown, only for his hopes to hit a shattering halt. On the eve of his fight on 31 March 1973, with 27-year-old world number seven Ken Norton, a characteristically confident Ali told *Radio Times*, 'He's so-o-o slow. He's big [6ft 3in] and strong, but I don't expect him to give me the trouble your Joe Bugner did. Joe's got fast legs.' Ali couldn't have been more wrong. In his hometown of San Diego, Norton, a tremendous puncher who'd KO'd 24 of his 31 opponents, broke Ali's jaw in the 11th round of 12, before taking the National American Boxing Federation title on a split decision. Ali had been beaten for only the second time in his career, but it was a painful defeat in every sense.

Nevertheless, after initially considering retirement, just six months later Ali faced the muscled ex-Marine Norton in a bitterly fought rematch in California. There, calling on all his pride and courage, Ali proved he was by no means a has-been, snatching a controversial split verdict in a thrilling 12-round battle that had seen some furious exchanges. At 31, though, no longer the superathlete of yesteryear, time was visibly running out for him. Just how long he could go on producing such monumental efforts remained to be seen. Even so, the ambition to regain his title was as keen as ever.

Against Lubbers, watched by a crowd of 35,000, Ali dished out a lot of punishment, yet whilst victorious on a unanimous decision his failure to nail his man raised serious doubts about his chances of being able to beat George Foreman, now the undisputed champion after dethroning Frazier in a brutal fight lasting only two rounds in January of that year. If anything, the Lubbers fight was most notable for the interview Ali gave to Reg Gutteridge during the interval between rounds, the ITV man leaning through the ropes of the ring to gain what is believed to be the only interview of its kind.

As Ali was facing up to the Dutchman, Brian Clough was coming to the end of a week in which he had, as Roger Hermiston put it in *Clough and Revie: The Rivals Who Changed the Face of*

English Football, 'just packed more turmoil and controversy into seven days than most football managers would fit into a lifetime'. After the bitter departure from the Baseball Ground of he and Taylor on Tuesday, then the storm over his comments about a certain Polish goalkeeper on the Wednesday evening, on Thursday Clough had taken himself off to see Mike Yarwood at Talk of the Midlands in Derby. Yarwood, Clough's principal impersonator, had once dubbed the verbose manager 'The Great Chatsby', and Clough, a serious man but one capable of laughing at himself, was a big fan.

The night after failing to be amused by a 'clown', some light relief was most welcome. But on the Saturday, Clough was in defiant and combative mode once more. Throughout the footage of Ali delivering his calling out, the studio camera cut back several times to a giggling Clough clearly enjoying the fact that his reputation had reached as far as across the Atlantic. 'Well, are you going to stop it?' Moore asked the beaming Clough when it ended. 'No, I want to fight him,' came the tongue-in-cheek but typically rebellious reply. It wasn't Ali that Clough was really in a mood for trading punches with, though. Ali may have jested he'd had enough of Clough's chatter, but Sam Longson wasn't kidding. And Clough wasn't quite ready to be silenced yet. Far from it.

The day before, the 14th Dalai Lama, the spiritual leader of Tibetan Buddhists, arrived in Britain for the start of a ten-day tour, the 38-year-old speaking of the need to have compassion and of his admiration for, amongst others, Chairman Mao, having 'developed respect for my former enemies'. Clough had no such feelings for Longson. That afternoon, while ITV showed exclusive live coverage of Ali continuing his comeback trail towards another title shot, Clough made an extraordinary comeback of his own.

Minutes before the kick-off of Derby's home game with Leicester City, Clough appeared inside the Baseball Ground, striding into the directors' box and sitting just a few seats away from Longson. Resounding applause broke out, which Clough, standing up, milked for several minutes. Longson responded by flinging his arms aloft as though the acclaim had been for him rather than Clough, but he was misguided. Fans had made it very clear where their loyalties lay. A large crowd had demonstrated outside, with banners – 'Clough In, Directors Out' and 'Clough is King' – demanding their former ruler be restored to his throne. Chants of protest had continued inside.

In an uneasy atmosphere, Derby won the match 2-1, John McGovern heading a second-half winner, but Clough hadn't been there to see it. Shortly after the kick-off, he'd made his exit from the ground, and though pursued by a waiting press pack he had briskly outpaced them all before reaching his chauffeur-driven Rolls Royce and being whisked home. But his day's adventures and travels weren't over yet. There was still a 130-mile journey to make from Derby to London, accompanied by his wife Barbara and Peter Taylor. That evening, straight after *Match of the Day* had featured highlights of the action (both on and off the pitch) at the Baseball Ground, Clough appeared on Michael Parkinson's chat show.

In an engaging, honest conversation with the blunt Yorkshireman, Clough, the forthright north-easterner, true to form, offered an opinion on every topic broached: his parents, Football League secretary Alan Hardaker, the hierarchy at the Baseball Ground – if Clough was to return 'the people who run Derby would have to be replaced with people of integrity'– hooliganism, and even what made him laugh.

When his host bemoaned the unhealthy 'hysteria' that had developed in the wake of both Clough's dismissal and England's World Cup exit – one newspaper the day after the Poland game had headlined its front page with, 'End of the World' – Clough countered that hysteria was perhaps the wrong word, but football after all was, he said, an 'outlet' for enjoyment, relaxation, as well as frustration, and 'life at the moment – and life always has been – it's not a bed of roses for anybody'.

The previous seven days certainly hadn't been for Clough. Yet throughout his appearance he gave no impression whatsoever of any trauma endured. There was positively nothing hysterical or unhealthy about him. Dressed in an immaculate light-grey suit with matching lilac shirt and tie, Clough was articulate, passionate and witty, and seemed perfectly at home in the environment of a television studio with a vast captivated audience to play to.

In December 1971, six months after his defeat by Joe Frazier, Ali had been similarly at ease when he'd first appeared on the BBC TV programme. Many viewers consider the boxer on his *Parkinson* debut – he went on to appear four times in total – as the greatest chat show guest British television has ever seen. Then, besuited in powder blue, the youthful, handsome Ali charmed his host, those watching at the Mayfair Theatre and millions of TV viewers with his fierce intelligence, comic timing and verbal dexterity. At one point towards the end of their hour-long talk (most of it coming from the boxer's mouth), Ali recited from memory his own epic, clever and extremely humorous rhyming poem predicting just what would happen the next time he met Frazier. It received loud and cheerful appreciation from the audience and had Parkinson wiping away a tear or two of laughter.

That next time wasn't actually until over two years later on 28 January 1974, when Ali, keeping out of trouble and denying Frazier any decisive blow for much of the 12-round bout, gained revenge for the first encounter loss, receiving a unanimous points verdict from the judges. Watching that night at Madison Square Garden, one of the most famous arenas on earth and in those days *the* boxing venue, had been a fully paid-up member of the Ali Fan Club, there to witness a man he believed could legitimately be called a genius.

Ever since 1963 when Ali, then called Cassius Clay, had been sent sprawling to the canvas by Our 'Enry (Cooper) in a fight at Wembley Stadium, the British had enjoyed a special relationship with the Kentucky-born boxer. Many a footballer, in particular, hailed the prizefighter as his hero. In the 'Focus On' feature in the weekly magazine *Shoot!*, when asked the question, 'Which person in the world would you most like to meet?', the majority of players gave the same reply: Muhammad Ali. Had he been asked, Clough might well have named the boxer, too. If so, on that January in the Big Apple, he got his wish.

Before Clough visited New York – jetting off with his club, Brighton, in a relegation scrap and on the eve of a match at

Cambridge United – there'd been a suggestion he might pen a piece about the fight or, more to the point, about a post-fight 'The Greatest meeting The Greatest' stunt for the *Daily Mail* (who were funding Clough's flight), but it came to nothing. He went there chiefly to enjoy a sporting spectacle. Clough had never seen a big fight at close quarters before and it proved to be a hugely visceral experience – 'the force of it all, the power with which two big men struck each other' – that left a deep impression.

The next day, at one of Ali's press conferences close to the ring where he'd battled the night before, Clough introduced himself, only for the boxer, his bruised face puffed and sore, to declare he had no idea who Clough was. But far from having his ego dented by Ali's puzzlement, Clough merely felt completely overawed by the entire event. 'It was like a king meeting a beggar,' Clough recollected in his autobiography. The two chatted, Clough explaining what he did for a living and Ali informing him rather flatteringly that, 'Football managers are grey men. You ain't old enough to be a manager – you should still be a player,' but Clough simply couldn't get over the aura of the man – his immense physical size, his engaging and polite manner. 'By the time we finished the chat and he said, "So long and thanks very much," the sweat was trickling down my back and I was shaking,' Clough said. 'I was supposed to be famous, good at what I did, a bit of a public figure, recognised almost wherever I went back home in Britain. In the presence of Ali, I was nobody, and rightly so.'

Peter Taylor, in his own book, *With Clough By Taylor*, delivers another version (presumably related to Taylor by Clough): 'He met Ali who taunted, "Hey, you a football player in England? You wouldn't last two minutes over here. You're too small" – which only goes to show that the champ had never heard of soccer. He thought the only kind of football was gridiron which, of course, is played by giants.' Regardless of which version was most truthful, and despite the two 'meeting' again (Clough in the audience when Ali, in a much angrier mode, appeared on Parkinson's late-night show for a third time, lost his temper with the host, and Clough put up his hand offering to 'referee' between the two), it was this first encounter that lingered most vividly in the memory of the Middlesbrough motormouth.

Ali didn't just have one more crack at Frazier but two, also winning 'The Thriller in Manila' on 1 October 1975 on a technical knockout after dumping 'Smokin' Joe' to the floor in the 14th round. By that time, Ali was on top of the boxing world once more, having, aged 32, defied all the odds to outwit and outfight defending champion George Foreman in 'The Rumble in the Jungle' on 30 October 1974, thus becoming only the second man to regain the heavyweight title. A fearsome fighting machine – his trainer called him, 'a monster' – Foreman was considered invincible. But Ali, regarded as a faded force, a shadow of the mercurial youngster who shocked the world a decade earlier, defied the passage of time, taunting the champion with his famous 'rope-a-dope' policy before flooring Foreman with a left-right combination in the eighth.

From the moment he first became world heavyweight boxing champion at the age of 22 years and 39 days, Ali had confounded his critics. He'd done it once more. And would do it again. After beating Foreman, Ali continued fighting for another seven years, during which time he lost his crown to and then regained it from Leon Spinks, making him the first heavyweight to win the belt three times.

In Clough's later view, Ali 'committed the cardinal sin of staying in boxing too long, taking one or two fights too many'. Maybe so, but the fighter still regarded by many as the greatest of all pugilists, was the man that, as he confessed in his autobiography, Clough would have loved to have been – 'that big, that quick, that fit, that talented, that famous'. For all their obvious differences, they did possess many mutual qualities. Ali dubbed himself 'the people's champion' and Clough might well have done likewise. Indeed, one of Clough's Nottingham Forest players Martin O'Neill would one day say of him that, 'He [Clough] was England's version of Muhammad Ali; a more charismatic man you could not meet.'

Over the years following his 1973 column, Clough, too, would experience what it was like to be completely written off. But, as with Ali, he would ride the punches, come back from the ropes, and carry on fighting, determined to defy the detractors time and time again. And also like the heavyweight boxer, that man with whom he shared a remorseless will to win, Clough, the Ali of the Midlands, would prove just what a champion he really was.

CLOUGH SOUNDS OFF Muhammad Ali, formerly Cassius Clay, steps back into the boxing ring this week against the Dutch heavyweight Rudi Lubbers, a fight you can see live on *World of Sport* on Saturday via satellite from Jakarta in Indonesia. Brian Clough, never at a loss with advice, assesses the former World Champion, and sends him this message . . .

CARRY ON FIGHTING ALI...
WE CAN'T DO WITHOUT YOU

I KNOW, as a football manager, how success brings no relief from pressures and problems; and when you're at the top there's only one way you can go—down.

Nothing else pleases the knockers more than to see the big boy dumped on his backside. And that's the way it is with Muhammad Ali.

He has had 25 fights since he won the Heavyweight Championship in 1963—that is an average of one fight every four months, if you don't count the three years when he was forbidden to enter the ring because he refused to join the U.S. Army. And as those dancing legs start to pedal a fraction slower than they used to, people are saying he is finished, over the hill, ought to pack it in and get himself a chat-show on television.

I couldn't disagree more. Boxing is at such a low ebb at the moment that in my opinion the sport can't do without Ali. My message to him is: "Keep on fighting. Carry on until you can't give us one ounce more pleasure.

Anybody who plays sport at any level shouldn't pack it in until they've exhausted their capabilities, because I think it is essential to play as many times, to box as many times, to try as many times as you possibly can.

When you retire, you're retired an awful long time. The average retiring age for a sportsman, depending on what sport he is in, is around 33. That is half a man's lifetime and he has still got a long way to go.

Why people want to retire I will never know, because the alternative to playing is what I'm doing, and that isn't an alternative . . . it's purgatory.

There is a dividing line, of course. There is also something pathetic about a champion or great performer in any field having fallen past his peak and being on the verge of ridicule. This is much more

likely to happen in an individual sport, like boxing or tennis, than in a team-game like soccer.

Muhammad Ali wins or loses on his own, with nobody around him to cover for him. When he does decide to call it a day it is going to be the hardest decision he'll ever make in his life.

I think Ali will carry on until he has had one more crack at Joe Frazier, and one more crack for the world title. Then I don't think he'll go near a gymnasium again. He'll never want to go and see fights again.

I believe he has done a lot of his fighting purely for the

money; he has gone into the ring when he didn't really have to fight at all, and I'd put this week's fight against Rudi Lubbers in that bracket. Joe Bugner lumbered to a points win over Lubbers in January and the Dutchman just isn't in the same class as Ali.

You've got to admire a bloke like Ali, who isn't one of these boxers who sit on their last purse and only get up to fight when the time limit for retaining their titles is running out. He has taken on anybody who'd fight him; he hasn't ducked anything, and that takes courage.

It is the same sort of courage he showed when he

KMP033103-3/31/73-SAN DIEGO, CALIF.: ALI-NORTON FIGHT
-Muhammad Ali bites his lip as he starts to leave the ring with one of his handlers who is near tears after Ali lost a 12-round non title bout by a split decision to Ken Norton of San Diego. It was reported Ali's jaw had been broken in the first round of the fight. It was Norton's 31st win against one loss in his pro career. (UPI) oas/gw

made a stand about not going into the forces. I think that was remarkable. He could have gone into the army quietly and never seen the butt of a rifle, let alone Vietnam. He would have been given some gentle job back home and the whole business would have been forgotten.

But he stuck to his principles to the point where he was prepared to go to jail rather than into the Army. I think his motives were good—and if more people had done the same thing, the Vietnam war would have been over a lot quicker.

Any war is bad. I don't think anything throughout

history has been solved by people dropping bombs on each other. All war brings only misery, death, poverty and famine and it takes people like Muhammad Ali to fight that small bunch of politicians and generals who cause all this bloodshed.

It is a contradiction, really, that a man who makes money knocking the hell out of somebody else should be prepared to go to jail in the cause of peace. But I don't see boxing as a vicious, cruel sport and Muhammad Ali has shown many times, that he is not interested in the killer-punch. Two years ago he deliberately spared Buster Mathis, who staggered through a last round like a lump of jelly; one punch would have flattened him.

Boxing, of course, can be dangerous, but I don't believe it is any more so than other sports. In soccer, you'd be surprised how many players of 30 and 35 end up with their knees and ankles swollen by crippling arthritis.

And what sport can demand more courage of a man than motor-racing, where it is not your fists against somebody else's: it is you against a machine? Knowing the dangers, I don't know how a racing-driver can climb into a car before a race. He is the one who's punch-drunk, not the boxer.

Ali has made as many fans with his mouth as he has with his fists. I think he is a very under-estimated man in this respect, and this applies to everybody who talks a lot.

People tend to say: "Oh, can't he talk?" But they never listen to *what* he says. Through all his boasting and drum-banging, he has come up with some beautiful lines on politics, on violence and on the state of the world.

But above all, he has brought art to a sport lacking in finesse. Boxing, without Muhammad Ali, is like a cake without the icing.

26

27 October–2 November 1973

With football gates still falling, much of the blame is put on the way the game is being played. The open, attacking game has been replaced by a boring, over-defensive spectacle. Brian Clough tells how the game can be given a much-needed shot in the arm – with the injection of a ballet dancer or two ...

WHY I'D LIKE TO SIGN NUREYEV

THERE were times when I considered making an offer for Rudolf Nureyev to join Derby County. I don't know how much I could have got him for, but the grace and poise of a man like Nureyev is, to me, what football should be all about.

I believe it is not a lack of goals or an emphasis on defensive soccer which has taken the spark out of the game in the last few years. It is the crying need to put beauty, art and creation back into the sport ... instead of the boring, computerised stuff we see these days.

A lot of people go on about changing the rules, as if there were a magic solution which would suddenly produce five goals a match and bring the crowds pouring back through the turnstiles.

My view is that any change of the rules would turn the game into an absolute farce. For instance, changing the offside rule so that you couldn't be offside between the goal line and the edge of the penalty area would, to my mind, be lunacy and I don't think it will ever be changed. Nobody's quite *that* daft in football.

Imagine that, one day, instead of eating a potato you were offered a little pill which contained the ingredients of a potato, and all you had to do was swallow it. Changing the rules of football would be like that.

You might as well scrub the game altogether and take a pill. I want to see the potato … I want to see it steaming, I want it scalding hot, I want it cold, I want it in its jacket, I want it roasted, I want to smell it, feel it, let it burn my tongue.

That is the way I want my football, and the rules don't dictate the way the game is played. The people in it do.

The only thing I will even listen to about changing the game is to split the season into, say, four parts and award an extra point or two to teams scoring a certain number of goals in each stage of the season. This would encourage teams to be interested, consistently, in playing positive football.

The game today has changed out of all recognition compared with the way it was played eight years ago when I was out there on the pitch.

It is more difficult to play attacking football because managers are close to perfecting sound defensive systems. Why? Because it is the easy thing to do. We have so much pressure in our jobs that we take the easy way out. We know that it is easier to get a no-score draw than to go out and win 5-0.

Today, clubs fear losing and this is why the game has deteriorated so much as entertainment. This is what I mean about playing Rudolf Nureyev. I think entertainment is watching gracefulness; a muscular, strong, athletically built man delivering perfection on the football field, something which, incidentally, hasn't been seen in the England side for years.

But it is seen at Derby. I pick players because I think they have this poise and quality … and I buy them accordingly.

I buy Colin Todd because I see a graceful athlete. I buy Roy McFarland because I see balance and pure skill. I buy David Nish because he carries his body like no other full-back in the country … ghosting effortlessly across the pitch.

When you play people like this, you are going to get goals anyway but, more than that, you are going to be entertained. Goals are essential – the cream on the trifle – but a game can be just as entertaining when a team wins 1-0 as it is when they stick six into the net.

Soccer is about incident, excitement, suspense, end to end; it doesn't matter how many goals are scored if a bloke can push his way out of the ground when it is all over and feel drained.

I am always preaching to my players that people are born with certain gifts. If you're religious, you can say God gave them to you. If you're not, you've simply acquired them; but, however they came about, I believe they are there to be shared.

If you have a special gift for talking or performing, you've got to give it to others. This is a cynical, cash-conscious world, but I am saying that anybody, player, manager or whatever, who puts money before a desire to share his skills is sick.

Normally, we have no time to think about this because we're so obsessed about making a good wage, we've got so many money people on our backs that we never say to ourselves 'I am going to go out there and enjoy giving people pleasure'.

There is one sure way to bring about this attitude to our game: to take a lead from the England side. The international side should be our North Star – and a few months ago we couldn't rustle up 25,000 fans to go and watch them play at Wembley.

I believe that Alf Ramsey *is* adapting now. He is beginning to pick more entertaining squads. He is doing it slowly and he is doing it too late, but it is happening, and the rest of football will reflect what he does.

He has got the fireworks show there ... he has got the bonfire built ... he has got the best Guy ever seen – but he hasn't struck the match since 1966. Alf can give us a lead – then it is up to every manager and player in the country to show us what they can do.

Exciting football doesn't come from a few clever strokes of the pen in the rule book ... it comes from the heart.

3–9 November 1973

Next Tuesday ITV brings you recorded highlights of one of the evening's European soccer ties. Here, Brian Clough looks at the differences in the game here and on the continent and says we've got one big lesson to learn – we've got to think big ...

WHY I WISH I'D TAKEN THAT JOB IN BARCELONA

WHAT do you think was the biggest clanger I and my partner at Derby for six and a half years, Peter Taylor, have dropped since we started in football management eight years ago? Making a mistake buying a player? Choosing the wrong team for a vital match? No. It was a decision we made three and a half years ago not to manage Barcelona. We were offered the job and turned it down because we wanted to finish what we had come to do at Derby.

Although we've had pleasure and success, and brought together one of the finest teams in Britain, the chance of being in charge of a club like Barcelona should have been irresistible.

We would have been operating under perfect conditions – in a sophisticated, professional set-up which makes almost any English league club look pathetic in comparison.

I don't want to discuss Derby here, but I believe some of our other clubs are too small-minded, too petty and too old-fashioned for their own good.

Too many people at the top – directors and chairmen – are small men with narrow minds, who treat the game as a hobby. They have as much knowledge of running an efficient and dynamic machine – which is what a football club is – as they have of running a sweet shop.

At Barcelona we would have had the stadium, the players, the money, and the backing of a really skilled board of directors.

I don't know whether Lord Stokes is as interested in soccer as he is in making motor cars, but he's an example of the sort of high-powered business mind I would like to see having a bigger hand in our clubs.

We've always had a very smug attitude towards running football clubs. It seems to me that the English, more than anybody, need about 100 years before they are prepared to accept that someone can do something better than them.

Thus, it may be a number of years yet before we can match some of the magnificently organised European clubs – like Barcelona – who have the courage and big thinking to pay an incredible £900,000 for Johan Cruyff. Or like Juventus of Turin, run by the giant Fiat car firm and with the same business spirit. Or like Real Madrid, where the stadium is used seven days a week, all day, because they encourage its use by sports outside soccer. If a lad turns up at Real's ground wanting to do a spot of sprinting, they'll supply a coach, look after him all the way and get him on their side. What do we say to the public? Stand up in the rain for 90 minutes, push off and come back for more in a fortnight.

We'll get round to it. Chelsea are planning this sort of organised European-style club now, and there's even talk of a multi-sport complex in Derby, to serve the East Midlands.

The boardroom isn't the only place where European and British clubs differ. There are sharp contrasts on the field, too. When you watch even the poorest Spanish and Italian sides in action, see how the players kill the ball dead, where an English player would need two attempts to get it under control. The have an inbuilt, basic skill because they play on bone-hard grounds, even when they're kids. They *have* to control the ball before they can do anything else with it, and the hot climate has meant that, over the years, they have learned to distil their movements on the field so that they need to use the minimum of effort, like a ballet dancer.

We were shocked into realising that skill was a basic part of football when the Hungarians came to Wembley 20 years ago and thrashed us 6-3. We should have learned our lesson then, but it has taken a long time for our game to evolve to absorb this new style. I think we are reaching a stage now when we have blended the European style with our own. I believe this gives us a lead as far as spectator enjoyment of the game is concerned. The top English clubs now play a beautiful fusion of the basic, tough British temperament – getting stuck in, if you like – and the refined, delicate ball-play of the Europeans.

The way we play soccer is now something we can be proud of. All we need is young, vital, courageous people in all our boardrooms. Then there won't be a country in the world to touch us.

* * * *

In *Cloughie: Walking on Water*, Clough contradicts the *TV Times* column, stating that it was actually he and Peter Taylor who were turned down by the Catalan club rather than the other way round. 'I had been interviewed for the job of Barcelona manager along the way. You don't turn down the chance of at least talking to a club of that magnitude if you've any sense,' Clough wrote. 'But I think I blew my chances when I was asked how I would respond to a situation in which more than 100,000 fans were waving white handkerchiefs in my direction. "I'd have learned enough Spanish to be able to tell them all to piss off," I said.' Despite Taylor's insistence to the Spaniards' hierarchy that Clough would have the Barça supporters 'waving flags and dancing the flamenco by the time he's finished', it can't have been any great shock when no offer of employment was forthcoming.

Whether or not Johan Cruyff would have still packed his bags and headed for Spain had the Clough-Taylor combo been in charge at the Camp Nou, one can only speculate. On 13 August 1973, Barcelona had emptied out their bank account to the sum of £922,300 to sign the Dutchman, a world record fee for the player dubbed 'the European Pelé' and regarded as the finest footballer on earth. Earlier that year, at the end of May, Cruyff was at the forefront of an Ajax side that claimed Europe's most coveted club trophy, the European Cup, for a third year running, beating

Juventus 1-0 in the Red Star Stadium, Belgrade. The Italians, of course, had overwhelmed Derby at the semi-final stage otherwise Cruyff would have encountered Clough that evening in Yugoslavia.

Only a month before the final, *TVTimes* had run a feature titled, 'How Ajax Cleans Up'. The pun was of its time. To the majority of British football fans, before they learned to pronounce it as 'Aiy-ax', Ajax shared a name with a brand of household cleaning products. Now, mispronunciations notwithstanding, the Dutch club were recognised as the undisputed masters of Europe. And many of those British followers, via their TV screens, had been fortunate enough to witness their dominance unfold. 'In the mid-50s, in the early days of European soccer, playing away was like the old Wild West, when a pass back to the goalkeeper in the San Siro Stadium was greeted with a screech of 60,000 garlic-scented whistles,' Jimmy Hill observed in the 30 December 1972 issue of *Radio Times*. 'Now, with hardly a week passing without European soccer on television, British fans are as wise to the skills of Johan Cruyff as they are to Joe Royle.' The skills of Johan Cruyff sparkled from the start.

Born within sight of Ajax's De Meer Stadion, where his mother worked as a cleaner, Cruyff, aged just seven, would watch the club teams of 10 to 12 year olds. 'One day they had a man short, and I was picked,' he recollected. 'After that, I always turned up with a suitcase and hoped for it to happen again.' At ten he was playing for the Ajax youth team, and his star rose rapidly. The youngster – whose father, a greengrocer with a spectator's passion for the game, died when Cruyff was 12 – soon worked his way up through the system. Having left school at 16 to sign on as a professional, within a year, in November 1964, at 17 Cruyff was making his first-team debut for the Amsterdam club, getting the consolation in a 3-1 defeat against GVAV. In his first full league season, he was top Dutch scorer with 33 goals. It took less than 20 months before he was earning his first international cap for Holland, in a European Championship qualifier versus Hungary, netting once more in a 2-2 draw in Rotterdam. And though he gained an unwanted place in the history books in only his second game for his country – becoming the first Dutch international to be sent off, in a friendly against Czechoslovakia on 6 November 1966 – Cruyff was already being recognised as one of the hottest prospects on the continent.

It was in the following month that English fans got their first glimpse of his audacious gifts, too. On a fog-bound night in Amsterdam, in the first leg of a European Cup second-round tie, the 19-year-old scored one of five goals as Ajax, 'the white-shirted Dutchmen flitting like ghosts through the mist and through the defence of Liverpool' as one reporter described them, shocked Bill Shankly's side 5-1. Seven days later, at Anfield, Cruyff found the back of the net twice as Ajax drew 2-2 to go through 7-3 on aggregate.

From the outset, Cruyff was utterly single-minded. 'At 18, I did things my way,' he said. 'I felt like a professional. I was living like a professional, but the club was like an amateur.' It didn't take long before Ajax caught up. Offering long and generous contracts, they cultivated a young professional force, and reaped the dividends. Diamonds like Wim Suurbier, Barry Hulshoff, Ruud Krol and Arie Haan were all unearthed from the youth ranks. Johan Neeskens was plucked from RCH Heemstede. Piet Keizer, a skilful left-winger, there since 1961, emerged as one of the great talents of Dutch football. Between 1965/66 and 1972/73 Ajax won six Dutch league championships, as well as the Dutch Cup on four occasions.

Much of that success was down to the coaching of Rinus Michels. In charge from January 1965, replacing Vic Buckingham, the Englishman who had first spotted Cruyff, Michels built on a foundation that Buckingham had laid, developing the 'system' of Total Football – more a state of mind than a tactical approach – whereby all the outfield players in the team, in Cruyff's words, 'knew what to do – with or without the ball – whatever the situation'. Equally comfortable in possession and capable of switching to any position on the pitch, they played 'as individuals but within a team framework'.

Ajax couldn't have been further from the rigid structure most sides operated; deploying instead an inventive, intelligent, free-flowing formation that made their players extremely difficult to man-mark. Relegation candidates when Michels took over, the club were transformed by this footballing revolution, welded into a near-perfect soccer unit. Inevitably, Cruyff, with his inbuilt leadership and outstanding vision, was pivotal to it all.

In 1971, a year in which his artistry earned him the title of European Footballer of the Year (he would also be chosen in 1973 and 1974), a first European Cup winners' medal also came Cruyff's way when Ajax, captained by Serbian Velibor Vasović, overcame Greek champions Panathinaikos 2-0 at Wembley. Beaten 4-1 by AC Milan in the 1969 final, the following season Ajax had had to suffer fierce rivals Feyenoord becoming the first Dutch club to claim club football's biggest prize, 2-1 victors over Celtic. But this now was their time. It was a final refereed by Wolverhampton's Jack Taylor, a man who would later play a small but significant part in Cruyff's career path. Though Michels departed shortly after, Barça-bound, declaring, 'I have achieved everything that I could – it is impossible to do better,' Romanian Ştefan Kovács continued and expanded on the Total Football philosophy.

If anything, Ajax became an even more potent force. In 1972, as Cruyff scored his 250th goal in senior football, he and his teammates not only claimed a domestic league and cup double, they also swept aside Argentina's Independiente 4-1 on aggregate in the two-leg Intercontinental Cup – Cruyff netting in the sixth minute of the 1-1 first leg before being injured by an outrageous tackle from forward Mircoli – as well as retaining the European Cup. The holders' opponents in Europe's glamour club clash were Inter Milan, who'd knocked out Celtic on penalties in their semi-final. Winners of the tournament in 1964 and 1965, the Italians were renowned for their defensive sturdiness, but on 31 May 1972, in Feyenoord's De Kuip Stadium, not even the most desperate rearguard action could halt a rampant Ajax. In a game described as great propaganda for attacking football, the night belonged to the dashing Dutchmen and, in particular, Cruyff, whose two second-half goals won him the man of the match accolade and his side, now captained by Cruyff's firm friend Keizer, a second successive success in the world's most important club tournament.

At one time an out-and-out frontman, Cruyff now occupied a new role, striking from deep and creating as many chances as he took. 'Most of the time I do things that I feel should be done,' Cruyff explained. Utilising one of his greatest assets, his speed, the Dutchman would take the ball up to a man, look as if he was strolling, then suddenly burst past him with incredible acceleration and ball control, leaving his marker tackling a shadow. Whippet-thin but exceedingly strong, with a natural ability to wrong-foot every opponent, Cruyff was almost unstoppable at times.

At the end of the 1972/73 season, as Ajax, now under coach George Knobel, headed for that hat-trick of European Cup wins, Cruyff, at 26, captain of club and country, was nearing his zenith. Another year on, and he would prove that what he could do at club level, he could replicate in the international team. But by the time of the World Cup finals in West Germany, Cruyff was no longer sporting the famous white shirt with the broad red stripe down the centre and, on the back, the number 14 he'd made his own.

In their path to the final, Ajax had scored 14 goals against the champions of Bulgaria (CSKA Sofia), West Germany (Bayern Munich) and Spain (Real Madrid – themselves six times winners of the trophy). However, the 1-0 victory over their Italian opponents in Belgrade – secured by an early looping header from another rising Dutch wonder kid, Johnny Rep – was to prove the pinnacle of that great side's achievement. Furious when, in a ballot organised by Knobel to select a captain for the coming season, his teammates opted for Keizer, Cruyff decided to leave the club, eventually linking up again with Michels in Spain, where together they would inspire Barcelona to a first national title since 1960. Johan Neeskens would join him the season after. More of Ajax's world superstars would follow in exiting the Amsterdam club, and unsurprisingly it marked the end of a golden era. It would be 22 years before Ajax became European champions for a fourth time.

Cruyff, hailed as 'El Salvador' ('the saviour') by the Catalan public, would stay with the Spaniards for five seasons. Many years later, reflecting upon his career, he said that if he had one regret it was that the opportunity to play for an English club never arrived.

His experience of a cold winter night at Anfield in 1966 – the sheer goosebumps-inducing passion of the home fans – had left a lasting impression. It was something he himself would have liked to savour regularly.

Brian Clough, in November 1973, was also expressing regrets. He wished he'd taken the job with the Spanish giants four years earlier. There were more regrets yet to come. By the time his *TVTimes* column went to print, Clough had signed up to take charge of another club beginning with B – one a whole world away from the noise, passion and partisanship of La Liga – and, though he didn't readily admit it, was very quickly wishing he hadn't.

10–16 November 1973

Brian Clough has never been afraid to speak his mind, so now, as a weekly contributor to ITV's *On the Ball*, what are the thoughts of pundit Clough on the perfect world of television? Here he fires off a few rounds at TV soccer coverage …

I'D LOVE TO SEE A SOCCER RIOT IN THE STUDIO

I was down in London to record my bit for *On the Ball* recently and Brian Moore and I were having a quiet beer before going in front of the cameras.

I said to Brian, 'One day, just as you're about to begin your match commentary, I'd love some nutcase to come along and kick your microphone away. Or when somebody has scored a goal, I would love your slow-motion machine to break down, leaving you to describe the goal all over again, without a picture to refer to. Or just as you're saying how well Arsenal are playing, wouldn't it be interesting if one of the other side's supporters got into your commentary box, grabbed the mic and told everybody how you were talking a load of rubbish?'

I've been working regularly for ITV now for three months and apart from the tedious journeys up and down the motorway every week, and having my face powdered once every ten minutes, I'm enjoying it immensely.

But this is the point I was making to Brian Moore: compared with being involved in a football club, either as a player or as a manager, compared with the sweat and the toil and the sleepless nights, working on television is like having a holiday in heaven. It's all so easy. Everyone is convinced that they are right.

With a few exceptions I have had to record my slot for *On the Ball* a couple of days beforehand. I must say I prefer the occasions when I've done it live. When I'm recording, I sit there in the studios with a good lunch inside me talking my way through some film of Günter Netzer. I sit back and start talking, and if it's not right we do it again. And if it's not right we do it again, and again. I make mistakes, but they are never seen, they're disqualified with one quick flick of a finger.

In contrast, the 22 blokes out there on the pitch are really up against it. They make their mistakes in front of up to 50,000 people and they can't go back and say, 'Sorry, I'll kick that again'. When Derby County let in two late goals against Sunderland in the League Cup last month*, I couldn't say to the players, 'Never mind, let's have another go. We'll get it right this time and they won't score.'

These TV people are skilled, they work hard, and they know their stuff, but they don't know they're born. And the danger is that that they can devote so much attention to making it all nice and smooth and flaw-free that they can fall into the trap of making football look easy, too. I've seen myself do it already and I'm trying my best to keep a check on it.

What we must do when we are showing soccer on television is to inform the public just what is going on, and just how difficult a game it is to play. Suppose we're talking about an attacker who has just banged the ball over the bar from three yards. The first thing you're bound to say is, 'How the hell did he miss that? What a bloomer!' What I want to get across is why he missed it. And nine times out of ten it's because it was an almost impossible shot to reach because the player had four defenders about to slice him in half and had his back to the goal.

Or if we're watching a film clip of some brilliant play – say a defender whipping the ball away from Martin Chivers's toes – I want the viewer to know that he isn't simply watching competent play – he's watching a genius at work.

I'm very seldom nervous on television, but one of the few things I do feel uncomfortable about is having to sit down in a bare studio to talk to this one-eyed god in the corner … the camera. I would prefer to stand up, walk about, never mind if you see a few cables or stray television cameras hanging around. It's not a beauty show is it? But the technical boys in the studios say it's not practical – they can't cope with me standing up. I wonder what they'd do if they had to deal with 11 snarling blokes on the football pitch?

They want it to look just right because they want television to look so smooth and simple. But let's not make the game look like the same well-oiled machine. That's my job – to try to bring in a bit of truth.

* On 8 October, in their League Cup second-round tie, Derby, with Clough still in charge, were held 2-2 at the Baseball Ground by FA Cup holders Sunderland. The replay at Roker Park three weeks later ended 1-1 before Derby (now with Dave Mackay at the helm) suffered a Halloween nightmare two days later, losing the second replay, again at Roker Park, 3-0 to the Second Division outfit from Wearside.

❉ ❉ ❉ ❉

Motorway journeys and face-powdering aside, Clough approached his career as a television performer with the same energy, enthusiasm and expertise that he brought to football management. *On the Ball* host Brian Moore found his Saturday lunchtime companion 'a stimulating man to work with' and admitted that Clough's work on ITV had 'amazed me by the consistently high quality and its superb professionalism'. Dissatisfied with a recorded piece, Clough would always insist on trying again – enlisting the help of industry professionals to make an improvement.

Moore, the Kent-born Gillingham fan, had joined BBC Radio in 1961 and commentated on the 1966 World Cup Final before, two years later, moving into television, recruited by Jimmy Hill, then head of sport at LWT. From August 1968, as well as presenting and commentating on the Sunday highlights programme, *The Big Match*, Moore had hosted *On the Ball*, with the ex-Fulham player, Hill, appearing alongside him in the studio as a ground-breaking analyst.

In March 1973 Hill, two months before the channel switch that opened the door for Clough to indirectly move in the opposite direction – Hill signing a contract with the BBC to front its Saturday evening highlights programme, *Match of the Day* – found himself forced to defend his TV role in a *Radio Times* article. Another Jimmy, Greaves, himself later to bring his own big personality into broadcasting, forming a successful combination with Ian St John on *Saint and Greavsie* from 1985 to 1992, had retired at the end of the 1970/71 campaign, the forward admitting that, in his last season with West Ham, he wasn't enjoying the game, so got out. That enjoyment was ruined by the increasing physical demands on the best modern players, the glut of fixtures meaning that 'they're playing too much soccer'. Another added strain, though, was bearing down on the top professionals: over-exposure on television.

'Too much is talked about football away from the game,' claimed Greaves. The pressure came from 'all the ballyhoo which surrounds the sport'. The likes of Hill, Greaves thought, should carry the can. 'Ten years ago, if a player had a bad game, he could go home and forget it,' Greaves noted. 'Now he can't. He has it stuffed down his throat on Saturday night or Sunday afternoon and people like you [Hill] slow it down, analyse it, and show it again.'

Hill argued that he'd much rather present skill than repeat a game's less savoury incidents: 'I seldom put the heat on players in talking about their performance; players are praised nine times for each time they are criticised – and that only happens when they have been violent'. He disagreed that TV's highlighting of individual incidents had an adverse effect. Some film of Birmingham City's Bob Latchford missing a simple chance from two yards had been repeated. Latchford later scored in the same game, 'and as far as I know,' Hill said with some sarcasm, 'he didn't go home and put his head in the gas oven because we screened his mistake.'

Six years later, Hill, now the familiar face of *Match of the Day*, held to that position. In a November 1979 issue of *Match Weekly* magazine, he reiterated his feeling that slow-motion replays, first introduced in 1969, were only of benefit in getting to the 'truth' of an incident, and didn't believe the scrutiny of pundits was detrimental to a player's confidence. Hill certainly didn't set out to persecute individuals. 'It's when a particular kind of foul or form of misbehaviour is occurring so regularly that it shrieks out for strong comment in the interests of the game that I will speak up,' he insisted. The effect Hill's views had on any one player were inconsequential, he still believed; if it pointed the game in the right direction, it had to be worthwhile.

The game, in Clough's view, though, could move forward much better without television's guiding hand. Or rather, its scrutinising eye. In February 1974 claiming 'I would like to see TV commentators – including myself – on the dole,' Clough had proposed a six-month ban on televised soccer, simply to prove once and for all whether or not it affected attendances. He didn't believe it would. Nearing the end of the decade, however, with television coverage still a burning issue, Clough, now managing Nottingham Forest, was fanning the flames in a different direction.

In the same *Match Weekly* article, arguing for the prosecution, Clough expressed his certainty that the medium *was* having a harmful effect – it is 'slowly strangling football,' he wrote – and threatened the game's long-term future. He called for a complete blackout for a trial period of anything up to three years 'to see if it would have a favourable reaction'. He was now convinced that gates would go up as a consequence.

'Don't get me wrong, I enjoy football on television as well as the next man,' Clough asserted, confessing that, were he not so directly involved in the game as a manager, he'd fall into the same trap as many – 'Can you really blame a man for getting his feet up, pouring a glass of Newcastle Brown and sitting back to enjoy his football in comfort?' he said. But those that did so, he felt, were missing out on the live product, 'the excitement of a crowd, the sense of anticipation'.

Whilst foreseeing real trouble ahead unless some curb was placed on the amount of football shown, Clough's biggest bugbear was, like Greaves's, the manner of television's coverage: the way the game was portrayed, not the fact it was being portrayed. Action replays – a pet hate – 'analyse and, at times, crucify players,' Clough stated. 'One split-second error of judgement and it's beamed to millions of homes.' Referees, too, got a raw deal: 'They have to make decisions amid a flurry of sweaty bodies ... but if they are wrong, heaven help them.' Television, exposing players and officials to searching analysis 'doesn't seem to allow anybody to be human,' Clough complained. Forwards were slated for not hitting the target or goalkeepers for dropping a clanger as if they'd committed some criminal act.

Hill was astonished at Clough's attitude. 'For a straightforward, hard-shooting guy, I would have thought he'd have been in favour of establishing the truth, however much it hurts,' Hill countered. 'Unless I'm mistaken, it's that shattering honesty with players – whoever they are – that keeps Brian and Forest on top. Why, I ask, does he reveal it in the dressing room and his personal dealings with the press and not like it on the box?'

Broadcaster Michael Parkinson, who'd once written a regular sports column for the *Sunday Times*, was a stern critic of football but took an even dimmer view of its representation on TV. Reprinted in the Everton versus Ipswich Town match programme of 15 April 1978, a week before Nottingham Forest got the point they needed to guarantee the league title with four matches left to go, was an article originally published in, of all places, a school magazine, Shrewsbury's *Apocalypse*, in which the forthright chat show host maintained, 'If you ever go to a football match that *Match of the Day* are televising and then watch *Match of the Day* at night, there's no relation to what happened, absolutely not, it's cosmetic.

'If a game's boring, show it and say it's boring. If a player's bent on the pitch, if he's kicking people, pick him out and show him, don't gloss over it, because until you tell the truth about football you will not get people educated to appreciate what's good in it. What you see in television football in my view is just pap; it bears no relation at all to what the game is about.'

In *Cloughie: Walking on Water*, Clough echoed Parkinson's sentiments. 'I don't want anybody trying to tell me that it's any better than I can recognise with my own eyes,' he wrote. He hated what he saw as a constant preaching to viewers about what they should be seeing and thinking, especially as 'a lot of the time I'm watching something nowhere near as good as they want me to believe'. What the football highlights shows needed to find, as Clough, at his enigmatic and prickly best, told John Motson in a 1979 interview, was 'a happy line where it's entertainment, a little bit educational, a little bit instructional, and [they] get off everybody's back'.

Match of the Day was failing, in Clough's opinion. 'You and your colleagues are turning us off from family entertainment on a Saturday night by lecturing us at the moment,' Clough accused the BBC commentator. 'I think you're becoming too deep. I think you're setting yourselves up as judge and jury. I think you've gone over the dividing line where you have a contribution to make to one of being dogmatic, overbearing, boring, and you can keep going. I know it's difficult to justify a none-none, for example, or to bill it as "Match of the Day", but if that's what you get when you take your cameras to a ground then show the none-none. Don't try and justify it or pick things out and bore us all to tears with your lectures.'

Clough loathed the dissection of the game by so-called experts. Football wasn't a corpse requiring a weekly autopsy on the slabs of the press and TV. The pillorying of officials, in particular, was 'nothing short of criminal,' Clough said. If there was, say, a disallowed goal, an offside decision, a controversial incident, 'then surely our job is to report that as fairly as we can?' Motson defended. After all, weren't these topics for discussion? Didn't viewers need clarification? And, Motson put it to his interviewee, 'when you used to work for us, Brian, and in a panellist capacity, *you* used to talk about games and voice an opinion'. 'As a critic. Far more qualified than you, or any of your colleagues,' Clough retorted. 'Where we used to look forward to going home and sitting in an armchair watching a bit of football, being entertained,' he went on, 'we're not seeing as much football as we should, and we're getting too much of that [chat] – and I suggest you shut up and show more football.'

Clough's career as a tough-talking TV critic had undoubtedly been one of the more extravagant chapters of his footballing life story. The challenge, and the recognition it brought, thrilled him. At one time he seemed to need television as much as he needed football, and the two lives were inextricably bound. Michael Parkinson admitted that Clough fascinated him. 'He was opinionated, he was funny, he was irreverent, he was articulate, and he was bright, too,' Parkinson said. And, as such, 'he was absolutely made for television'.

Ultimately, though, as Clough later emphasised in his book, television was just a platform the manager had used to expound his views on the one thing he knew best and loved most of all: football. Talking about the sport was something he was really rather good at. But, when it came to the actual day-to-day involvement, the playing of the game, the coaching and the management of a club and its players, that, in the end, was where he truly excelled.

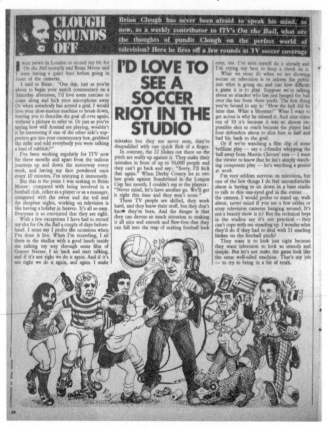

17–23 November 1973

What should England be doing now that their World Cup hopes are dashed? Not moaning about it, says Brian Clough. Among the 16 teams going to Munich is one which will need all the support we can give them …

SHOW THE WORLD
WE'RE STILL CHAMPS

ENGLAND are out of the World Cup. We've stopped crying, we've wiped our eyes now. But I'll still be going to Munich next June with a rosette pinned firmly on my lapel – a blue-and-white one.

After all the sadness and soul-searching we've gone through since that Wednesday night last month, we seem to have lost sight of the fact that we *have* got something to cheer for next year. Scotland!

They may have had the luck of the draw so far as the qualifying round was concerned, but the main thing is that they're there, and I think they possess all the ingredients to spring surprises when the competition begins. They might even get the chance to stick a few goals past the Poles, and that would warm any Englishman's heart.

At their best, Scotland have a blend of tenacity and skill which could unsettle the walkabout style of the South Americans and continentals. But only if the English help them.

We're knocked out and that's that. But many of the star players in the Scottish side, like Bremner, Lorimer and [Joe] Jordan of Leeds, [George] Graham and [Willie] Morgan of Manchester United, and [Colin] Stein and [Tommy] Hutchison of Coventry, play every week in England. One of the struggles Sir Alf Ramsey had was getting the England team together for regular training sessions, hoping against hope that, occasionally, clubs would put their country first and themselves second.

What we should do is say: Scotland now carries the flag for British football in Munich – let's bend over backwards to help them. We should release Scottish international players in the English league as often as manager Willie Ormond wants them and allow him to build and mould his squad in lengthy training sessions.

We should offer them everything: training facilities, practice games, all they want to get into shape. But will we do it? That's another matter. It needs big men in English soccer administration to agree, say, to cancel fixtures to help the Scots.

Scotland's record doesn't exactly make them favourites. They've blown hot and cold over the years. They reached the World Cup finals in 1954 and 1958, but they haven't been seen at the run-in since. In fact, Willie Ormond probably still has nightmares about 1954. He was a member of the Scottish side which went down 7-0 to Uruguay in Basle, and the Scottish press gave him such a roasting that it put him out of international football for five years.

'The gentle snowflake' they called him, which is about as big an insult as you can throw at a footballer.

In their last six matches, Scotland have won only once – and that was the vital match which pushed them through to Munich, when they beat the Czechs 2-1. But a couple of defeats didn't do them any harm. They gave England a scare or two in May when they went down 1-0 and Alf had to admit that they were 'the best Scots we've met'.

They are building up to Munich well. After last week's game against West Germany at Hampden Park, they play a return match against the World Cup favourites in March, then England can do them a good turn by giving them a hard game in the Home Internationals tournament in May.

I'd like to see them get through to the final and win. But if they get knocked out in the first round, it doesn't matter. The important thing is that we have someone out there, rubbing noses with the world's best.

* * * *

As Belgian referee Vital Loraux sounded his full-time whistle and the death knell on England's World Cup dreams on 17 October 1973, ITV commentator Hugh Johns described the national team's exit on the evening as 'one of the blackest days they've ever had'. In the immediate aftermath, a fog of despair and disbelief enveloped the nation's football followers. Just how the English game had gotten into such a hole and was now to climb its way out of it became an almost constant subject of some passionate debate.

'It is a football match, not a war. Let us keep our sense of perspective,' Football League secretary Alan Hardaker had said in a radio interview four days before Ramsey's side faced the Poles. 'Everybody is getting hysterical. If we do lose, the game is not going to die. It will be a terrible thing for six weeks and then everybody will forget about it.' Six weeks later, though, the gloom had barely lifted and no one had forgotten it. A forensic examination was still being undertaken. Inquests were being held. 'After that World Cup failure, what now for English football?' ran a headline in the 8 December issue of *Shoot!*

Hardaker had slightly changed his tune. 'Now I believe the way we lost will do nearly as much good as if we had won,' he told the magazine. 'And defeat could provide more advantages in reconstructing the game than victory.' England had no divine right to be at the World Cup finals, Hardaker stressed. Less talking was what was needed. 'People must stop blaming each other and concentrate on putting things right,' the curmudgeonly Yorkshireman said.

Reigning secretary since 1957, Hardaker, renowned for his autocratic rule – 'the great dictator' was one nickname; 'football's godfather', 'a cross between Cagney and Caligula', and 'the league's answer to Idi Amin' were others – had himself come under attack, his stubborn refusal to postpone top-flight fixtures in the lead-up to the match seen in certain quarters as a chief obstacle to England's progress. Jimmy Hill believed the powers-that-be should have helped Sir Alf Ramsey a lot more. All fixtures involving Poland's players had been postponed on the weekend before both the game in Katowice in June and prior to the Wembley clash. The England manager hadn't enjoyed the same luxury as his Polish counterpart.

How were players thrown together after only two or three days' training together expected to instantly gel? While it was understandable that fans thought first of their clubs and the national side second and that the football hierarchy inevitably gave preference to domestic competitions, Hill referenced the huge increase in league attendances in the season following England's 1966 triumph as the prime example of how international success could benefit the game at club level. 'They rose dramatically and interest in the game was never higher,' Hill argued.

Don Revie didn't think the picture was as black as was being painted. 'Why all this crying about English football being in the doldrums?' he asked. Yes, qualification would have boosted gates but the performance versus the Poles – a 'wonderful advertisement for our football,' the Leeds boss felt – was one of the best he'd seen by a national side, and rushing into drastic changes in our style of play wasn't necessary.

Even a Northern Irishman, Derek Dougan, didn't see too much wrong with the English game. In 'their most attacking display that I can remember in my entire career', England simply hadn't had the bounce of the ball against the Poles. 'Football – just like life itself – has an element of good luck,' Dougan reasoned. 'And Poland had all of it that was going on the night.'

Dougan only wished that Ramsey had had his team playing like that two or three years earlier. Following the Poland game, the England manager had refused to comment on his own future. In Revie's opinion, he deserved 'a massive vote of confidence' and he hoped Ramsey would remain in charge of the team 'until after the next World Cup at least'. But he was clearly living under the shadow of the axe.

A 1-0 defeat at Wembley on 14 November 1973 – Italy scoring their first-ever win in England when Fabio Capello netted the game's only goal in the 87th minute, steering the ball over the line after Peter Shilton had parried a shot from Chinaglia – only intensified the feeling that Ramsey was nearing the end. He and his team came under concerted attack in the press. 'L-Plate England' cried the *Daily Express*. 'Alf's final humiliation' blazed *The Sun*. 'Whole-hearted England are no match for Italian finesse' observed the *Daily Telegraph*. And though Ramsey still declined to discuss his future plans, Stan Seymour, a Newcastle director, wasn't in any doubt what they should be. 'It is time that he [Ramsey] handed over his job to Brian Clough,' Seymour stated in a *Daily Mail* interview.

The Wednesday had been declared a national holiday in the UK – not because of the football, but because earlier that afternoon the marriage of Princess Anne, the Queen's only daughter, and Captain Mark Phillips took place at Westminster Abbey. It just happened to be Prince Charles's 25th birthday, too. Later in the day, however, England's football players somewhat blighted the celebratory mood.

It was a familiar tale. England dominated the match for long periods but, despite peppering the Italian goal, lacked the killer instinct, unable to find a way through Italy's superbly organised defence. It was a game in which Bobby Moore equalled Billy Wright's record of captaining England 90 times. The friendly also marked the 108th and what would prove the final international appearance of arguably the greatest England defender of all time. In his previous international, Moore had skippered the side that lost 2-0 in Turin in a match to mark the Italian FA's 75th anniversary, meaning Moore's final two England appearances were against the same country – Italy – and both ended in defeats. After the Wembley match, Moore reckoned England couldn't really win regardless of the result. Had *they* scored three minutes from the end as Italy did, they would have been dismissed as lucky.

Three days later, Clough's *TV Times* column went to press. The likelihood of Sir Alf Ramsey pledging allegiance to a flag bearing Saint Andrew's cross or his heart being stirred by the strains of bagpipes was zero. 'I'd sooner anybody beat us than the bloody Scots' was a catchphrase attached to the England boss. 'Alf hated the Jocks,' according to Allan Clarke. That loathing even extended to him refusing to wear Paisley patterned pyjamas. No, there'd not be a hint of tartan on Ramsey's person the following summer, never mind a blue-and-white rosette pinned to his lapel.

The Scots could manage just fine without his support. West Germany was on the horizon and, despite a poor run of results, after a 1-1 draw against the World Cup hosts in Glasgow on the same night England were losing to Italy, there was every cause for optimism about the prospects for Willie Ormond's men at the finals in '74. Sir Alf might not be joining them but thousands of staunch Caledonians would be there, donned in Highland regalia, waving their Saltires and singing 'Flower Of Scotland' in the bona fide belief that their country's footballers could better the world's finest.

Meanwhile, the way ahead for English football remained uncertain. With the country in the midst of industrial and economic misery – the knock-on effect of war in the Middle East – and, the day before the Italy game, entering its fifth and final 'state of emergency' under the prime ministerial rule of Edward Heath, it was a bleak time all round. With a full-scale energy crisis looming, restrictions on the use of electricity and power cuts soon to be a feature of everyday life, no one was laughing except sellers of candles.

England had had setbacks before and overcome them. At the World Cup in Brazil in 1950 their all-star team was beaten by the almost unheard of United States side, 1-0. Three years later, the Hungarians led by Puskás the 'galloping major' humiliated them at Wembley by winning 6-3 – in Alf Ramsey's last international appearance – and then, in May 1954, 7-1 in Hungary. In 1958 they failed dismally at the World Cup finals in Sweden. But they'd bounced back to conquer the world in 1966. In Mexico in 1970 they'd been extremely unlucky. This latest disappointment was surely just that, not the end of the world. Yet it had hit the nation hard. Clough could urge the English to unite in their support for the Scots all he liked, but the hurt at their own failure to reach the tournament was still being felt deeply. It would be quite some time yet before they finally got over it.

24–30 November 1973

Football's most controversial manager, Brian Clough asks …

WHERE HAVE ALL THE GOALSCORERS GONE?

BACK in the 1927/28 season Dixie Dean, an Everton player, scored 82 goals. The year before, George Camsell of Middlesbrough stuck in 75.

Today, if a player scores half that number we regard him as a goal machine, a genius. British football these days is suffering a chronic shortage of that magic commodity, natural goalscorers – men who are born, not taught, to be prolific scorers.

I thought Ted MacDougall had that magic when he scored 46 goals for Bournemouth in the 1971/72 season, but since he moved to Manchester United and West Ham, he hasn't shown that innate ability. Last season John Richards of Wolves almost convinced me he had it. He was England's top goalscorer with 36 goals in all competitions (27 in league games), a remarkable feat. But this season he has managed only a handful of goals.

MacDougall and Richards are the sum total of possible natural goalscorers in the league today, apart from one man who should have been wearing an England shirt against Poland in October – Newcastle's Malcolm Macdonald. He's my last hope.

He's chunky, arrogant and attacks goal like a bull; some say he's bigheaded. But he's resilient and skilful, he tackles ferociously and behaves like a thoroughbred who's prepared to do the donkey work. He's a master of the art of shielding the ball, which is a brave and thankless thing for a centre-forward to do. While he has his body between an opponent and the ball, he knows he's going to get clobbered. But Macdonald sticks it out and seems to have the uncanny talent for scoring. He scored 31 in the 1971/72 season, 28 in 1972/73, and he's well up to that standard this year. I would say, and only time will really tell, that Mac has the knack.

I really believe people like Macdonald are born to score goals. I think it's the same in any creative field. Like great writers, painters and musicians, they must have the seed sown early on. You can either score a goal or you can't.

As a player I scored 251 goals in 274 matches, a scoring record that still stands. If football continues to be the tight, give-nothing-away affair it is today, that record will stand for 1,000 years. Goals were like a drug to me, and I'm sure it was the same with players like Macdonald, Dixie Dean, Arthur Rowley (the all-time highest scorer, with 434 Football League goals) and Jimmy Greaves (357 in his league career).

I sometimes ask myself how I did it, how I scored my goals. But I can honestly say I don't know. I concentrated so hard on scoring I shut everything else out of my mind. I was unaware of people around me, ignorant of what defenders could do to me, unafraid of what the people might say if I missed. At the precise moment of scoring, I thought only of putting the ball away. There are few moments in life when you are so engrossed in what you are doing that everything else is shut out. If you work in a factory or an office you do your job, but you are conscious of things going on around you. For me, scoring was like stopping breathing.

I was suspended in space, in another world. The goal went in and my heart was pumping away, and suddenly I realised somebody was clapping, putting their arm round me, we were one up. It was an extraordinary feeling of detachment.

When Walter Winterbottom was England team manager 11 years ago, he took great interest in researching the physical qualities of goalscorers. 'There has been a wealth of work done on the subject of why certain people make better sportsmen than others,' he says. 'But the one thing on which everyone agrees is that some skills *are* inborn. Research has shown that there are two vital factors. The first is anticipation – the ability to read a situation quickly and so gain time to carry out a job on the field. This can be learned by experience. The other factor is built-in at birth, and that is the speed of muscle reaction.

'Scientists have found that players from warm countries like South America, Italy and Spain have faster muscle reactions than those from colder countries. This is why so many South American players appear faster than the North Europeans. But there are exceptions – brilliant ones like Puskás, Finney and Greaves. They had the magic combination of anticipation (which put them in the right place at the right time) and fast muscle reactions (which enabled them to strike the ball so fast that they didn't allow the goalkeeper the luxury of knowing which way they were going to shoot).'

You might think it's curious that my partner, Peter Taylor, who was a goalkeeper in his playing days, is a better judge of a centre-forward, or a goalscorer, than I am. It's probably because he spent so much time trying to anticipate which way a forward was going to put the ball past him, and so much time fishing it out of the back of the net afterwards, that he knows instinctively whether or not a player has a special scoring gift. As a goalscorer myself (I never went more than four games without scoring), I'm a better judge of goalkeepers, because I spent so much time trying to bang the ball past them. A great goalscorer gets to know a keeper's flaws very quickly – and then exploits them.

But there isn't much of this talent about in British football today. It could be that we are not recognising the natural goalscorer these days. In our obsession to find all-round, superbly fit players who can do everything – so-called utility players – we may be producing too many bland and uninteresting footballers.

Somehow, perhaps by changing our attitude, we must start to find these born stars and feed them into the game. They don't have to be able to explain their art. They don't have to measure their own muscle reactions to the nearest 1,000th of a second.

Some of the great players of the past – Tommy Lawton, Raich Carter, Wilf Mannion and Stanley Matthews – will all be household names for the next 100 years. But they couldn't talk about football to save their lives. They just went out there and did it.

1–7 December 1973

Brian Clough wants *you* to sound off …

TELL ME WHAT'S WRONG
WITH FOOTBALL

SOCCER supporters seldom get the chance to express their views about the game publicly. So this week I'm giving you the chance to do the talking. Everybody is talking about soccer-sickness. Why is the game so negative? Why can't we feel safe on the terraces? Why don't players respect referees? Why does it take half an hour to get into a ground? The plain fact is that ten years ago three and a half million more fans attended league matches over the season. Where have they gone? This week, I've prepared a questionnaire which could provide important answers. All you have to do is fill it in and post it to me at *TVTimes*. I'll assess your answers and discuss them in this column in the New Year.

1. *Soccer gates have dropped by three and a half million since 1963. What do you think is the most important reason? (Please tick one).*
A. Hooliganism
B. Increased prices
C. Negative football
D. Bad behaviour on the field
E. You have a wider choice of things to do on a Saturday
F. Other reasons

2. *What are facilities like at your club? (Delete where not applicable).*
A. Do you find it easy to get in and out of your ground? Yes/No.
B. Is car parking a problem? Yes/No.

C. Are the toilets adequate? Yes/No.

D. Are you satisfied with the refreshment services? Yes/No.

E. On the whole, do you think you get a good view of the match? Yes/No.

F. Is the club programme informative enough? Yes/ No.

G. Is the sound quality of the public address system good? Yes/No.

H. Does the public address system provide a good news and entertainment service? Yes/No.

I. Does the club run good transport to away games? Yes/No.

3. *How close do you feel to your local club? (Delete where not applicable).*

A. The club makes you feel as if you really belong to it.

B. The club's only interest is in taking your money.

4. *What is your opinion of your fellow supporters? (Please tick).*

A. Your club's fans are a credit to the club.

B. They are an embarrassment.

5. *What are your feelings on the subject of hooliganism? (Delete where not applicable).*

A. Have you personally witnessed violence on the terraces? Yes/ No.

B. Is hooliganism a real problem? Yes/No.

C. Has the subject of crowd violence been blown out of proportion by the press? Yes/No.

D. What would you do with soccer hooligans? Please explain briefly ...

6. *When would you personally prefer to see a football match? (Please tick).*

A. On an evening during the week.

B. On Friday night.

C. On Saturday afternoon.

D. On Saturday night.

E. On Sunday afternoon.

7. *What is your assessment of soccer in Britain today? (Delete where not applicable).*

A. Do you think it is far too defence-minded? Yes/ No.

B. Is it bold and attractive? Yes/No.

C. Is there too much football played in Britain today? Yes/No.

D. Overall, would you say that going to a match was value for money? Yes/No.

8. *Players have come in for a lot of criticism lately. What do you think? (Delete where not applicable).*

A. There is a lot of bad behaviour on the field? Yes/No.

B. Does bad behaviour on the field lead to violence on the terraces? Yes/No.

C. Do players readily accept the referee's decisions? Yes/No.

D. Do you think refereeing standards have fallen? Yes/No.

9. *Would you make any changes in the game, given the chance? Please tick any innovations you would like.*

A. Referees should be employed full time and paid well.

B. The offside rule should be relaxed to encourage attacking play.

C. More substitutes should be allowed.

D. The game needs two extra linesmen to help the referee.

E. Other suggestions …

10. *How does television affect soccer today? (Delete where not applicable).*

A. Instead of going to a match, have you ever stayed at home to watch recorded soccer on television? Yes/No.

B. Is there too much soccer on television? Yes/No.

C. Is soccer discussed too much on television? Yes/No.

When you have answered this ten-part questionnaire, please answer these two questions about yourself by deleting where necessary:

I am under/over 25.

I support a club in Division One/Two/Three/Four.

Then send your completed questionnaire to:
BRIAN CLOUGH SURVEY,
TVTimes
247 Tottenham Court Road,
London W1P 0AU

8–14 December 1973

In 1967 Leicester City shook the soccer world by selling Gordon Banks to Stoke. They reckoned that they could afford to sell the best goalkeeper in the world and put their trust in a teenager who was in their reserve team ...

BORN TO TAKE OVER AS NUMBER ONE

WE may have oil troubles, worries about rising prices, and trouble in the factories. But there is one thing we have never had to worry about – goalkeepers.

England have always had a remarkable tradition of top-class men between the posts – Bert Williams, Frank Swift, and the best of them all, Gordon Banks. But now that Banks has retired, who carries the flag for the great British goalkeeper? I believe that the man who has filled his place in the England side during the last year will do more than that. Peter Shilton, in my opinion, is *even better* than Banks.

Like the great goalscorers I was talking about in this column a fortnight ago, brilliant goalkeepers are born, not made. They know, instinctively, how to position themselves for any type of ball, how to time their run when they are coming out to narrow the angle to a forward who has burst clear. They have an almost god-given command of their penalty area.

Every country produces its top-class men, but Britain hatch more excellent men in goal because we play in such a variety of weather conditions: snow, sleet, driving rain, frost, fog, and sunshine. We play on pitches as soft as foam rubber and as hard as steel and the goalkeeper has to put in a performance right where it counts.

The most important asset a goalkeeper can possess is a calm but commanding temperament, the ability to keep control when everyone around him is losing theirs, the frame of mind to say, 'Nothing is going to put me out of my stride.'

Banks had this quality to a superb degree. A lot of very talented keepers, when they make a mistake, allow their nerves to collapse. But Banks could turn a mistake into magic.

Shilton has such a dynamic temperament that, during training sessions in the week, he questions and re-examines every shot which goes past him. Was I six inches out of position? Should I have punched that ball? This is the sort of thing he asks himself, so that by Saturday afternoon he has built up his determination to such a pitch that he can say, 'I cannot be beaten.' Then he transfers this gritty concentration to the pitch by stopping the unstoppable.

I think there is nobody to touch Shilton in the league, now that Banks has gone. Jennings of Spurs and Northern Ireland has all the skills, agility, perfect handling, but he doesn't have Shilton's iron resolve. Clemence of Liverpool, for all his brilliant reflexes, is occasionally inconsistent. [Ally] Hunter of Celtic and Scotland and [Gary] Sprake of Birmingham and Wales don't match up, either.

Unlike other players on the field, goalkeepers mature, they build on their natural ability by gathering experience, and they don't usually become great players until they're in their late 20s. Banks didn't blossom until he was 29 or 30. But I've only ever seen one great *young* goalkeeper, and that's Shilton. He is still only 22 and he's by far the greatest in the world. And he has had more to do in the last few years than most – at Leicester he hasn't had the best people in front of him and he has had to pull out everything he knows.

If I had to find the slightest fault with him I would say it was his slowness in distributing the ball – sometimes putting a man under pressure with a throw – but I'm finding flaws in someone who is near-perfect.

* * * *

'The confidence of the entire team hinges on the keeper,' wrote Brian Moore in a 1978 issue of *Look-in* (the magazine dubbed 'the Junior *TVTimes*'), 'and that is why men like Shilton and Clemence are worth their weight in gold.' At the time the pair, long regarded as the two best English goalies in the country, were spreading confidence throughout the team at the Football League's two leading clubs, and for several years had been the subject of some debate as to which of them was most worthy of wearing the number-one jersey for the national side. Successive England managers had struggled to fully make up their minds.

Since April 1974, when Shilton, then at Leicester City, won his 20th cap in a friendly with Argentina, failing to stop a last-minute penalty as the visitors claimed a 2-2 draw, it was Liverpool's Clemence who'd largely ruled the roost, and the goalmouth, a regular under, first, new national team manager Don Revie and then Ron Greenwood. Shilton only appeared sporadically during this period – for a European Championship qualifier in April 1975 when, by now a Stoke player, he had little to do as England eased to a 5-0 Wembley win over Cyprus; and two Home Internationals in April 1977, in the second of which Leighton James's 44th-minute penalty gave Wales their first victory in England for 41 years and their first-ever at Wembley.

It was Shilton himself who conceded the spot kick, pulling down James in the box following a mistake by Emlyn Hughes. By the time of Shilton's next cap just under a year later, against the same opposition (though with a happier outcome this time as Greenwood's side won 3-1 in Cardiff), Shilton was on Nottingham Forest's books. There, under Clough, the Leicester-born keeper's priceless role in a meteoric success story that saw the club move from the relative obscurity of the lower reaches of the Second Division to the pinnacle of the First brought him widespread acclaim. At the end of the 1977/78 season, his fellow pros voted him the PFA Player of the Year.

England's 6-3 humbling at Wembley in 1953 by the great Hungarian side had opened eyes to new possibilities about how the game could be played. 'It was the day the masters were publicly scolded and fiercely punished by the pupils,' according to John Motson. The Magyars' football had seemed revolutionary at the time. England captain that famous afternoon, Billy Wright, admitted to being amazed, for example, by the way the visitors' keeper Grosics had come out of the penalty area to play the ball like a full-back. It took some years but Gordon Banks, in Wright's opinion, was the first English keeper to play like an extra defender. He read the game like a fine tactician. Even when the ball was well away from goal, Banks, ever alert, would dart around his area, putting himself in the correct position.

Shilton saw himself in the same mould, controlling the goal area with ruthless efficiency. 'I prefer to see myself as a fifth defender, another sweeper if you like, rather than a man who makes last-ditch saves,' he told *Look-in* in 1977. 'Facing play, I can use that advantage, together with my experience, to guide defenders out of trouble.'

At Forest, Shilton's performances proved beyond doubt that a top-class keeper could mean around a dozen points a season to his club. Clough reckoned Shilton was 'worth at least 15' to his side. Yet on the international stage it was still Clemence, the best of pals with Shilton off the pitch, who, for the most part, remained in the leading role. When Shilton, brought in for a friendly in November 1978 against Czechoslovakia, earned high praise after the 1-0 Wembley win, Clough was critical of Greenwood's method of rotating goalies. 'It's no condemnation of Ray Clemence,' he said. 'But we just happen to think that Peter is the best there is.'

In spite of that, the rotation went on – Manchester City's Joe Corrigan was another given an occasional try-out – and it wasn't until the 1982 World Cup finals that Shilton finally established himself as the perfect fit for the number-one shirt. While Clemence had been the first-choice in the bulk of the qualifiers, it was Shilton guarding the net as England sealed their passage to Spain on a nervy November night in 1981 with a 1-0 Wembley triumph against the Hungarians. The following summer, the Forest keeper played in all five matches as Greenwood's team exited after the second round.

Over the next eight years, under Greenwood's successor, Bobby Robson, Shilton was virtually immoveable, wearing the yellow jersey with distinction and cementing not only his position as England's top keeper but probably the best there was in world football. It was an ambition that had been burning ever since June 1965 when the then 15-year-old, after winning his first England schoolboys cap and helping the Leicester Boys' side to reach the final of the English Schools Trophy, signed apprenticeship forms with his hometown club, Leicester City, resisting overtures from both Manchester United and Arsenal.

At Filbert Street he was understudy to a master. Gordon Banks had everything: superb positional sense, intelligent distribution, good handling, an almost uncanny sense of timing and, above all, guts – the courage needed to dive at the feet of a goal-hungry onrushing forward running at full pelt. Shilton couldn't have asked for a more inspiring teacher. Able to study Banks at close quarters, he learned rapidly.

The following spring, with Banks on England duty, the 16-year-old, on the strength of a performance he gave when taking over from Banks in a testimonial game for Alex Dowdells, a former Scotland coach, became the youngest player ever to don the shirt of his local club, making his first-team debut in a 3-0 home win over Everton on 4 May 1966. The 6ft tall youngster was still a junior at the time. From then on, Shilton barely looked back.

One year later, increasingly pressuring Banks for his place but feeling a regular spot wouldn't be his while Banks was at the club, Shilton handed in a transfer request and was determined to leave. However, so convinced was he of Shilton's exhilarating potential, Leicester boss Matt Gillies, who'd acquired the then unknown 22-year-old Banks from Chesterfield for just £7,000 in 1959, surprisingly decided to sell the England international instead, the keeper now generally accepted as the world's finest going to Stoke City for £50,000.

Accepting many of Banks's qualities and adding techniques of his own, Shilton quickly established himself as a fixture for the Foxes and one of the country's most outstanding young prospects.

In September 1967 Matt Busby again tried to take the keeper to Old Trafford – without success. The following month Shilton even managed to get his name on the scoresheet, Southampton goalkeeper, Campbell Forsyth, misjudging Shilton's long punt upfield during Leicester's 5-1 win at The Dell on 14 October 1967 – and by the end of 1967/68, in his first full season in the first team, Shilton had featured 35 times as the East Midlands club finished 13th in the First Division table.

There were heartaches on the horizon, however. Leicester, after a run to Wembley that included a 1-0 fifth-round replay win at Anfield in which Shilton pulled off a 40th-minute penalty stop from Tommy Smith, suffered a narrow FA Cup Final loss – a fierce first-half drive from Manchester City's Neil Young proving decisive – and relegation in 1969. But yet more attempts to prise away the keeper failed. At the end of that campaign West Brom's £100,000 bid was rejected.

The following summer, Shilton was part of a 28-man provisional squad Sir Alf Ramsey announced ahead of the World Cup finals in Mexico, but a week before the tournament kicked off, when the final 22 players were confirmed, he was one of six returning home. But his first full international cap wasn't long in coming: on 25 November 1970, Shilton made his England bow as Ramsey's side saw off East Germany 3-1 in a friendly at Wembley, a dipping 25-yard drive by Vogel catching Shilton off his line for the visitors' goal.

The 1970/71 season was a memorable one all round for Shilton, with Leicester at the end of it heading the Second Division table to gain their place back in the top flight and the keeper's heroics earning him yet more admiring glances from hopeful suitors. Clough was one of them. Having never made any secret of his admiration for Shilton, it was in June 1971, soon after the campaign's conclusion, that the Derby County manager first showed his hand, putting in a £200,000 bid. Yet as huge a sum as it was, the newly promoted Foxes weren't tempted; they turned it down. Clough would have to wait a little while yet to get his man. Further offers, from Everton and Arsenal, also followed but Shilton still wasn't going anywhere.

In the Potteries, Banks, England's keeper in the World Cups of 1966 and 1970 (discounting the quarter-final with West Germany) and most likely the next finals if he were to maintain his incredible consistency (and if England qualified), was still regarded as the king of the goalies in British soccer. Ramsey had never had to think twice about who would be his last line of defence since he first selected Banks back in 1963. Billy Wright believed Banks's main quality was confidence; it was, he said, 'the greatest thing a goalkeeper can possess because it spreads to the rest of the defence'.

With his wonderful anticipation and split-second reactions, he made goalkeeping seem simple at times. The spectacular stop – 'miraculous' the Brazil boss Mário Zagallo called it – from Pelé's header during the World Cup in Mexico almost defied belief. In December 1971, on the way to helping Stoke win the League Cup, the first major honour in the club's history, Banks's penalty save from West Ham's Geoff Hurst in the semi-final second leg with only three minutes left in extra time was, the *Daily Mail's* Brian Scovell wrote, 'one of the greatest saves of his distinguished career'. The following autumn, though, for the then 34-year-old, tragedy was waiting just around the corner.

On 22 October 1972, as Banks was travelling back after a session on an injured shoulder with the Stoke physio, his car was involved in a head-on collision with a van near his home, and shards of glass from the shattered windscreen badly damaged his right eye. The accident cost him the sight in the eye and would ultimately cut short his career. In August 1973, Banks, who just prior to his injury had signed a new six-year contract with Stoke, was forced to admit he would never play again.

It was a sad loss to the game. But, with his retirement at international level a door was unexpectedly opened. Shilton, now with five full caps to his name, was considered a firm favourite to step into Banks's boots once again. Up in Merseyside, however, Liverpool fans thought differently: the Reds's custodian, Ray Clemence, was the man they wanted to see between the sticks. Bill Shankly's shrewd purchase from Scunthorpe, Clemence was still only 24 but had the assurance of a veteran and, like Shilton, was a talented shot-stopper with a tremendous future ahead of him.

Sir Alf Ramsey agreed. For his 100th match as manager, the England boss handed the Anfield club's keeper, along with teammate Kevin Keegan, his international debut in the World Cup qualifier at Cardiff. But Shilton was soon back in favour. After Clemence was retained for the return game with Wales at Wembley, another Liverpool teammate John Toshack putting one past him as England struggled to a 1-1 draw, the Leicester player returned, featuring in a 5-0 win in Glasgow to celebrate the Scottish FA's centenary, then all three Home Internationals. A stupendous save Shilton pulled off from Kenny Dalglish at Wembley in the 1-0 conquering of the Scots – making a flying leap and clawing away the Celtic player's goalbound left-footed volley – was one of the finest seen in the championships. 'That's a wonderful sign for England's World Cup chances; to see a goalkeeper replacing Banks with that ability,' enthused ITV's Jimmy Hill. But those World Cup chances were soon to receive the most painful jolt.

The subsequent defeat and draw in the two matches against Poland were devastating blows. A spectator for much of the fateful evening in October, Shilton had been caught cold by Domarski's shot. Hit low with pace, the ball went under the outstretched leg of Emlyn Hughes before taking a slight jump on the Wembley turf and skidding beneath Shilton's body. Shilton, for a big man, was amazingly agile. His reputation was built chiefly on his excellent understanding of angles and lightning-fast reflexes. Nevertheless, many felt that the keeper was too slow to get down and certainly couldn't be absolved of at least some of the blame for England's failure.

Some doubts were raised as to whether Shilton was a worthy successor to Banks. Had he the necessary reserves of nerve needed to make a great performer? Shilton, Brian Moore observed, 'looked edgy and unsure in an England jersey, a shadow of the very mobile brick wall he had become, week in and week out, for Leicester City.' His current club boss had no worries, however. 'Peter has a thing about him,' Jimmy Bloomfield said, 'that perfection is not enough.

He is always striving to go one degree beyond it.' No one trained more often or more enthusiastically in the quest to improve.

'The fact is that to err is human: in football as in any other branch of life,' Brian Glanville stated, 'and a goalkeeper's errors are punished more cruelly than those of any position on the field.' Such was their importance, *Target* magazine in a 1972 feature, alliteratively titled 'Salute to the Super Savers of Soccer', described them as 'the men who literally have the balance of a match in their hands'. One off-moment, an odd gyration of the ball, a single lapse, the briefest gaffe, or a crucial miscalculation could affect the result of a game. Any wonderful saves that might have gone before were forgotten for this lone, glaring glitch.

Despite his disappointments, Shilton never lost his firm belief in his own ability. He enjoyed another tremendous year, his 11th, at Leicester. On 3 April 1974, only a Liverpool side at their best denied the Foxes an FA Cup Final appearance, winning 3-1 in a semi-final replay at Villa Park. That same night, with QPR's Phil Parkes making his debut, England played out a meaningless goalless draw in Portugal, meaningless but for the fact it was Sir Alf Ramsey's final match in charge. Aside from Banks, Shilton and Clemence, Parkes was one of just four other keepers who represented England in the 1970s: Corrigan, Bonetti and Jimmy Rimmer (who played only the opening 45 minutes of a USA Bicentennial Tournament clash with Italy in New York's Yankee Stadium in 1976, conceding twice, before being replaced by Corrigan at the break as England netted three times in the second half to win 3-2) were the others.

It was in the summer of 1974, though, that Shilton, having declined a new contract, put in another transfer request. Again, Manchester United and Arsenal showed interest but this time were unwilling to match what they considered an excessive asking price. Derby, now managed by Dave Mackay, were also keen. But, just like his predecessor Banks, seven years previously, it was to Stoke that Shilton eventually headed, a long drawn-out saga coming to an end on 21 November when the Staffordshire club forked out a staggering £325,000, a world record fee for a goalkeeper.

Ambitious Stoke had now spent three quarters of a million pounds recently on new players. Shilton was just one more big signing in an attempt to bring major success to the Potteries. It was a bold plan that ultimately failed. After two successive fifth-place finishes, an anticipated title challenge in 1975/76 never materialised. The following season, depleted following the sale of several top players, Stoke were relegated and so began the 1977/78 campaign in the second tier.

At the end of June 1977, Manchester United were yet again in the hunt for Shilton, but his high wage demands (reportedly £100 a week) then Tommy Docherty's sudden sacking prevented any move from materialising. Now Clough, anticipating that the ambitious Shilton wouldn't be willing to linger too long in the lower reaches, was ready to pounce. Though he already had a highly talented keeper and a very fine prospect in John Middleton, Clough wanted experience in goal that Middleton was too young to provide. Forest were planning success for today, not tomorrow. After their storming start to life in the top flight, a 3-0 defeat at Arsenal prompted Clough to make a bid for the man he considered as the complete package.

'Well, there's an old saying that the Mountie always gets his man,' wrote Brian Moore in *Look-in* in March 1978, 'and Brian Clough should have become an honorary member of the Canadian Mounted Police, if only for persistence.' That persistence had paid off. Having failed to lure Shilton firstly to the Baseball Ground and then to Leeds, Clough made it third time lucky, taking the keeper from Stoke to the City Ground for a £250,000 investment.

On 17 September 1977, the day before he turned 28, Shilton made his Forest debut in a 2-0 home win over Aston Villa and, with their new number one installed, Clough's side only conceded 18 times in their remaining 37 matches on the way to league title glory. Despite Stoke City's chairman Thomas Degg telling Clough before his purchase of Shilton, 'You do realise he'll put you in the workhouse. He's earning a fortune and he'll want at least a ten per cent pay rise,' Clough would later say, 'I'd have paid a million for him if I had to.'

Whatever the fee, few would argue that it was a bargain. There was little question, too, that, of all Clough's masterstrokes in the transfer market, the capture of the keeper he'd long regarded as 'by far the greatest in the world' was the biggest and best of his entire footballing career. With only a Second Division championship medal to his name when he signed for Forest, but a hoard of silverware including successive European Cup-winning medals by the time he left, it's probably safe to say that Peter Shilton regarded it as rather a profitable move as well.

CLOUGH SOUNDS OFF

In 1967 Leicester City shook the soccer world by selling Gordon Banks to Stoke. They reckoned that they could afford to sell the best goal-keeper in the world and put their trust in a teenager who was in their reserve team.

BORN TO TAKE OVER AS No.1

WE MAY HAVE oil troubles, worries about rising prices, and trouble in the factories. But there is one thing we have never had to worry about—goalkeepers.

England have always had a remarkable tradition of top-class men between the posts—Bert Williams, Frank Swift, and the best of them all, Gordon Banks. But now that Banks has retired, who carries the flag for the Great British Goal-keeper? I believe that the man who has filled his place in the England side during the last year will do more than that. Peter Shilton, in my opinion, is *even better* than Banks.

Like the great goalscorers I was talking about in this column a fortnight ago, brilliant goalkeepers are born, not made. They know, instinctively, how to position themselves for any type of ball, how to time their run when they are

Gordon Banks, Peter Shilton, 1970: now the understudy carries the flag

coming out to narrow the angle to a forward who has burst clear. They have an almost God-given command of their penalty areas.

Every country produces its top-class men, but Britain hatch more excellent men in goal because we play in such a crazy variety of weather conditions: snow, sleet, driving rain, frost, fog, and sun-shine. We play on pitches as soft as foam rubber and as hard as steel and the goalkeeper has to put in a performance right where it counts.

The most important asset a goalkeeper can possess is a calm but commanding temperament, the ability to keep control when every-one around him is losing theirs, the frame of mind to say: "Nothing is going to put me out of my stride."

Banks had this quality to a superb degree. A lot of very talented keepers, when they make a mistake, allow their nerves to collapse. But Banks could turn a mistake, into magic.

Shilton has such a dynamic temperament that, during training sessions in the week, he questions and re-examines every shot which goes past him. Was I six inches out of position? Should I have punched that ball? This is the sort of thing he asks himself, so that by Saturday afternoon he has built up his determination to such a pitch that he can say: "I cannot be

beaten." Then he transfers this gritty concentration to the pitch by stopping the unstoppable.

I think there is nobody to touch Shilton in the League, now that Banks has gone. Jennings of Spurs and N. Ireland has all the skills, agility, perfect handling, but he doesn't have Shilton's iron resolve. Clemence of Liverpool, for all his brilliant reflexes, is occasionally inconsistent. Hunter of Celtic and Scotland, and Sprake of Birming-ham and Wales don't match up, either.

Unlike other players on the field, goalkeepers mature, they build on their natural ability by gathering experience, and they don't usually become great players until they're in their late 20's. Banks didn't blossom until he was 29 or 30. But I've only ever seen one great young goalkeeper, and that's Shilton. He is still only 22, and he's by far the greatest in the world. And he has had more to do in the last few years than most—at Leicester he hasn't had the best people in front of him and he has had to pull out everything he knows.

If I had to find the slightest fault with him I would say it was his slowness in distributing the ball —sometimes putting a man under pressure with a throw—but I'm finding flaws in someone who is near-perfect.

6

15–21 December 1973

The Cinderellas of the Third and Fourth Divisions, plus the remaining non-league teams, battle for a money-spinning place in the third round of the FA Cup with the big clubs on Saturday. *World of Sport* will keep you in touch with the latest scores throughout the afternoon. It's one of the few days when the small clubs get the limelight, though one of these has had a publicity boost lately – Brian Clough's Brighton. So what's life like below the top? And how is he planning to get back up there? …

MY FOUR WAYS TO MAKE BRIGHTON ROCK

SIX weeks ago my partner Peter Taylor and I were at the top of the tree, brushing shoulders with the best teams in the world at the head of the First Division. Now we're about 60 places down the league with Brighton. I must say the sea air is doing me a power of good, but, brother, we've got a long way to go.

Being involved in the Third Division doesn't make me change my approach to the game. Whether I am with Ajax of Amsterdam or the late lamented Accrington Stanley, the basics of football and management remain the same.

This is crunch week at Brighton because when I arrived I gave myself until Christmas to impress my ideas upon the players – to get my personality across and to let them know exactly what I wanted of them.

Team discipline is the first of my requirements. For home as well as away matches I insist on taking the players to a hotel for the night before the game, just as I did at Derby. If we have an evening match, we book into a hotel in the afternoon and have a two-hour nap. I make sure the players eat the right food before a game – steak, a few chips and rice pudding. I want the players to arrive at the ground for training on time in the morning. I don't want to see their hair creeping down their necks. All I really ask is that they behave like a team of professionals, and when you have 17 professionals on your books discipline is the priority. No team can apply the talents until it is disciplined properly.

After that I make myself absolutely available to my players. No shirking, no inhibitions, no hiding round corners, no closing the door of the manager's office. Everything out in the open. I believe in literally wading in among the players, undoing their bootlaces, living with them all the time they are with me. Every time they take a lung full of air, I want half of it.

So I get the players to observe my rules, know where they stand with me. Then comes the third vital thing, and this is where the football manager sinks or swims: getting the maximum in ability and effort from each player. Of course, in the Third Division you have to bear in mind that the standard of the end product is not going to be as high as it was in the First, but confronted with a new set of players, the manager has to be a brilliant judge, putting his finger on the things a player does right, the things he does wrong, the things he will never be able to do and, most of all, recognising pure talent. A good manager should be able to spot that like a full moon.

It shows immediately, the first morning in training; it sticks out as if a player's leg were covered with plaster. I look for the player who instinctively finds space for himself, gives himself time to play the ball, the player who times his tackling with precision, a player with composure under pressure. Then comes the final and most nerve-racking aspect of management – employing these skills on the field. In other words, choosing the right team, getting the right blend of aggression and skill, defence and attack, to win matches.

That's the way I do it and I don't care whether a player likes it or not. At times I am brutally honest with a player, but he has to learn to accept my assessment of his ability. It's like a patient who goes to a specialist and might not like his diagnosis. At Derby I laid down exactly what I wanted, and in the early days some of the players didn't like my approach. But ask them now, ask them why they've got big houses and big cars, and they'll say they owe it to me.

As a spectacle, the Third Division isn't a great deal different from the First. It's not an over-physical division as some people think – the roughhouse tactics have gone out of football overnight, from the top of the First to the bottom of the Fourth, and it's the best thing that has happened to soccer in a generation. In the Third there is no lack of excitement and enjoyment, there is simply a lack of the finest skills, and this means that you will see more mistakes during a game.

It is my job, and my belief, that Brighton won't be in the Third Division for very long, but while they are there, one of the things Peter Taylor and myself will have to contend with is a certain amount of stick from other managers in the game. This is the penalty I have to pay for saying too much and I accept this. I know that a lot of people think I'm too big for my boots. For the past few years we have been the envy of most managers up and down the country. They were waiting, praying perhaps, for us to fall flat on our faces or, as one football writer once said, for the bubble to burst. We had just won the First Division championship and I told that gentleman at the time: this isn't a bubble, there are foundations, the castle has been built, and it will live for 100 years while we're on the drawbridge. That's how it's going to be at Brighton, despite the obstacles people are already putting in our way.

We hadn't been in the Third Division for one week when we had two refusals of help from managers we had spent many hours with when we were at the top. At Derby we were never too busy for the Third and Fourth Division managers. We played our fair share of testimonial matches with our full first team, we loaned our fair share of players, our feet never left the floor. But in that first week at Brighton I spent seven hours asking a favour of a manager regarding a player, and at the final second he turned me down.

I'll tell you this much: when we get back up there, and we shall, we'll remember these people who were once in my office at Derby guzzling champagne and who now won't take a phone call from us.

At Brighton, we do our training on the nearby playing fields of the University of Sussex, and after a session the other day I went back to the canteen for a cup of tea and got chatting to some of the students. I told those lads that when they left university they would go away with degrees, bits of paper which will always be a measure of their ability. In football, I told them, there are no diplomas, there is only success. And after nine years as a manager I have two little round medals which represent my achievements – a Second Division championship medal and a First Division championship medal. I had two replicas made in solid gold and gave one to my mum and one to my wife Barbara.

But unlike the student who can wave his degree about for the rest of his life, the football manager can't keep polishing his old championship medals. He has got to go on winning if he wants to stay in a job.

* * * *

'I have often heard it said in football that it is better for a manager to start at the bottom. That the best bosses begin at the foot of the ladder. And do you know what I think about that kind of theory? Bunkum. A load of old rubbish.' In 1971 Clough, the dynamic young manager of Derby County, was reflecting on the deprivations of life he'd experienced at Fourth Division Hartlepools, and didn't recommend it to anyone. 'I would say that the ideal place for a manager to start a career would be as high in the league as possible,' he said. 'Because the higher the club the better the players, and that is what a manager needs most. Good, skilful players.'

On Thursday, 1 November 1973, when Clough joined Brighton and Hove Albion as their new manager, he wasn't exactly beginning at the bottom again, but not far off it. Unless results improved, the club, with just four wins from their opening 14 games, were staring relegation to the basement level of English football squarely in the face. In 1971/72, Brighton, referred to by Peter Fay in *The Official Football League Yearbook 1972/73* as 'the team from the south coast holiday playground that had laboured too long in the soccer backwaters', had entered the river of the Second Division after promotion from the Third in the runners-up berth behind runaway champions Aston Villa. Another year on, however, 22nd and out of their depth, and they were back in the third tier once again. Their poor league form at the start of the next campaign, coupled with a fall at the first hurdle in the League Cup – Albion losing at home to Charlton Athletic – had predictably cost Pat Saward his job. But even though the sports editor of the local paper, the *Evening Argus*, speculated that Saward's replacement might well be the former Derby boss – 'Could the club afford Brian you-know-who?' – most fans scoffed heartily at its likelihood.

Clough had stressed that he wasn't opposed to managing outside the top flight provided the set-up was right, but after the heights he'd reached in the East Midlands surely a struggling Third Division outfit on the south coast was the last place he'd choose as his next destination. Wasn't it? No, it wasn't. Whether he liked it or not, for Clough the reality was he was out of work and needed a job – fast! And the top clubs weren't exactly beating a path to his door. So once Peter Taylor, initially approached about the possibility of Clough and him taking over, told his partner that the position was theirs if they wanted it, talks got underway and though it took six days of non-stop negotiations between Clough, Taylor, Albion chairman Mike Bamber and vice-chairman Harry Bloom, the pair finally agreed to come on board, Brighton's astonishing coup pulled off on Halloween night in a Derby hotel.

The following day, when the announcement was made that the duo had signed a contract at the Goldstone Ground, property developer Bamber, an ambitious and rich young chairman, described it as the greatest of his life, promising that Brighton would soon be a force in football. Not that soon, though. Clough and Taylor were quickly made aware of the monumental task ahead. 'They were casual, almost amateurish, joking about their plight instead of being concerned,' Taylor wrote in his autobiography, *With Clough By Taylor*, on first meeting the Brighton team at a hotel in Lewes. 'Brian thrust his chin at them, challenging, "Go on, punch it! Show me you're capable of positive action." I wanted to wade in, too, but decided that the best course was wholesale replacement.'

Gates, which had dwindled to just over 5,000, were given an instant boost by the partnership's arrival. Over 16,000 – three times that season's average attendance – turned up for their first game in charge, at home to York City. Banners greeting the new manager and his assistant flowered on the terraces as the twosome received a rapturous welcome from the Brighton crowd. But the match with York ended 0-0 and three league games later the home supporters still hadn't seen a goal, Brighton ending 0-0 in their next Goldstone encounter following a 2-2 draw at Huddersfield and a 1-0 win at Walsall. When Isthmian League side Walton & Hersham turned up for an FA Cup first-round replay, all that was expected to change.

The first encounter had resulted in another goalless stalemate. Prior to the clash, the last away cup tie Clough had witnessed from the dugout had been Derby's European Cup semi-final first leg versus Juventus in April. That one in Turin had ended in rage and frustration, and accusations of cheating on the Italians' part; this one in Surrey's stockbroker belt concluded in relief. The home side, the Amateur Cup holders, hurried and harried the visitors from the word go, having much the better of the chances against a shot-shy Albion, and it was only keeper Brian Powney who earned Clough's XI a second chance. Had referee Gordon Kew not disallowed a 'goal', adjudging that Walton centre-forward Russell Perkins had jumped at Powney seconds before a hard and high punt upfield from captain Dave Bassett had bounced into the net, Albion would have been behind after only several seconds. Clough, according to *The Observer*, spent the match 'prowling the touchline', the subject of screamed abuse from the locals in the 6,300 attendance, mostly upset at him for coaching his charges instead of remaining seated.

At a windy Goldstone Ground the following Wednesday afternoon – the match kicking off at 1.45pm as the country's power crisis meant floodlight use could not be guaranteed – it was screams of jubilation that were coming this time from the Walton & Hersham faithful in the 9,857 attending. From 1-0 up on 20 minutes through a header from the rangy Perkins, a PE teacher, 26-year-old joiner Clive Foskett hammered a quick-fire hat-trick for the amateurs in the game's last eight minutes, and a cup upset became a total humiliation and a national shaming for Clough. The 4-0 scoreline was the worst defeat suffered by the club in the FA Cup since they'd first entered the competition as Brighton United in 1898/99.

If Clough reckoned the display was too bad to be true, three days later it got even worse. At home to Bristol Rovers, the early promotion favourites looking to establish a new Third Division record of remaining unbeaten in the first 19 games of the season, Albion were sliced apart by fast, accurate passing and the faultless finishing of two of the league's sharpest strikers: Alan Warboys and Bruce Bannister. Between them, the 'Smash and Grab' duo – Rovers's marketing team had used the slogan in a 'Wanted' poster featuring the pair, and the nickname stuck – plundered seven goals, with Gordon Fearnley getting another. At the interval the visitors were 6-1 up. By full time, the score was 8-2. Worse still for Clough, it had all been captured by ITV cameras.

Emerging grim-faced from an hour-long dressing-room inquest after the match, Clough told reporters, 'This has been the worst experience of my entire football career.' He looked shell-shocked, visibly shaken. 'I feel sick,' he said. 'We were absolutely pathetic. Our side hasn't enough heart to fill a thimble and this was the most humiliating 90 minutes I have endured.'

His misery was understandable: it was the Seagulls's heaviest-ever home league defeat. Ironically, in the worst defeat in the club's history – 9-0 in a Second Division match against Middlesbrough on 23 August 1958, the season's opening day – Boro's centre-forward that afternoon, netting five times in what was also the Teessiders' all-time record league win, had been none other than Clough.

As 'ashamed for the club and the town of Brighton' as he said he was, Clough surprisingly laid the blame at his own feet. 'I have become larger than life, larger than the players, larger than Brighton – and that is wrong,' he confessed. 'They don't know how to cope with me.' So what was the remedy? 'I have to come down to their level. They put on their shirts, look at me and wonder whether they are doing *that* the right way.'

It had been a shattering week, yet on the Sunday a much calmer Clough bravely fulfilled a punditry gig on LWT's *The Big Match*, albeit with a slightly forced smile. 'There was a lot of speculation as to whether you would turn up today,' said host Brian Moore. 'Obviously they were wrong and they don't know me,' Clough replied.

It was patently evident that the Albion players weren't yet that sure about the true character of their newly installed manager, either. Or of Peter Taylor, for that matter. After the briefest honeymoon, no one was under any illusions. If the marriage was to be a success there was still, as Clough put it, 'a long way to go'.

When Clough next watched his Brighton side take on Bristol Rovers, on 27 April 1974, as the curtain came down on the campaign, in certain respects they had at least made some progress. Albion fared much better, gaining a 1-1 draw at Eastville against a side that sealed promotion from the third tier in second place behind Oldham. Yet even those who suspected that his stay by the seaside was just a sojourn as he waited for a bigger fish to come along cannot have predicted that that second game with Rovers would be Clough's very last in charge of the south-coast club.

22 December 1973–4 January 1974, Christmas and New Year double issue

1973 – a year of turmoil in British football, and in the thick of it has been our own columnist Brian Clough. Here he examines the shape of soccer to come, and throws in his own wish for a much happier New Year …

LET'S MAKE '74 CHAMPAGNE YEAR

WHAT will football be like on New Year's Eve, 1983? Well, apart from the odd certainty – like Brighton riding high in the First Division – and one or two imponderables (will Alf Ramsey still be trying to get the England team to find the net as he works up to the 1986 World Cup on the Moon?), I believe that the game itself will be vastly different in many ways.

The biggest and best change in football will be that it will become a young man's game, from the boardroom to the pitch. The average age of a First Division football manager today is 45. Not long ago they went on till they were 65, but I think this figure will fall below the 40-mark in the next ten years. This summer, for the first time, the Professional Footballers' Association held a management course at the St Helens College of technology, in Lancashire, with young, intelligent men like Paddy Crerand, Ian St John, and Bobby Charlton sitting behind a desk as pupil-managers.

Young management means young men at boardroom level, too – and I can see us clearing out the dead wood of the men who treat football like a game of tiddlywinks. There has been a contemporary trend for players to think that they are over the hill by the time they reach 30. But I predict a reversal of this. If we have younger managers, people who know how to get the best out of a player and how to use his particular abilities, it will mean that players will last longer. We will go more for brains and less for brawn, and mature players of 33, 34 and 35 will be giving the game greater composure and grace.

What about football itself in Britain? We've seen fear creeping into it – the chronic fear of losing, and this has created boring, methodical football, reflected at its worst at international level. The influx of young, creative people at all levels of the game will do more for it than any artificial stimulants, like giving points for goals and changing the rules.

I think we'll close the gap in ball skill between ourselves and the continentals. We will encourage, develop and demand skill from our players because, if it comes to a choice, people would rather see skill than goals. The Italian league is the only one in Europe which showed an increase in attendances last season, and they have the most defensive football in the world. But, as we saw at Wembley in November, they have an abundance of skill.

We'll get the players – we might even get round to importing a few continental ones – and we'll have the people to watch them, in comfort. One day, certainly before 1984, one rich First Division club is going to announce that their ground will be converted to seated, covered stands all round the pitch. Once one team does it, the rest will follow.

It will certainly cost more for the average fan – a pound or two admission for each match – but I think he'll be prepared to pay for more comfort and better facilities. Youth, skill and facilities: it sounds good and I really think that it can happen in the next few years.

This last year may have been one of self-examination for English soccer – but it's been a hell of a year for me personally. I started it leading Derby in the European Cup, I signed for ITV in August, and ended up in the Third Division with Brighton in November.

We had a lot of Christmasses at Derby, and they didn't always come at the end of the year. The champagne flowed in the dressing room, and I built up my own stock of the stuff – the best I could get – at home. And I'd earned it.

Now I'm going to get it coming through the taps at Brighton, despite the hammerings we took last month. Which brings me, at this festive time, to ponder over what to send Sam Longson, the chairman at Derby, for Christmas. I could think of a million things – like balloons with a few well-chosen words written on them – but I'll be nice, and offer him the present he might least like to receive – Brighton's success.

To Sam, with love: two points from sunny Brighton. Merry Christmas, and a Happy New Year.

✳ ✳ ✳ ✳

A decade on, some things definitely hadn't changed. In early 1983 the football versus TV conflict was still to be resolved satisfactorily. 'All those housewives dancing with glee at the prospect of no football on TV next season are wasting their time,' a *Football Monthly* article had stated confidently. 'There is no real danger of our number-one game not appearing on the box next winter.' Yet as obvious as it was that the sport and television needed each other too badly for the situation to be allowed, in the springtime of that year the threat of football being wiped altogether from the small screen was very real indeed. Negotiations between the Football League and the TV companies went well into extra time.

It was only after months of uncertainty that the big question was finally answered: there would be football on television in 1983/84. Not only that but the season would mark a significant shift in the way the game was beamed into the nation's living rooms. A bold new experiment – a package drawn up between the League and the TV chiefs – was put on the launching pad in a bid to restore football's flagging fortunes and revive it as a spectacle.

After a diet of many years consisting of mainly recorded highlights, when results were already known, the TV viewing public had demanded something different; now, armchair football fans could look forward to a veritable feast for the eyes: the enticing prospect of seeing the top English clubs 'live' in action, with five league games each for ITV (scheduled for Sunday afternoons) and BBC (to be broadcast on Friday evenings), plus alternate rounds of the FA Cup as well as the usual edited clips. ITV would have exclusive coverage of the Milk Cup Final, too. *Match of the Day* was also switching back to what John Motson termed 'the programme's rightful slot' on Saturday evenings.

No one could gauge the effects of this innovation. Live games were likely to threaten a club's gates only when they staged the transmitted match, though critics maintained that overall they would actually be less damaging to weekly attendances – tele-presenters were so skilled in their art that the edited package could easily pass for the real thing or, worse, become a more satisfactory substitute for it. Young fans weaned on many hours of recorded football could be disappointed by the real thing – no commentary, no goals every three or four minutes, and no action replays.

'If a club can prove that attendance drops as a direct result of live TV coverage, then compensation is assured,' said Jimmy Hill, now enjoying a popular partnership with ex-Arsenal keeper Bob Wilson as co-host of the BBC's highlights show. He hoped that, on the contrary, attendances as a whole would pick up because of the interest generated. (They needed to. The total attendance on 27 August was the lowest-ever for the first day of a season, although First Division crowds were larger than the previous season.)

For most people – as the theme of the Football League's commercials emphasised – there was no substitute for 'being there'. The basic audience for televised football, the market researchers advising the League insisted, was comprised almost entirely of people who also regularly attended matches. There were not, they said, millions sitting at home waiting to switch on the telly but refusing to go to the genuine article. A minority might possibly exist whose appetite was satisfied with one televised game per weekend – but they weren't regarded as football supporters in the traditional sense. And one game on Friday night or Sunday afternoon was hardly unbearable competition for the other 45 on a Saturday afternoon. At least for an experimental season, the game's major figures were happy to accept the situation. There were others, though, still in the anti-camp. Brian Clough was one.

It was perhaps ironic then that when the new era of ITV's *The Big Match – Live* kicked off it was Clough's Nottingham Forest that featured. Somewhat ironical, too, that the game – a First Division encounter on 2 October 1983 – took place at White Hart Lane. On Saturday, 10 September 1960, when ITV had first offered people at home the chance to watch a live Football League fixture – a dour 1-0 win for Bolton at Blackpool – the experiment had been deemed so dull a failure that the following week Arsenal withdrew permission for the cameras to cover their match against Newcastle, and Spurs quickly followed suit, refusing to host cameras for a home clash with Aston Villa. Under the weight of disinterest, the deal collapsed and ITV abandoned the project altogether.

On that Sunday afternoon in October 1983, though, the fare was much better. It was, as commentator Brian Moore enthused at the full-time whistle, 'a game that's really been a credit to both sides; tremendous entertainment and a really dramatic finish to it.' A header from Spurs's Mark Falco touched over the line by Steve Archibald right at the death gave the home side a 2-1 win, and 30,596 were at the ground to witness it. The TV audience was recorded as five million.

Forest's beaten goalkeeper was a Dutchman, Hans van Breukelen, whom Clough had picked up a year earlier after Peter Shilton had left the East Midlanders for Southampton. Of the 22 players in the two starting line-ups in north London, van Breukelen was the only foreigner on the field, but over the previous five years, following the 1978 World Cup finals in Argentina plus the cessation of a longstanding Football League ban on overseas players, a trickle of imports from outside the British Isles had become a fairly steady flow. Once Spurs manager Keith Burkinshaw, still in charge of the club five years later, had taken the plunge on two of the Argentinian cup-winning squad, Osvaldo Ardiles and Ricardo Villa – Burkinshaw's audacity described by the press as 'shattering new ground in the game' – others followed suit, shopping abroad with varying degrees of success. Clough's first foreign purchases

– Swiss midfielder Raimondo Ponte, Norwegian defender Einar Jan Aas and German striker Jürgen Röber – each made only 21 appearances for Forest before being moved on again.

It was largely because of Clough that no highlights exist of the debuts on English soil of Ardiles and Villa. On the opening day of the 1978/79 season, with Clough's newly crowned champions Forest entertaining Spurs, both BBC and ITV had hoped to film the game for their respective highlights show. Clough denied access to their cameras. That season, while Forest went on to take over Liverpool's mantle as European champions, it was the Anfield club, dethroned the season before, who regained their First Division crown, finishing with a record total of 68 points, eight ahead of their nearest rivals, Forest. It was Liverpool's third title success under the stewardship of their County Durham-born boss, Bob Paisley, and the sixth major trophy in five years under his management.

On New Year's Eve 1973, after a 1-0 win at Chelsea two days before, Liverpool, managed by Bill Shankly, had ended the year second in the First Division behind eventual champions Leeds. Ten years later, on 31 December, three weeks after a 4-0 beating at Coventry City in which Terry Gibson hit the first hat-trick past the Reds in 11 years, another 1-0 victory away from home, at Clough's Forest, meant that Liverpool, now under the tutelage of Joe Fagan, entered 1984 sitting right at the head of the table. In between, in nine years in charge, from the then 54-year-old's appointment as Shankly's replacement on 26 July 1974 to his retirement at the conclusion of the 1982/83 campaign, Paisley had not only matched but exceeded all expectations as his side dominated both English and European football.

The haul of silverware – including six league championships, three European Cups, the UEFA Cup and three League Cups – had the Anfield trophy cabinet needing reinforcement. The one-time second-in-command had proved himself second to none. Shankly may have been the messiah of Merseyside, the man who walked on water, but his former assistant, with the club since 1939, had stepped into Shankly's shoes and given the club an even firmer footing in football's history books. While the fortunes of almost every other club had fluctuated – successes erected on shifting sands – Liverpool had solid foundations beneath them.

After 1978/79, Liverpool sealed three more league titles, their only barren year coming in 1980/81 when Aston Villa broke their monopoly. Ron Saunders's side were the last club to be champions under the two-points-for-a-win system, in place since the Football League's formation in 1888/89. The following season, after a proposal was given the thumbs-up by the League chairmen and managers, three points was the new reward for being victorious, however that victory might be achieved.

The game was as much in need of a booster shot as ever, but for the most part the authorities had resisted the use of 'artificial stimulants'. Scrapping the offside laws and having America-style shoot-outs at the end of drawn matches were two ideas mooted but rejected. Nevertheless, with the country suffering an ever-worsening recession – yes, some other things hadn't altered since 1973 either – it was perhaps a little fanciful to think that the consequence of a new points system would be far more attack-minded football which, in turn, would inspire the crowds to flock back to the terraces.

Most of those terraces were now bordered by high metal fencing, erected in an attempt to combat hooliganism, a scourge which was still very prevalent in 1983 and which would only worsen as the decade progressed. 'People sitting on their backsides do not cause trouble,' Football League secretary Alan Hardaker had said in August 1973, calling for all-seater stadia as a means to beat the troublemakers. Ten years later, the troublemakers were still on their feet and on the loose at grounds that, in the main, had seen little by way of improvement for far too long. Sadly, Clough's vision of fans watching football in the luxury of covered, seated stands was only realised after the nightmare of Hillsborough in 1989, when Clough's Forest were Liverpool's opposition on that ill-fated afternoon.

It was also in 1981/82 that Aston Villa, with a 1-0 win over Bayern Munich, became the sixth successive side, after Liverpool (three times) and Forest (twice), to keep the European Cup in

England. Dominance by English clubs in Europe, however, didn't convert to success at international level. The national side was still playing with a different currency, one with a poor exchange rate.

By the last day of 1983 it wasn't Alf Ramsey still trying to get the England team to find the net, but another former Ipswich boss, Bobby Robson. And football hadn't quite joined the space age yet. It was Mexico in 1986, not the Moon, that was the target (and eventually reached, but only after England's rocket fell to earth attempting to make the much shorter flight to France for the Euros in 1984). Before Robson, both Don Revie (painfully discovering the huge chasm between club and international management) and Ron Greenwood (despite commendable efforts) had failed to elevate the national side into the highest ranks of world football and make England a real force to be reckoned with again.

Although, under Greenwood, they'd qualified for the 1980 European Championship finals in Italy, after one draw, one loss and one win England were soon on their way home back to Blighty. Two years later, with the sagging fortunes of football at the top level in need of revival, England's appearance at the World Cup finals gave an injection of genuine interest the national game required. Yet the team at the time was, as John Motson put it, 'riotously unpredictable', and despite pre-tournament promises in song that 'this time we'll get it right' they didn't; sorely lacking a cutting edge, goalless draws in their round-two games with West Germany and hosts Spain meant an exit from a competition in which they'd begun in the most explosive manner – Bryan Robson scoring after 27 seconds versus France – and really should have finished higher placed.

Until Robson's goal on 16 June 1982, Martin Peters was the last England player to score in a World Cup finals, with the second in the 3-2 quarter-final defeat by West Germany in 1970 on, what Geoffrey Green termed, 'the day a blazing Mexican sun burned a hole in our hopes'. Before 1982, the last time they'd actually qualified for a World Cup had been 20 years earlier. True, England were making the finals of major tournaments once more, but their report card still read 'Must try harder'.

By 1980, perhaps sensing that the ship had sailed, Clough openly admitted, 'I'm no longer interested in the England manager's job.' The money he was earning at the City Ground – reportedly £60,000 per annum (the highest wage in the league) – might have done a little persuasive talking as well. Clough and Brighton had long since gone their separate ways. But during the 1979/80 season they became reacquainted as the south-coast club, now under the management of Peter Taylor's successor Alan Mullery and with Mike Bamber still chairman, played their first-ever campaign in English football's top flight. It was the Seagulls, then in 21st place, who pulled off a remarkable 1-0 win in Nottingham on 17 November 1979 to bring to an end Forest's 51-match unbeaten streak on home soil.

In four successive seasons in the First Division, under Mullery, then Mike Bailey, followed by Jimmy Melia, a 13th-place finish was as high as Brighton rode, but at the end of 1982/83 they also graced Wembley in the FA Cup Final against Manchester United, and but for a miss by Gordon Smith (the Scottish striker's low, weakly struck shot coming off the knees of United keeper Gary Bailey) with virtually the last kick of the game in extra time, they would have won it, too. Level at 2-2 at the end of that first meeting, Albion were soundly beaten 4-0 in the replay five days later, the winning margin the biggest in an FA Cup Final for 80 years. And by New Year's Eve 1983 they were also back in the Second Division once more, their relegation after coming rock bottom of the division compounding their cup final disappointment.

Clough was right. Although it would be a further ten years still before the face of football began to change forever with the birth of the Premier League era and the first instalments of serious television money, a decade on from his column the game *was* vastly different in many ways. It was a ten-year period that had seen admission prices go up, wages rise and transfer fees spiral. Club shirts were now emblazoned with the names of sponsors. The League Cup was backed by, of all things, the Milk Marketing Board and had been rebranded accordingly. While England now had a manager, after Alf, Don and Ron, with more than three letters in his forename, Fulham had a boss who had originally been bought for the club by the now England chief Bobby Robson way back in 1968 – Malcolm Macdonald. And on 19 November 1981, it was none other than Supermac who'd become the first paid director in English football.

If the terraces at many grounds were still in a decrepit state, playing surfaces on the whole had greatly improved – even the notoriously difficult-to-maintain pudding at Derby County's Baseball Ground. At other grounds, undersoil heating, to combat the winter weather, had become popular. In 1981 QPR had even dug up the grass at Loftus Road and installed a synthetic pitch. Luton, Oldham and Preston would also go on to try an artificial turf. Fond as Clough was of a quote or two about how and where the game should be played – 'If God had wanted us to play football in the clouds, he'd have put grass up there' and 'We had a good team on paper. Unfortunately, the game was played on grass' – what he would have said about Astroturf and plastic, from his 1973 perspective, one can quite easily imagine.

Clough certainly hadn't seen that one coming. There was something else that he, even at his clairvoyant best, could probably never have imagined either as he projected forward ten years. On New Year's Eve 1983, Leeds United beat his hometown club Middlesbrough 4-1 at Elland Road – but, after going down in 1981/82 under Allan Clarke, they were a now a mid-table Second Division side managed by another former player, Eddie Gray. It had taken nearly a decade and their relegation as the third-worst team in the top flight, but Clough, the man who in August 1973 had called for the demotion of the West Yorkshire club to the second tier, albeit for disciplinary reasons, had finally seen his wish fulfilled.

5–11 January 1974

Who is the best footballer in England; the best young player; the best team? These questions will all be answered on Sunday night when the results will be announced of a members' ballot of the Professional Footballers' Association. Meanwhile, Brian Clough makes his choice …

MIGHTY MICK,
MY PLAYER OF THE YEAR

IT is my guess that when the Professional Footballers' Association declares the winner of their first Player of the Year award, the man who picks up the trophy won't be one of the great international stars such as Bobby Moore, Martin Peters or Colin Bell.

The players themselves will choose somebody who doesn't steal the headlines, a grafter who slogs away partially unnoticed for 60 games, an unsung, one-hundred-per-center. A player's player.

There are quite a few blokes around who could fit the bill. I had a couple at Derby – John McGovern and Henry Newton, and there's always that man I raved about in this column the other week, Newcastle's Malcolm Macdonald. But my choice – a man who could be the managers' player as well as the players' player – is someone who has never worn an England senior shirt, whose talents are often ignored in contrast to the glittering names playing around him: Mick Jones of Leeds United.

Jones is playing in the most difficult position in football – centre-forward. He gets his fair share of goals, he shirks nothing, he takes an incredible number of knocks, and he's always suffering injuries. This can mean two things in football. Either a man is injury prone – and this is a real problem for some players – or, like

Jones, he is suicidal in his determination to get into the thick of it. Jones puts his foot where a less courageous player would pull it out. Jones puts his head into a goalmouth where another man wouldn't even go into the penalty area.

I often think that soccer should take a lesson from ice hockey – and football clubs like Chelsea – and, instead of simply noting the players who score the goals, should recognise 'assists' as well. That way, the man who laid on the goal gets some of the credit – officially. Mick Jones plays in the enormously talented shadow of Allan Clarke, who gets the goals and pinches the limelight at Elland Road. But I would like to know how many 'assists' Jones has chalked up in his career. I would guess that if Leeds scored 70 goals in a season, and Jones scored ten of them, you could credit him with 30 or 40 'assists' … and some important ones, too.

Remember the 1972 FA Cup Final? Who ripped past the Arsenal defenders with that snorting, loping run, pulled the ball back from the goal line and put over a beautiful centre for Allan Clarke to head the winning goal? It was Jones. And at the end of the match, who had his face screwed up in agony after dislocating his elbow in another of those kamikaze leaps into the penalty area? It was Jones.

Managers warm to these types of players. They never cause you a discipline problem, and when it comes to the team sheet, the name writes itself automatically, it flows from your pen. Sometimes players like Jones are paid a terrible injustice because the manager doesn't realise just how much he puts into a game.

On a wet Saturday night when you're sitting at home after losing a match in the afternoon, when you're feeling depressed and you're going over the game in your head, that's the time when you suddenly think, 'God, that poor devil went through fire and water for me today.' That's when you get it into perspective.

I have often heard Don Revie talk about his greatest team – his Madeleys and his Coopers and his Charltons – but I doubt whether penny for penny he has ever spent a better £100,000 than when he forked it out to buy Mick Jones from Sheffield in 1967.

In the Young Player section the choice is more difficult. There haven't been that many outstanding young players rising to the surface in the last year. A few names spring to mind: Trevor Francis and Bob Latchford of Birmingham City, Gerry Francis of Queen's Park Rangers, Leighton James of Burnley.

But I can't see further than one youngster who made 22 first-team appearances at Derby last season, who played in the European Cup, and all at the age of 17. Young Steve Powell would get my vote because, in addition to his undoubted skills, he has matured to such an extent in 1973 that it is a certainty that he'll become one of the great footballing names of the future. If we're looking forward to the World Cup in 1978 we should be grooming players like Powell now.

My First Division team (on 1973 form) is: P. Shilton (Leicester City), C. Todd, R. McFarland (Derby County), E. Hughes (Liverpool), D. Nish (Derby), B. Bremner (Leeds United, captain), T. Brooking (West Ham), P. Osgood (Chelsea), A. Clarke, M. Jones (Leeds), M. Macdonald (Newcastle United). If the usual five 'international' substitutes were allowed, they would be: P. Jennings (Tottenham Hotspur), B. Moncur (Newcastle), M. Dobson (Burnley), R. Marsh (Manchester City), M. Channon (Southampton).*

Whoever wins the awards on Sunday night, the most pleasing thing about the whole affair is that, for the first time, players are asserting themselves as a unit. Once, anyone who played football for a living was considered thick and stupid, unable to put two intelligible words together. It is slowly dawning on people that many footballers are educated, talented men.

That's what I mean when I say I'm pleased that the players are now beginning to behave like a professional body, and the more we hear the voice of the players the better. Because players *are* football.

* * * *

Clough was in the right ballpark; it wasn't Mick Jones, however, that became the inaugural recipient of the PFA Player of the Year trophy (the award actually made on Sunday, 3 March 1974) but another loyal servant from Revie's Leeds United side, Norman Hunter. The previous day, the Gateshead-born defender was in the United line-up that had drawn 1-1 at home to Newcastle in the First

Division. It was the West Yorkshire club's 32nd league game of the season and they'd lost just one of them. The dependable England centre-half had been United's best player in many.

For much of his career slated for an uncompromising approach – 'Our Norman came home with a terrible leg last night – all bruised and bleeding. The trouble is, he doesn't know who it belongs to,' Hunter's wife supposedly once joked to her neighbour – Hunter was much more than a mere leg-biter deployed to break up opponents' play by fair means or foul; he was very often assured in his ball control, accurate with his forward passing, shrewd with his strategic positioning, even majestic in his tackling. And now he was commanding a fresh respect.

Before Leeds's game with Liverpool on Saturday, 20 October 1973, the same afternoon that Clough was putting in his defiant show at the Baseball Ground before Derby's 2-1 win over Leicester City, the two teams had formed a guard of honour for Hunter, who was also presented with an ornate silver salver from United chairman Manny Cussins to commemorate his 600th appearance for the club, made in a League Cup loss at Ipswich. 'Whatever harsh words are applied from time to time to Hunter's forthrightness,' wrote *The Times*'s Tom German after a New Year's Day home draw with Spurs, 'he really is a sustaining pillar.' A performance in another drawn game, 0-0 at Everton, prompted the *Yorkshire Post*'s Terry Brindle to extol Hunter's 'unswerving combativeness' as he 'covered, chased and tackled with the intimidating sureness that makes strong men quail and in doing so typified real professionalism, the aggressive spirit which meets adversity with bared teeth.'

To Don Revie's mind, the PFA award was overdue vindication for the player, whose aberration versus the Poles had clearly been forgiven by his fellow Englishmen and perhaps even earned him extra brownie points from the Scots. 'I do not think he has been given anything like sufficient credit,' Revie said of one of his favourite sons, 'for the ability he possesses, and his great dedication and will to win.'

It was in the October clash with Bill Shankly's reigning champions, the sternest examination of Leeds's title credentials thus far, that Mick Jones, evading challenges from Ray Clemence and Tommy Smith, had headed in at the near post Peter Lorimer's swerving centre from the left flank for the game's only goal. The previous week, as United recovered from falling two behind within 19 minutes at Leicester, Jones had reached the 100-goal mark for the club since joining from Sheffield United. 'Jones, perhaps more than most because of the very nature of his play, is the type of player who draws heavily on energy and takes a regular buffeting from defenders yet still pounds away in uncomplaining fashion,' wrote Don Warters in the *Yorkshire Evening Post*. 'This season, however, he is gaining the kind of reward his endeavours deserve.'

He had been in fine goalscoring form. But Jones, unlike his teammates Madeley, Hunter, Bremner, Giles and Clarke, didn't even make the PFA team. Clough might have recognised Jones's unselfish, unstinting work as leader of the Leeds line but it clearly wasn't enough to warrant the votes of his fellow pros. As fulsome as his praise for the forward was, Clough did do Jones a slight disservice: the fair-haired Yorkshireman, first spotted at local league level with Dinnington Miners Welfare, in fact, won three caps for England, all in friendlies, the first two in May 1965 as a Sheffield United player when Sir Alf Ramsey's side beat West Germany 1-0 in Nuremberg then, four days later, overcame Sweden 2-1 in Gothenburg.

It was a further four and a half years though before he earned his last cap for his country, Jones's first while at Leeds, in England's first international of the 1970s, at Wembley against the Netherlands on 14 January. It was a forgettable night. Starting in the same XI as his Elland Road teammates Cooper, Charlton and Hunter, Jones was replaced on 73 minutes by West Ham's Geoff Hurst as the home side, slow-handclapped and jeered by their fans, struggled to a goalless draw with a quality Dutch team featuring Cruyff, Van Hanegem, Krol and Keizer, one England had beaten 1-0 in Amsterdam just two months earlier.

At Elland Road at the time, Jones was now partnered up front by Allan Clarke, Revie jumping in ahead of Arsenal, Manchester United, Spurs and Everton to hand over a British record £166,000 for the Staffordshire-born striker in July 1969. The Jones-Clarke combination had been unlocking defences with relative ease ever since.

If the slender, wiry Clarke, possessing what journalist and, later, United's public relations officer Peter Fay perfectly described as a 'ghostly and aristocratic presence' in the opposing penalty box, the burlier Jones provided a far more robust threat to defenders. But he was anything but just a brave workhorse. Skilful on the ground and a brilliant header of the ball, able to hold up the play until help arrived or go on mazy runs by himself, Jones made an ideal target man. Like the clinical executor alongside him, Jones had a keen eye for a half-chance in front of goal, often scoring exciting individual efforts.

On 7 August 1968, 11 months after he'd joined the club from the Blades for £100,000, becoming Leeds's first six-figure signing, it was Jones's goal that gave United a 1-0 home win over Hungary's Ferencváros in the first leg of the 1967/68 Inter-Cities Fairs Cup Final, and in due course the club's first European trophy following a goalless return game. In the 1970 FA Cup Final with Chelsea, ultimately lost 2-1 in an Old Trafford replay, Jones had netted in both games, his 84th-minute goal at Wembley, rifling home a low left-footer after Clarke had hit the post, looking like a game-settler before Ian Hutchinson levelled two minutes later. Two years on, the deadly duo enjoyed better fortune. In the Centenary Final, as the West Yorkshire club won the trophy at the third time of asking after failures versus Liverpool and Chelsea, it was Jones, evading Bob McNab's flailing tackle near the byline on the right of Arsenal's penalty area, who delivered the fine 53rd-minute cross on the turn, which Clarke, flinging himself forward, dispatched past Bob Wilson's deputy Geoff Barnett from 15 yards out for the match winner.

The abiding image of the afternoon, however, came after the full-time whistle; in the final seconds of the game, Jones, bearing down on goal in Leeds's last attack, took a tumble on the famous turf, landing awkwardly in an innocuous challenge from the diving Barnett. Helped off the pitch by physio Ian Adams, it was several minutes before the number nine, a dislocated left elbow heavily bandaged, his shoulder hunched and his face contorted with suffering, was able to ascend the 39 steps and collect his winners' medal to the biggest cheer of the afternoon. The whole of Wembley rose to him.

It was typical of Jones that in such a state he should insist on the climb to shake hands with the Queen, though he admitted afterwards that, had he realised he was keeping Her Majesty waiting, 'I'd have thought twice about going up to the Royal Box'. When he fulfilled his ambition, albeit extremely gingerly and with the assistance of Norman Hunter, the Queen inquired, 'Are you in pain?' 'I thought I should be as polite,' Jones related years later. 'Yes, Ma'am, a little,' he told her.

Jones's determination and willingness to go beyond the pain barrier was symptomatic of the man. In the courageous centre-forward, Clough saw a footballer who was the archetypal model professional, a player of all-out endeavour, totally committed to his club's cause and, more importantly, one exempt from the roughhouse tactics and snide, underhand mannerisms Clough found so disdainful in some of Jones's teammates. But Clough, when Leeds manager, never got to select Jones for his side.

After featuring in both the heartbreaking 1-0 final defeats at the conclusion of 1972/73 as Sunderland became the first Second Division club to lift the FA Cup for 42 years, then AC Milan benefitted from some highly questionable refereeing decisions in the Cup Winners' Cup, Jones opened the new campaign with renewed vigour. 'Jones is much more penetrative and eager than he was towards the end of last season,' the *Yorkshire Evening Post's* Don Warters reported. 'He is quicker to the ball, more direct when in possession, and is prepared to take on defenders.' But a nagging knee problem, first picked up in training, was taking its toll.

Absent for a few matches in November, after his return Jones missed a further three games following the goalless draw at Goodison Park on 19 January. He made a goalscoring comeback in a 2-0 triumph before 60,025 at Old Trafford. But after two FA Cup ties with Bristol City (Leeds surprisingly exiting the competition

1-0 at home in a replay), Jones only started three more league fixtures, with young Scot Joe Jordan occupying the central striking role for the season's remainder. The 57th-minute opener versus Manchester United, his 14th league goal of the season, was not only Jones's last of the campaign it was the final one he ever registered for Revie's side.

Just 18 months later, after intensive physiotherapy following an operation failed to alleviate his troubles, the 30-year-old Jones had no option but to call it quits. An attempt at reserve-team football had proved too painful; the bone under his kneecap had flaked away and Jones recognised that the end had come.

Don Revie regarded Allan Clarke – 'a killer with a gentle touch,' he called him – as 'a finisher to rank with the greatest anywhere', but Jones, with 111 goals from 312 appearances, had an impressive record, too. In both Leeds's title wins under Revie, it was Jones who top-scored with 14 goals. They prospered in each other's company, developing a tremendous understanding from almost their first game together. In 'Jonah' – 'the best striking partner I played with for either club or country' – Clarke knew he had the most complementary companion. They were a near-perfect pairing. 'We were compared with Toshack and Keegan of Liverpool, Radford and Kennedy of Arsenal, Chivers and Gilzean of Tottenham, and Osgood and Baldwin of Chelsea,' wrote Clarke in his autobiography, *Sniffer*. 'None of them touched us.'

* For the record, it was Ipswich Town defender Kevin Beattie who took the PFA Young Player of the Year award, whilst the full PFA Team of the Year selected was:

Pat Jennings (Tottenham Hotspur), Paul Madeley (Leeds United), Roy McFarland (Derby County), Norman Hunter (Leeds United), Colin Todd (Derby County), Billy Bremner (Leeds United), Tony Currie (Sheffield United), Johnny Giles (Leeds United), Mick Channon (Southampton), Malcolm Macdonald (Newcastle United), Allan Clarke (Leeds United).

2–8 February 1974

Thousands of soccer fans answered the Brian Clough questionnaire in *TVTimes* recently, and on Saturday in *On the Ball* Clough is hoping to discuss the results with Brian Moore. Here we give you an at-a-glance guide to the main results and Clough's first reactions to them ...

CLOUGH ASKED AND YOU TOLD HIM ... SOCCER VIOLENCE? BLAME THE PLAYERS

WHY are the fans staying away from football? What are conditions like at your club? What is the extent of hooliganism in football crowds? How would you change the game? I asked you for some answers, and the response was enormous.

The most worrying problem in football, of course, has been falling attendances, and 49 per cent of fans who answered my survey blamed negative football for this. What a damning statistic about the way we play our national game! We can't afford to ignore information like this.

It was encouraging to see from the survey that most fans were happy with conditions at their clubs, and especially that 97 per cent thought they got a good view of the game. Great progress has been made in improving grounds, and I can think of four First Division clubs – Burnley, Sheffield United, Chelsea and Newcastle – where terrific new stands have just been finished or are being built. That figure of 97 per cent shows that clubs are making a real effort, costing millions, to look after the fans.

The question which asked if your club made you feel as if you belonged, or was only interested in taking your money, produced an interesting generation gap among fans. 73 per cent of the under-25s said their clubs did make them feel part of them, but 54 per cent of the over-25s said the clubs' only interest was in taking their money. I think this was a predictable answer. Younger fans associate with clubs whether or not they are well looked after and encouraged. The over-25s who are more cynical, want to be made to feel they are part of a club, and I think their response shows that they feel they are right out in the cold as far as having a say in how the affairs of their clubs are handled.

The next figures staggered me. 70 per cent of fans said they had personally witnessed violence on the terraces, but two out of every three of the under-25s said that they thought the subject had been blown up out of proportion by the press, while two out of every three over-25s said they thought it had not. This amount of violence is very worrying.

I left a space for fans to suggest what they would do with soccer hooligans, and there were some bloodthirsty ideas. 'Amputate below the knee.' 'Hang them publicly at half-time in the centre circle.' 'Set them on Brian Clough.' 'Put them to a work in a sewage farm on a Saturday.' These were some of the strong answers, but more fans thought that convicted hooligans should have to report to a detention centre on matchdays, a most sensible idea.

The fans made it clear that hooliganism was a real problem, but they went further than that in the survey. 65 per cent said that bad behaviour on the field led to violence on the terraces, and I think they are dead right. If the people you hold in high esteem, the star players, behave badly, it can only have a bad effect on youngsters in the crowd.

The police in New York are widely believed to be corrupt, and one of the results is that people there have no respect for law and order. So, on the same score, if a player acts like a thug on the football field, he will bring out the thuggery in the crowd. If, on the other hand, he played the game fairly, as it should be played, and wore the mantle of a star as it should be worn, the young fans would take a lead from him. It works like that all through life. If I turned up at a Brighton training session roaring drunk, the players would also start turning up the worse for drink, and I wouldn't blame them.

One more interesting fact to emerge from the survey was on the question of when fans would personally like to watch a football match. Although Saturday afternoon was the first choice, with a 53 per cent vote, 26 per cent chose Sunday afternoon, and this poll was conducted *before* Football Association secretary Ted Croker gave his blessing to Sunday soccer. I must say that I love my Sunday lunch, and look forward to putting up my feet on a Sunday afternoon, but I'd gladly spend it on a touchline somewhere if it were going to make our game healthier. There are problems to overcome, but I am sure that Sunday soccer is inevitable; it's as certain as spring follows winter.

On the subject of referees, 85 per cent of fans said they thought players did not readily accept a referee's decision, and I agree that this is one of the plagues of football. It happens chiefly because football is a professional game with an awful lot of money at stake, but I always tell my players to accept the official's decision, utterly and completely.

A majority of fans – 63 per cent – said they thought refereeing standards had fallen, which is a sad statistic. People tend to think that standards are falling whatever they are talking about, and when it comes to referees, I don't see the point in arguing about it. They are the men who must have the moral courage to make decisions and stick to them, and that's that.

However, people do seem to be most concerned about referees. In the next question, which asked fans to say what changes they'd like to see in the game, 40 per cent chose the suggestion that referees should be paid well and employed full-time. This must come, as surely as Sunday football; it's only a question of time. 28 per cent felt they would like to see a change in the offside law, to encourage attacking play. I feel that we *can* have attacking play within the framework of the present rules.

In the space left for other suggestions, many people attached notes suggesting that the pitch should be re-drawn, with bigger goals, two penalty spots (one for minor, one for major offences), and semi-circular penalty areas. Some wanted 'sin-bins' for perpetual offenders, cameras behind the goals to assist the referee. Quite a few said, 'Sack Alf Ramsey,' while there were a couple who said: 'Get rid of Brian Clough.' Well, you can't win them all.

The last question, about television and soccer, showed that 80 per cent didn't think there was too much soccer on TV, and 63 per cent said they didn't think it was discussed too much. (So I'm still in a job!)

The idea of this survey was to find out, not from managers and talkers like me, not from people who govern the game, but from fans who pay to get into grounds, what they thought about the state of the sport. When we sent a copy of the questionnaire and the survey results to Ted Croker at the FA and Alan Hardaker, the Football League secretary, they both declined to comment. Never mind. If all those fans cut out the survey, filled it in, stuck a stamp on it and sent it off, with nothing in it for themselves, the game can't be in that bad a state, can it?

23 February–1 March 1974

Two years at Hartlepools, seven at Derby, four months at Brighton: Brian Clough and his partner Peter Taylor have seen soccer management at the top and the bottom. But what makes a manager? This is Clough's recipe for a top management team ... and why he thinks Brighton is best ...

WE'LL SUCCEED
BECAUSE WE'RE THE BEST

WHETHER you are running a brewery, a vast multi-national company, a water-pistol factory or a Football League club, the essence of successful management is the same. There are three ingredients for successful management wherever you are: the ability to communicate, the gift of decision-making, and wholehearted involvement.

The combination of myself and Peter Taylor is the best football management team in the country. There is only one other manager to compare with us in our thorough approach to the job: Don Revie at Leeds. He earns laurels from me. Leeds haven't been out of the top-four places in the First Division for nine years and in that time they have won the FA Cup, been beaten in two finals, won the UEFA Cup twice, and narrowly lost the Cup Winners' Cup Final last year. In 1974 they'll win the league as surely as the sun comes up tomorrow.

We all have our own ways of doing things and, unlike me, Revie keeps very quiet about his job. But I am sure that those three qualities which I have spotlighted would come top of his list, too. Take communication with his players – Revie knows them inside out. He knows every shade of their ability. This two-way flow of understanding with them means that his will is literally transferred to the pitch. It's as if 11 Don Revies were out there playing.

You have to bear in mind that your ability to manage depends on the commodity you're dealing with. A manager in business would have his work cut out if he was trying to sell substandard goods, and in football it is harder to manage a club with indifferent players than one with star players. Bad players need good management more than good players, but the biggest secret is how to extract the very best from any player.

Wherever Peter Taylor and I have worked we have applied this rule: look at a player, then decide what things he is good at and what things he is bad at. Then develop, encourage and perfect his good points. Too many managers make the mistake of concentrating on improving a player's weaknesses. But that same player may have instincts for other aspects of the game which are worth exploiting.

The ability to make decisions is a rare quality. There are only a handful of people in any field you care to name who can make decisions. I know of one manager who used to ask other managers their opinion of a player before he had the courage to put his money where his mouth was and make an offer.

We rely on our judgement, and this includes the judgement to know when you've made a mistake. If I spent £200,000 on a player who did not live up to expectations, I would have no hesitation in dropping him – quickly. Many managers turn their backs to this sort of decision and these are the people who never find success. If you are not a man of decision, you might as well go and sweep the streets as be a football manager.

I often envy the business manager – he can go to a board meeting and tell his directors that in another nine months they'll be ten per cent up on sales. But we in football are not dealing with crates of machine tools – but with human nature, and we have to sit on a touchline 50 or more times a season, watching our decisions succeed or fail in front of thousands of people.

I can best illustrate the third quality – having total involvement – by talking about my days at Derby. We built up one of the greatest sides of all time, and when it established itself, there was not a lot more we could tell them. They knew what we wanted and they went out and put it into practice. And that's when we made the mistake of being complacent. A surgeon might remove so many toenails that he could probably take them out blindfolded. But the day he thinks he can is the day he makes a mess of it.

Three or four times at Derby I thought I could relax before a game, have a big lunch and a few beers and leave the players to themselves, and, curiously, on those occasions we lost the game. We knew we were playing inferior sides, we knew we could beat them with our eyes shut, but this attitude had a strange way of rebounding.

At about this time the captain, Roy McFarland, accused me of not spending enough time with the players and I accepted what he said – but I made sure he never had the chance to say it again. On matchdays we got to the ground at 10am and made sure everything was perfect. We ate with the players, breathed the air they breathed right up to the kick-off. We even did up their boots.

I apply the same philosophy at Brighton. I walked out of the Goldstone Ground the other day for a beer and a sandwich and I saw two of my apprentices walking into the ground. One of them had his hands in his pockets, and I said, 'Oi, get 'em out, lad.' Now if I hadn't been there, on the job, watching, I wouldn't have seen that. What will putting his hands in his pockets do to that boy's footballing skills? I'm not sure it makes any difference at all. But it could be that putting your hands in your pockets reflects a lazy state of mind which could show on the pitch, and I'm not going to take that risk.

No manager can find lasting success without the three qualities I have outlined. There are 92 managerial jobs in the Football League and, for various reasons, 800 managers have changed or quit their jobs (me and Peter included) since World War Two. Quite a turnover isn't it? But there is a gift in management – it's not something you can just play at. And I think we've got it. Watch Brighton and you'll see what I mean.

2–8 March 1974

This Saturday, live from a Wembley Stadium packed with 100,000 Football League Cup Final followers, you can see the finals of the *On the Ball* Penalty Prize: four boys bidding for the *TVTimes* Trophy. Brian Clough considers the penalties of success ...

YOU SHOULD *NEVER* MISS A PENALTY

CYRIL Beavon, 36 and three years retired from professional football, represents the sort of player who makes up the backbone of our game. A solid full-back for Oxford United, he never won an international cap – he didn't even open a boutique. But after five years at Wolves, he went on to set a club record at Oxford with 508 first-team appearances in 12 years.

It seems a bit ironical that his son Stuart, at the age of 15, is doing something this Saturday that his dad never achieved in his long career ... appearing at Wembley. Having scored ten goals out of ten shots in his heat against Gordon Banks, Stuart is favourite to lift the *TVTimes* Trophy in the *On the Ball* penalty competition against the three other contenders, Jim Grattan, 15, from Belfast; north London boy Steve Brennan, 15; and 14-year-old Barry Grainger from Yate, Gloucestershire.

Penalty taking, it seems, runs in the family. Cyril Beavon was Oxford's regular spot kicker, slotting in a regular half-dozen goals every season. He only missed one in his career. 'That was against Reading, years ago. The pitch was like treacle pudding and the ball was almost impossible to kick. When I hit it, I don't think it even reached the goal line. That took a bit of living down.'

Young Beavon could well be embarking on a soccer career himself. Recently, Arsenal invited him to take a look at their facilities with a view to signing him on as an apprentice. It looks as if the lad has the makings of a fine kicker of the dead ball: he plays for Oxford schoolboys, and takes all their corners, free kicks, and penalties. This is a skill far too scarce in our game today – it's the sort of quality which makes Derby's Alan Hinton an indispensable player.

Stuart has two penalty rules. The first is 'keep your cool'. He explains that 'if you're het up you can't take a decent penalty, and Wembley is going to be the biggest test of that. My other rule is, when I'm taking a kick, I always aim for one of the stanchions at the back of the goal. That way you get it near the corner without being too close to the post, and yet well away from the goalkeeper.'

Last year's Penalty Prize winner, Christopher O'Sullivan from Kensington, south London, relied on a well-rehearsed ritual when he took his kicks in the competition. 'Call it superstition if you like, but I think you have to feel psychologically right to take the kicks properly. And so, when I went to Wembley I had to have everything just right. I wore the old boots I had on in the previous rounds, and I left them covered with mud because I didn't want to clean them until I'd won. When I walked on to the pitch some of the crowd shouted at me, "Cor, couldn't you clean your flippin' boots?"

'But I knew what I was doing. I made my brother Michael wear the same coat he had worn when he had watched me in the heats, and I chewed the same brand of chewing gum.

'When I took the kicks, I went through the same moves every time. I wiped the ball on my shirt and turned my back to the goalkeeper. As I walked back I decided firmly which side I was going to shoot. Then I looked only at the ball. I gave David Best in goal no idea where I was going to shoot.

'I really think all the preparation I made gave me a lot of confidence and I was the coolest of all the finalists. I would say that applies this year – the coolest boy will win.'

A player should never miss a penalty. When Walter Winterbottom was England's team manager he worked out that it was impossible for any goalkeeper to reach a hard, accurate shot, banged into goal from 12 yards. A ball struck at 60 to 70 mph – the speed at which the ball travels from a powerful player's boot – takes one-third of a second to go from the penalty spot to the goal line. It takes that time for a goalkeeper's brain to send the message to his muscles to dive in a particular direction. And by the time he reacts, the ball is already nestling in the back of the net.

Of course, goalkeepers are aware of this and with experience they begin to move fractionally before the kick is taken. In some cases today, they move a long time before the kick is taken and get away with it. With goalkeepers doing this, the placing of the shot is important, and on our diagram*, it's those orange areas which give him practically no chance. They are the areas where the goalkeeper has the longest distance to dive, but the blue areas, close to the side of the goalkeeper's legs are deceptively difficult spots, too.

The yellow areas, however, do give the keeper a chance. Obviously, a shot going anywhere near the centre of the goal is a bad effort, but a ball placed between 3ft and 6ft high, even towards the corner, also gives him that sniff of a chance. Often, goalkeepers save powerful shots at this height when a lower or higher shot would have beaten them.

Statistics about penalties are hard to come by because referees, in their match reports, are not asked to state whether they awarded any penalties. They simply register the goals scored, players disciplined, etc. Over the last two seasons there have been approximately 60 penalties awarded in the First Division each season, and 80 per cent were scored. Most prolific scorer of penalty goals is Manchester City's Francis Lee. His 15 penalty goals in the 1971/72 season is the penalty record.

There has been quite a lot of discussion lately about the penalty kick. Some people are saying that any offence committed inside the area should warrant a penalty. And a month ago Jimmy Hill said on *Match of the Day* that any serious offence or misconduct, even if it is committed outside the penalty area, should warrant a penalty or a free shot from, say, 18 yards. I'm sure these are sincere suggestions for improving the game, but my attitude on this is the same as ever: misconduct cannot be cured on the pitch, it is a management responsibility, and changing rules does not change attitudes. It's thinking, not rules, which needs to change.

Finally, when you're watching the Penalty Prize on Saturday, I hope you never see the embarrassing sight I witnessed when I was touring Spain with Derby last August. A match between Atlético Madrid and the Russian side Dynamo Tbilisi finished level and they had to decide it on penalty kicks. Atlético's ace spot kicker limbered up to take his kick and – I'm not kidding – he took a 30-yard run up!

He scorched up to the ball, stubbed his toe on the ground, sent a clod of earth spinning into the air, and went screaming off the pitch on one leg, clutching his toe with both hands. The ball trickled towards the Russian goalkeeper like a dead Sputnik.

In the one-against-one situation of the penalty kick, the laws of nature, which say you can't miss, can go horribly wrong.

* The coloured diagram referred to in the column was accompanied by the following text: Clough's Law on penalties is 'aim for the orange areas'. The blue areas are, he says, deceptively difficult, also. A shot anywhere near the centre of goal, or the yellow area, is a natural save for the goalkeeper.

❋ ❋ ❋ ❋

On 8 August 1970, when Derby County won the Watney Cup, Britain's first sponsored football tournament, the opponents they beat 4-1 that afternoon at the Baseball Ground, Manchester United, had progressed to the final via the first-ever penalty shoot-out in a professional match on English soil. United's semi-final three nights earlier at Second Division Hull City's Boothferry Park, 1-1 after extra time, was decided by this new match-settling rule, with 'a penalty-taking session which,' the *Daily Mail's* Brian Taylor wrote, 'was one of the most exciting and dramatic features I have ever seen on a soccer field.'

Over the course of the following decade it was a method of determining victory for ties still level after 120 minutes that became widely employed. For both club and international fixtures, this footballing 'high noon' increasingly resolved the outcome of important knockout matches. In 1970 UEFA opted to use penalty kicks rather than the toss of a coin for matches finishing all-square in the three main cup competitions. At domestic level, in the FA Cup, penalty kicks were used in the 1972 edition of the short-lived third-and-fourth-place play-off. Drawn games in the initial rounds of the League Cup were being settled by penalties by August 1976. While earlier that summer, after the two countries were tied at 2-2, a shoot-out in the European Championship Final in Belgrade between Czechoslovakia and West Germany had famously spawned the 'Panenka' that gave the Czechs the trophy for a first time. Penalty takers could generally be divided into two classes: the blasters and the strokers. The Czech midfielder's audacious chip down the middle of Sepp Maier's goal took not just the German keeper but also everyone watching by total surprise: despite Maier going the right way, Panenka coolly lofted the ball over him for the win.

In Hull on 5 August 1970, in front of a huge pre-season crowd of 34,007, it was George Best who made the record books as the taker (and scorer) of the first-ever penalty of a shoot-out, placing the ball into the bottom left of home goalkeeper Ian McKechnie's net. But the dubious honour of being the first to miss in this new format went to Best's teammate Denis Law. After Terry Neill, Brian Kidd, Ian Butler, Bobby Charlton and Ken Houghton had all converted, Law, scorer of United's goal during the 90 minutes that cancelled out Ken Wagstaff's early strike for the Tigers, saw his kick kept out by fellow Scot McKechnie. It was catching: Wagstaff then flashed his shot wide. But after Willie Morgan slid home his spot kick, when keeper McKechnie, with no other City players offering their services, stepped up and slammed the ball against the bar and over, the top-flight visitors were through. 'Whether you regard it as excitement or comic opera,' watching YTV commentator Keith Macklin concluded, 'tonight history-making soccer has resulted in a win for Manchester United.'

It was at United's neighbours, City, in the late 60s/early 70s that Francis Lee was the undisputed penalty king of English football, the force and ferocity of his shots – Lee opting mostly for power and pace rather than placement – virtually guaranteeing a goal. He'd scored some crucial ones, too, most notably the decider in the 1970 European Cup Winners' Cup Final against Poland's Górnik Zabrze that earned City a first European trophy, Lee celebrating his 26th birthday by getting his side's second goal of a 2-1 win in Vienna two minutes before half-time. 'I put plenty of meat into the kick,' he said, recalling his winner shortly after. 'I always do, as I think this gives the goalie far less chance of saving it!' However, he did 'put it too close to the keeper for comfort,' he admitted.

Of the 15 spot kicks Lee converted in league and cup games during the 1971/72 season, the last came on 22 April 1972 as Malcolm Allison's side, with new acquisition from QPR, Rodney Marsh, scoring a wonderful individual goal then getting bundled over in the box for the penalty, beat Clough's Derby 2-0 at Maine Road in what was County's penultimate First Division match of the campaign. As it transpired, of course, the defeat didn't turn out to be too damaging; the two points gained from a 1-0 home win over Liverpool in their final fixture – John McGovern slamming a 25-yard effort past Ray Clemence – was ultimately enough for the Rams to secure the title, their 58 points one better than the Anfield club, Leeds as well as Lee's City who, at one point in March, had been four points clear at the top of the table before faltering.

On 29 April, just seven days later, Lee, then aged 28, made the last of his 27 England appearances, as Sir Alf Ramsey's side fell 3-1 to the West Germans at Wembley in their European Championship quarter-final first-leg encounter. His 77th-minute goal on the night – tapping into an unguarded net after Sepp Maier failed to hold a Colin Bell shot – equalised Uli Hoeneß's first-half strike, before two in the last five minutes from Netzer (a penalty conceded by Moore, which an unlucky Banks got his hand to but couldn't keep out) and Müller left England with a deficit that proved too difficult to pull back. With 11 days to go before the second leg in Berlin's Olympic Stadium, Lee collapsed from sheer exhaustion and spent almost a week recovering in hospital before a period of convalescence. He was never selected again. In all, Lee netted ten times at international level, though, ironically, on the two occasions he was asked to take penalties for his country he missed both times.

Joe Mercer, Lee's boss at Manchester City as the club won the league title (in 1967/68) for only the second time in its history, the FA Cup and League Cup in successive seasons, cited the explosive forward as his ideal penalty taker. As well as the belief he could beat any keeper, Lee had the two essentials for scoring from 12 yards: a strong nerve to withstand the noise of the crowd and the needling remarks of opposing players, and conviction to put the ball exactly where he'd decided he would. 'That's the real killer,' said Mercer. 'Players will change their mind. Once you decide what you are going to do, you've got to stick with it.'

In 1971/72 Lee 'was bubbling with confidence,' Mercer said, and had converted 11 penalties in succession to equal a Football League record set in the same season (1932/33) by Spurs winger Willie Evans and Sheffield Wednesday centre-forward Jack Ball. 'That year we christened him Lee Won Pen, City's Chinese penalty taker,' Mercer remembered affectionately. It was a nickname conferred upon the player who for five successive seasons was Bolton's top scorer before going to Maine Road for £60,000 in 1967 and who'd actually made his Bolton debut while still an amateur – and scored, from open play – against City. Lee's enthusiasm on the day had also resulted in his name ending up in the referee's notebook.

The football of the tough, chunky striker was as direct as the Lancastrian himself. 'His style at times borders on that of a wall of death rider,' observed the *Manchester Evening News*'s Peter Gardner in *The Official Football League Yearbook, 1972/73*. With amazing sprints of acceleration, Lee went hell-bent for goal and, Gardner said, 'by running straight at defences he can often exploit weaknesses or command fear – perhaps an unsophisticated ploy, but one that is oh so effective!' Opponents argued – some quite violently (as was the case with Leeds's Norman Hunter on 1 November 1975) – that many of Lee's penalties were forced, and took exception to the way he fell to the ground. He consistently 'conned' referees, they claimed.

The barrel-chested forward's tendency to go over a bit too easily in the box resulted in Lee gaining a fairly negative name for himself among certain cynical journalists, too. In Lee, as well as Mike Summerbee, Terry Brindle of the *Yorkshire Post* wrote in 1973, Manchester City had done 'as much as any team to legitimise this now prevalent form of deviousness'. That was diving. Though given that the majority of City's penalties were awarded for fouls on other players, it was perhaps a little unfair. Regardless, Lee wasn't overly concerned about it. He and George Best used to laugh at his reputation. 'Every footballer is a bit of an actor,' Best once said. 'You have to be, especially forwards.'

The sun might have already set on Lee's England career but the 1974 League Cup offered him the chance of another run-out on the Wembley turf, as City took on First Division rivals Wolves in the final of a competition they'd won four years earlier, beating West Brom 2-1 after extra time, a game in which Lee was acknowledged as the Manchester side's best player. It was thanks to yet another Lee penalty that City had squeezed past their neighbours from Old Trafford 4-3 in a two-leg semi-final. But on what turned out to be a huge letdown of an afternoon for Lee and his teammates, it was West Brom's Black Country neighbours who won the day, again by the odd goal in three, John Richards's late strike taking the trophy to Molineux for the first time.

It was also one of Lee's last games for City. A week before the next season's opening fixture, boss Tony Book splashed out £200,000 on West Brom's Scottish international midfielder Asa Hartford and the very next day agreed to sell Lee in a £110,000 deal – his destination, the Baseball Ground. Still believing he had a future at Maine Road, Lee was clearly unhappy with the move and departed the club on less-than-friendly terms.

If Lee's playing days were supposed to be in their twilight, however, no one told the Greater Manchester-born sharpshooter, who embraced his new challenge and, despite spot-kick duties being the responsibility of Bruce Rioch, still notched up 12 league goals as Dave Mackay's side, with a smattering of players still left over from the Clough-Taylor era, won the East Midlands club a second title in four seasons. In fact, one of Lee's dozen, scored away to his former employers on 28 December 1974, was possibly the most iconic of his career: a thumping right-footer from outside the box which flew into the top corner of Joe Corrigan's net and inspired the subsequently oft-quoted lines croaked out by *Match of the Day* commentator Barry Davies: 'Interesting … very interesting! Look at his face! Just look at his face!'

'A moment never to forget,' was how Lee later regarded his golden goal. He'd enjoyed a fair few down the years. One more season on, though, and Lee called it a day, though only after a very last Wembley appearance in August 1975 when league champions County beat FA Cup winners West Ham 2-0 to take the Charity Shield. It was a Lee penalty that had won Manchester City the trophy, 1-0 against Third Division champions Aston Villa in 1972 – cracking home on 70 minutes after Mike Summerbee's tumble in the area over keeper Jim Cumbes's outstretched hand.

It was in that summer of 1975 that Stuart Beavon did indeed embark 'on a soccer career himself'. Though rather than at Arsenal, it was with the Gunners's north London neighbours Tottenham that the Wolverhampton-born youngster signed as an apprentice, becoming a professional in July 1976. But Beavon found first-team opportunities limited at White Hart Lane. As, first, Spurs struggled to keep their place in the First Division and, then, following their promotion back to the top flight in 1977/78, they brought in the Argentines Ardiles and Villa to reinforce a midfield that already possessed the mercurial talents of Glenn Hoddle, Beavon failed to establish a berth in the side. In 1980, in search of regular football, the bright attacking midfielder decided to join Reading.

Beavon remained at the Berkshire club for over a decade, a virtual fixture in midfield, clocking up nearly 400 league appearances in the process. And, though not quite as synonymous with spot-kick excellence as Francis Lee, he maintained his early reputation as a Deadeye Dick from a 12-yard range. For all that, it wasn't until 1988, 14 years after his pre-League Cup Final shoot-out exploits, that Beavon made a belated return to Wembley and played his first-ever match at the stadium.

That high point came on Sunday, 27 March, when, with Reading gloomily facing impending relegation from the Second Division, they came up against top-flight hot favourites Luton in the Simod Cup Final and Beavon, only playing courtesy of a cortisone injection, got the chance to put them into a 25th-minute lead from the spot, with the scores level at one apiece.

At the time, no one had missed from 12 yards in a Wembley cup final – though Ray Graydon had seen his spot kick pushed on to a post by Norwich's Kevin Keelan in the 1975 League Cup Final, the Villa winger then put away the rebound and his cup-winning goal was recorded as a 'penalty' – and Beavon, who'd scored Reading's second in the semi-final shoot-out against Coventry, was determined not to break that record. He duly obliged but his old trick, well-established since the long-ago days of 1974 – look one way, put it the other – didn't quite work as usual: the Luton keeper Les Sealey went the right way; however, the end result was still the same. Reading went 2-1 up and on to register an unexpected 4-1 victory.

Perhaps Beavon's most widely known – and most viewed – penalty, nonetheless, resulted in a deliberate miss. When, in October 1989, an episode of Channel 4's football drama *The Manageress*, filmed at Reading's ground Elm Park and with the Reading players taking part in it, required an actor keeper to save a last-minute spot kick, Beavon was the man asked to take the dramatic penalty. Ten takes and retakes later, with the director finally satisfied, and Gabriella Benson's (actress Cherie Lunghi's) team winning 1-0 to seal promotion in the season's climactic game, Beavon's theatrics were done.

Still, so accustomed had he become to missing through his TV appearance, or so he later said, in Reading's next fixture, at home to Huddersfield Town, Beavon spurned an opportunity from 12 yards, costing the Royals victory, and although he regained his killer instinct from the spot just three days later in a 3-2 win over Fulham the 4-1 defeat at Leyton Orient that followed meant manager Ian Branfoot was collecting his P45 after his club's sorry start in the Third Division.

Whether or not the practice at failure at the TV company's insistence had had a derogatory effect or was just a good excuse, who knows. Gordon Banks often said, 'No goalkeeper should have a chance with a penalty kick if it is taken properly. The odds are very much on the side of the kicker,' but as Clough well knew deepdown, even the best could sometimes have an off day; on the odd occasion he'd been guilty himself of not making a spot kick count during his Boro and Sunderland days.

Ten years before Beavon's moment in the Wembley sun, it was a penalty that Clough had to thank for bringing the first major trophy – discounting the 1976/77 Anglo-Scottish Cup that Forest won – to the City Ground under his guidance. After the 1978 League Cup Final, dominated by Liverpool in one of the most one-sided games ever seen at the Empire Stadium, ended goalless, four days later, in the replay at Old Trafford, Forest somewhat fortuitously overcame Bob Paisley's side when winger John Robertson put away a 53rd-minute spot kick past Ray Clemence following Phil Thompson's 'professional foul' on John O'Hare, which the Liverpool players justifiably claimed – and BBC TV replays later confirmed – was actually outside the area. It proved to be the game's only goal.

Referee Pat Partridge's contentious decision, one of a number against the Merseyside club on the night, so enraged the Reds players, their subsequent frustrations led to stalwart Ian Callaghan receiving a booking for the first time in 849 games for the club – and what would be the only time in his Liverpool career – for a too-high tackle on Forest's Peter Withe whilst, immediately after the game, Anfield hard man Tommy Smith, playing in his ninth major final, was incensed, to say the least. 'Was the referee on their side tonight?' he angrily shouted at an interviewer. 'It's bloody ridiculous. It's terrible. He should be shot.'

Partridge himself wasn't shifting. When told that TV film suggested that Thompson's infringement was not in the box, he said, 'If the cameras show that, they're entitled to their view. But they weren't in line with the incident.' Predictably, Clough didn't care what any TV pictures revealed. He had no quarrel whatsoever with Partridge's verdict. 'It was a penalty,' the victorious Forest boss told reporters. 'The referee gave it and we stuck it in.'

In fact, as he related in his autobiography, such was the 'deep, intimate joy' Clough experienced at winning the trophy, television was exactly where he stuck it – right on top of his set when he arrived home. 'I gazed at it for most of the night and then gazed at it again next morning,' he wrote, 'wanting to clutch it tight and show the kids and everybody else in town and the neighbourhood and never let it go. That's the way I felt about that first trophy I won with Forest.'

16–22 March 1974

Brian Clough, 38 on April Fools' Day*, always preaches the advantages of young management, but he is very adamant about the virtues of the older player. Here, Clough picks his special team – the over-30s …

FINISHED AT 30? DON'T YOU BELIEVE IT …

THERE seems to be a notion in sporting circles that to make your way in sport, you have to be spotted before your milk teeth have started to loosen, you must reach your peak before you've got a beard worth shaving, and you're over the hill by the time you're 28.

To me, that's a load of nonsense, and to prove it this week I'm presenting my own team of so-called old-timers, 11 old crocks who I think could, collectively, take the shine off any top side.

Don't get me wrong, I believe in youth. At Derby, brilliant young players like John McGovern and Roy McFarland were the backbone of the side I took into the First Division, and I had no hesitation in playing in my first team a talented youngster like Steve Powell, who made his First Division debut when he was 16.

At Brighton, we're combing the country, like every other league club, for that teenager who's going to set our team alight. We have an intricate scouting network looking for these youngsters just about every day of the week.

It's a different story with the older player. Once you start to pass 26 and 27, people begin to shake their heads and say he's slowing up, he hasn't got long in the game.

Some people thought I was absolutely barmy when I paid £100,000 for Henry Newton from Everton just before I left Derby last autumn. He was 29 years old, they said how can he repay that sort of money when he's already on the way out? Anybody would think they issued footballers with a free pair of crutches on the National Health once they passed the age of 30.

I saw in Henry Newton a mature professional, a skilled footballer who played with his head and his heart as well as his feet. I also saw a man who would be playing top-class football for another six years at least.

I suppose I do have a personal axe to grind. I was cheated out of some of the best years of my career when I went down to a knee injury on Boxing Day 1962. I was 27, loved the game, and felt as if I could go on forever.

At 30 your life is less than halfway through, and you're conditioned to feel that you're too old for the game you love, just by current thinking.

So here, in praise of the older man, I present my British over-30s XI. Look at the names; they don't sound like Has-Been Academicals or Geriatrics United, do they?

Goal: Peter Bonetti, Chelsea, 32.

Defence: Bobby Moore, West Ham, 33; Alan Mullery, Fulham, 32; Billy McNeil, Celtic, 34; Frank McLintock, QPR, 34.

Midfield: Billy Bremner, Leeds, 31 (captain); Denis Law, Manchester City, 33.

Attack: Alan Gilzean, Tottenham, 35; Terry Paine, Southampton, 34; Geoff Hurst, Stoke, 32; Derek Dougan, Wolves, 36.

You can put B. Clough, Brighton, 37, on the list as substitute, and we'll take on the world.

---

* It is generally accepted that Clough was born on 21 March 1935, but he mentions in an October 1973 column about being 37 (when he would have been 38 if he'd been born in 1935) and, here, there is a further reference to him being 37, as well as being 38 come 1 April. Were he born in 1935, he would have been 39 by April 1974. Is there an argument then that Clough was actually born on 21 March 1936?

* * * *

'There was a time (and not so long ago at that) when a top-grade player who was moving into his late 20s/early 30s would be dropped like a hot brick. He would then begin the inevitable slide down the divisions. Not so today – for more and more clubs realise the value of having at least one 'old head' in their set-up.' In his *On the Ball* feature in a February 1977 issue of *Look-in* magazine, as Clough's TV pal Brian Moore looked at 'some of the Golden Oldies of English league soccer,' the not-so-long-ago time to which Moore was referring had been just a few years earlier when Clough had penned his column for *TVTimes*.

Every member of Clough's Old Crocks United – five Englishmen, five Scots and one Northern Irishman – had already enjoyed lengthy, distinguished, and honours-strewn playing careers. Yet, for most, there was still some considerable mileage on their respective clocks.

Chelsea's Peter Bonetti, a regular guardian of the Stamford Bridge goalmouth since making his debut, aged 19, in April 1960, had, on 24 November 1973, become the first person to play 600 league and cup games for the Londoners, keeping a clean sheet in a 4-0 home win over Southampton. By the time he donned his gloves for the Blues for a final time – playing his 600th league game on Monday, 14 May 1979 in a 1-1 draw at home to Arsenal – the keeper nicknamed 'The Cat' for his remarkable agility and graceful style had, man and boy, been part of the Chelsea picture for 21 years. He'd even had time to spend a brief period in the NASL with the St Louis Stars, joining on a free transfer following Chelsea's relegation from the First Division in 1974/75 before returning to the Smoke in October 1975 and, in 1976/77, adding a knowledgeable old head (and sure pair of hands) to Eddie McCreadie's raw, exciting young side that gained promotion from the second tier.

Capped for his country at under-23s and full level, Bonetti's seven-game England career is perhaps cruelly remembered only for his last international, on a steamy afternoon in León in 1970, when, as a late replacement for Gordon Banks, the victim of food poisoning, he let in three West German goals as England relinquished a 2-0 second-half lead and their hold on the World Cup. The keeper, an easy scapegoat, was held accountable for at least two of the critical strikes, especially the first when, diving to stop a drive from Franz Beckenbauer, Bonetti let the ball under his body when it looked like he had the shot covered.

Having won an FA Cup winners' medal a couple of months earlier following the replayed final versus Leeds, Bonetti added to his collection the season after when Chelsea came out on top in another final that required two games – in the European Cup Winners' Cup against Real Madrid – and over the course of the decade his long and sporadically successful tenure as the Mr Consistency in the Chelsea goal continued. On 11 March 1978 both he and fellow Chelsea pensioner Ron Harris became the first footballers to play 700 games in all competitions for the club in a 1-1 draw at Derby. But the following campaign as the Londoners, now managed by Danny Blanchflower after Ken Shellito's December 1978 dismissal, once again surrendered their top-flight place, marooned at the bottom of the division, Bonetti at 37 decided to retire and begin a new life with his family on the faraway Scottish island of Mull. A 5-2 disintegration at Highbury on 16 April 1979 – Arsenal's forwards getting in some sharp FA Cup Final practice against Petar Borota, the keeper Blanchlower had bought from Partizan Belgrade – consigned the Blues to relegation with five games still to play. When Bonetti faced the Gunners a few weeks later on that May evening, it marked the last of 729 appearances for the club, a total only exceeded in the Chelsea records by Harris on 795.

By the time of Clough's column, Bobby Moore, marshalling the back line in front of Bonetti as England lost their grip on the Jules Rimet trophy in that quarter-final in Mexico, had already sported West Ham's claret and blue for a very last time. For his final three years at Upton Park, the 1966 World Cup-winning captain had endured an edgy relationship with the club and its manager, Ron Greenwood, following an incident on the eve of an FA Cup third-round clash at First Division rivals Blackpool. On New Year's

Day 1971 Moore, along with teammates Jimmy Greaves, Brian Dear, 19-year-old forward Clyde Best and club physio Rob Jenkins, visited a club the night before the cup tie, which saw the Seasiders trounce the Hammers 4-0.

The result was to have a sensational sequel later in the week, as the East London club briefly announced that 'as a result of a breach of disciplinary rules,' fines had been imposed on the four players, and then revealed that the club captaincy had been taken from Moore, and that neither he nor Greaves would play against Arsenal at Highbury on 9 January, a match which a weakened West Ham lost 2-0. When Moore, after missing two games, played in a friendly versus Charlton Athletic, he commented simply, 'It's good to be back', but although he remained for a further three seasons with the club for whom he'd first played in 1958, his treatment had slightly soured the love he'd once felt.

In September 1973, still England captain though soon to be left out of the line-up for a friendly with Austria, Moore was pressing for a transfer, with Greenwood informing the player that he 'would not be against a move'. According to reports, it was Clough who was keen to bring Moore (and Trevor Brooking) to Derby and move Colin Todd to a midfield role. Unbeknownst to Greenwood, Clough had already met Moore (at The Churchill Hotel, just off Oxford Street), and sold him the idea of joining the league champions.

When a combined bid of £400,000 was made to the Hammers, Greenwood rejected it but agreed to put the offer to his board. But the West Ham directors were adamant the defender was not for sale, leaving a furious Moore accusing Greenwood of denying him a final tilt at a title-winning medal. The manager had already vetoed a move for the defender to Tottenham. It was no great surprise then when, on 5 January 1974, ironically in another FA Cup third-round game as West Ham struggled to a 1-1 home draw against Third Division Hereford United, Moore made his last appearance for the London club. He was injured in the match, replaced by substitute Pat Holland, who netted a last-ditch leveller, though it was ultimately to no avail; the Hammers suffered a calamitous 2-1 defeat in the replay four days later. Finally allowed to leave,

Moore wanted to go to Crystal Palace to team up with his old Upton Park mentor Malcolm Allison but, whilst remaining in the capital, instead joined Fulham, then in the Second Division, for just £25,000 on 14 March.

In three years with the club on the banks of the Thames, the undoubted highlight came on 3 May 1975 when the veteran of so many Wembley campaigns in an England shirt faced up to his former employers (now managed by John Lyall) in the second all-London FA Cup Final (after Spurs and Chelsea in 1967). Fulham's appearance – in their first FA Cup final – was cast-iron evidence of the unpredictability and appeal of the competition. For Moore, playing less than a year after transferring from east to south-west London against the club he led to so much glory, including their first FA Cup in 1964, there was an extra poignancy to the occasion: it marked a last-ever run-out at Wembley as a professional player. Billed as The Cockney Cup Final and potentially a classic Jack versus the giant confrontation, on the day a well-balanced West Ham side ultimately had too much class, authority and skill, winning 2-0. But most of the non-partisan support was with Fulham and, in particular, Moore.

Also in the Fulham side that May afternoon was Alan Mullery. In 1972, after eight years' service and over 300 appearances for Spurs, the deep-lying central midfielder, famously the first England player to be sent off (during a 1-0 European Championship semi-final defeat to Yugoslavia), had rejoined the Craven Cottage club where he'd made his debut in 1958, the same year that Moore first made his mark in the English game. On 26 January 1974, during Fulham's FA Cup fourth-round home tie with Leicester City, Mullery's right-footed volley, hit first-time from a cross by Les Strong and sent rocketing past a helpless Peter Shilton, would later earn the player the BBC's 'Goal of the Season' nomination. Although Fulham only drew the game then lost the replay 2-1 to the eventual cup semi-finalists, the following year, as wise old owl Alec Stock's 500-1 outsiders took a fairytale road all the way to the Empire Stadium before the Hammers finally put their Cup dreams to bed, Mullery was honoured with the coveted Footballer of the

Year award, a title bestowed on Moore in 1963/64. Both Moore and Mullery had proved the inspiration of Fulham's young squad.

Celtic's Billy McNeill was the one player in Clough's side who never plied his trade in England (though he would later manage Manchester City and Aston Villa); he was also the only one who spent the entirety of his career with the same club, remaining as centre-half with the Glasgow giants for 19 years, during which he got his hands on no less than 22 domestic trophies as well being the first Briton to ever lift the European Cup. Tough-tackling but technically superb, McNeill was a towering figure both at the back for his club and in the history of Scottish football. When he bid farewell to Parkhead (though Celtic, too, was another club at which he'd take charge, in two separate spells), retiring in 1975, the captain of the Lisbon Lions had clocked up a record 822 games. Astonishingly, of the matches he started in the green and white, he played every single minute, having never once been substituted.

Alongside McNeill in Clough's XI, fellow Scot Frank McLintock, captain and one of the major components of Arsenal's double-winning team of 1970/71, enjoyed something of an Indian summer after joining newly promoted QPR in June 1973. Bertie Mee made few blunders when he was in charge at Highbury, but the sale of McLintock must have been one. The centre-back still had many seasons of good soccer left in him, as the fans at Loftus Road discovered to their pleasure. The first to admit that his ageing legs weren't quite what they used to be, McLintock overcame that deficiency by using his vast experience to anticipate any move that much earlier and, along with another 'old timer' David Webb, performed brilliantly at the heart of the Hoops defence. Having helped the west London club to an eighth-place finish in his first season, in 1975/76 McLintock featured strongly as Dave Sexton's hugely entertaining side came within touching distance of the title, only pipped by a point by Bob Paisley's Liverpool.

The following May, when McLintock retired, the Glaswegian had 776 league and cup games as well as nine Scotland caps to show from a 20-year professional career. He also had the rather unenviable record of having lost in five out of the six cup finals in which he'd appeared. Two of those – the 1961 and 1963 FA Cup Finals – were with Leicester City, the club where he'd started his playing days way back in 1956. And it was at Leicester, a month after quitting, that McLintock began his managerial career, too, appointed as replacement for Jimmy Bloomfield, who'd resigned following six seasons in charge.

When McLintock had led out Arsenal for the Centenary FA Cup Final in 1972, captaining the oppositon that afternoon was Leeds's Billy Bremner. In June 1977, as McLintock started life on the touchlines at Filbert Street, the terrier-like Bremner was still playing as tenaciously as ever – but in the Second Division with Hull City. In September 1976, when that 'ten stone of barbed wire,' as *The Guardian's* John Arlott once brilliantly described him, left Elland Road after 16 years, the fiery little midfielder's service since joining the club from Scottish junior football as a teenager amounted to a staggering 770 outings – 586 league, 77 European, 69 FA Cup and 38 League Cup matches that brought him 116 goals. He'd achieved almost every major honour a player dreamed about in the game. But by his own admission, Bremner had become stale and bored at Leeds. Not yet ready to hang up his size-five boots, when Hull boss John Kaye – 'a genuine fellow, straightforward and honest' – and the club directors 'sold' the Tigers to Bremner, telling him his huge know-how and professional drive would be invaluable to the young City side, Bremner agreed to a move, viewing it as a new lease of life. The 33-year-old swapped West for East Yorkshire for a nominal £40,000 fee. Hull City hoped that his arrival would inspire a new and successful period for the club who'd never graced football's top flight. It didn't quite work out like that, but certainly got off to a good start. At the beginning of October, before 16,000 at Boothferry Park, Bremner lined up for his debut – against Clough's Nottingham Forest – and scored the game's only goal with a long-range free kick.

Bremner was skipper on the day that Denis Law donned a Scotland shirt for one last time – in the encounter with Zaire at the 1974 World Cup finals. Bremner's Leeds boss Don Revie called Law 'the finest finisher in English football since the war'. Yet of all the goals that Law scored in a career that yielded over 250 for both club and country, including at one-time more FA Cup goals (41) than any other player post-war, it is perhaps his final one in league football for which he is best remembered. Or rather, wrongly remembered.

On Saturday, 27 April 1974 when Manchester City's Law, the ex-Red Devil still so adored by United supporters, cheekily back-heeled into the net at Old Trafford nine minutes from the end of a derby which United needed to win to have any hope of avoiding the drop from the First Division, it sparked one of the greatest non-celebrations in football history; instead of the trademark one-hand-in-the-air, clutching-the-sleeve-of-his-jersey joy, the disconsolate Scot sulked off back towards the centre circle, refusing to acknowledge a strike that, to the best of his knowledge, had hammered the lid-sealing nail in his former club's coffin. Law was substituted almost immediately. When an ensuing pitch invasion from the home supporters resulted in the game's abandonment by referee David Smith, the scoreline stood and United, just six years after their European Cup triumph, had lost their battle against relegation. 'I have seldom felt so depressed in my life as I did that weekend,' Law later said. He needn't have been. Birmingham's win over Norwich that same day meant that City's closest neighbours were doomed regardless of the result in Manchester and, contrary to ITV's Gerald Sinstadt's commentary – 'So I suppose that is that. Denis Law's back-heeled goal has sent United down' – Law's match-winner was completely inconsequential.

The misconception has remained, however. 'Law scores the goal that sends United down' is still the default heading whenever a photo of the goal or Law's subsequent lack of celebration is posted online. After taking his international farewell later that summer, Law turned out for City two more times, albeit in the pre-season Texaco Cup, scoring in a 4-2 defeat at Sheffield United, then playing in the 2-1 home victory over Oldham Athletic, a match in which he was substituted by Barney Daniels. Rather than play reserve-team football, he decided to quit. 'I always wanted to call it a day while I am still on the top,' he said. He formally retired on 26 August 1974.

Law had 19 years of finding the net and yet it is still 'the one that I almost wished hadn't actually gone in' that he has never really been allowed to forget.

As Alan Gilzean made his international debut for Scotland on 7 November 1963 in a friendly match at home to Norway, the first of 22 caps for his country, Denis Law was his partner up front on the night. Law netted four times in the Scots' 6-1 victory. Though Gilzean didn't put his name on the scoresheet for the national side until his third game, when he did so it was quite momentous; a towering header, the only goal of the game, scored after 72 minutes, as Scotland beat England 1-0 in the 1964 Home Internationals before a mammoth Hampden Park crowd of 133,245. He also got two in his next game as Scotland came from two down in a friendly with West Germany in Hanover.

The Perthshire-born Gilzean was a Dundee player at the time. By the following year, though, he'd headed south of the border, Spurs's double-winning manager Bill Nicholson paying £72,500 for the striker he envisaged as the perfect foil for Jimmy Greaves. The Tottenham boss was right; together, the G-Men, Greaves and Gilzean, were an outstanding partnership, Greaves describing his 6ft tall fellow forward as 'possibly the best footballer I've ever played with'. Acknowledged as one of the game's most accomplished headers and possessing the deftist touch, the stylish Gilzean had the ability to trouble any defence. Over a decade later, during which he'd been part of the FA Cup-winning team of 1967 and then, after Greaves left for West Ham in 1970, had formed another formidable front pairing with Martin Chivers, as Spurs, in successive seasons between 1971 and 1973, won two League Cups and a UEFA Cup, the 'King of White Hart Lane', as the faithful dubbed him, gave up his crown. In 439 appearances for the north Londoners, the number nine had delivered 133 goals.

On the opposition side when Gilzean first registered for Scotland was Southampton's Terry Paine. The previous year, when he bagged three goals in England's 8-3 victory over Northern Ireland, Paine, a wideman of pace and cunning, became the first England winger to score a hat-trick in 70 years of the Home

Internationals. Appointed Southampton captain in August 1961 aged just 22, five years later Paine led the Saints to promotion and the First Division for the very first time at the end of the 1965/66 campaign. That summer he was also part of Alf Ramsey's World Cup squad, lining up alongside Jimmy Greaves and Roger Hunt as England won their second round-one game, 2-0 against Mexico. But Paine, though lasting the full 90 minutes, suffered concussion in the encounter, was replaced by Liverpool's Ian Callaghan for the 2-0 win over France, and didn't feature again in the tournament as Ramsey's wingless wonders went on to World Cup glory. Capped 19 times, Paine had also played his last time for his country.

His club career, however, still had plenty of legs. At Southampton, moving from the flanks to become a midfield mastermind, he was a player rated by team boss Lawrie McMenemy as the best long passer in the game. When Paine eventually left the Hampshire outfit in 1974 following the club's relegation back to the second tier, between signing in August 1956 as a 16-year-old amateur and his last match versus Burnley, he'd racked up a club record 713 league appearances.

Nevertheless, aged 35, Paine was still up for fresh challenges. During three years at Hereford United, he helped the side managed by (Coventry City's) future FA Cup-winning boss John Sillett claim its first Third Division title in 1976 and, earlier that campaign, on 25 October 1975 when he captained United against Peterborough, featured in a record-smashing 765th league game, exceeding the previous number held by Portsmouth's Jimmy Dickinson. By the time he concluded his 20-year career at the end of 1976/77, as the Edgar Street club, having won only eight matches, finished bottom of the Second Division and made an immediate return from whence they came, Paine had played in 824 matches in total.

Seven years after an exhausted Geoff Hurst had hit the ball as hard as he could for his net-bulging third goal that signalled England's greatest footballing victory – 'I thought if it didn't go into the net, at least it would reach the Wembley crowd behind that goal,' he said, 'and, while the ball was retrieved, I could have a little rest' – the World Cup Final hat-trick hero was putting his deadly feet and lethal head to good use in the Potteries. If Bobby Moore's West Ham departure was no real surprise, when his teammate agreed to a transfer to Stoke City in August 1972, it came as a big shock to many Hammers fans. In a career with the Londoners which spanned 14 years he made over 500 first-team appearances and, despite many thinking him crazy to leave, the Greater Manchester-born forward was seeking pastures new away from the bright lights of the capital.

Though Hurst's first season at the Victoria Ground was marred by a back injury, he still proved he had the ability to score goals in the top flight, something many critics doubted after his £80,000 move. After helping Stoke maintain their First Division status in 1972/73, the following season, when the Staffordshire club recorded a fifth-place finish, it represented a career high for Hurst. Something he and Stoke would match in 1974/75.

Before he'd ever been to The Dell, Terry Paine had a trial at Southampton's bitter rivals, Portsmouth. They never got back to him. Fratton Park was, though, the starting point on the extensive and often controversy-riddled footballing journey of Derek Dougan that also made stops at Blackburn Rovers, Aston Villa, Peterborough United and Leicester City before the lanky, long-striding Northern Irish striker eventually settled in the West Midlands with Wolves.

The Doog's very first league goal, in 1957 for Portsmouth, had actually come against his final employers. Wolves were also the opponents when Dougan, after posting a shock transfer request on the morning of the match, played in the Blackburn Rovers side beaten 3-0 in the 1960 FA Cup Final. Seven years later, on his home debut for Wanderers following a £50,000 move from Filbert Street in March 1967, Dougan smashed a hat-trick in a 4-0 thrashing of Hull City, netting nine in 11 games in total as the club clinched promotion back to the top flight after a two-year absence. There, in the next two campaigns, while Wolves struggled for a First Division footing, the forward firmly established himself as a cult hero on the Molineux terraces, finishing top scorer with 16 and 14 goals respectively.

It was a feat he repeated in 1971/72 whilst forming a lethal front partnership with winger Dave Wagstaffe and hitman John Richards, hailed as 'King John' by the Wolves supporters. That season, during the run to the first-ever UEFA Cup Final (an updated version of the Inter-Cities Fairs Cup in which Wolves lost over two legs to Spurs), Dougan, with his three goals in an away tie with Portugal's Académica de Coimbra, had become the first player to score a hat-trick for the Midlanders in a major European competition. After registering twice in a 3-0 victory over the East Germans Carl Zeiss Jena, he broke the club's individual scoring record in European competitions, too, taking him past Peter Broadbent's total of seven. He went on to net 12 goals in European competitions in all. In August 1972, when he hit Wolves's third in a 3-0 home win over West Ham (getting much the better of Bobby Moore on the day), Dougan also became the first Irishman to reach 200 Football League goals.

Dougan had already gained what he described as 'the greatest soccer honour I can contemplate' by captaining his country. All the same, it wasn't until 1973/74, his last full campaign before back troubles saw his game time limited and in due course he called it a day in 1975, that the Belfast-born centre-forward finally got a winners' medal (discounting the Texaco Cup of 1971) to add to his 43 full international caps (the first of those won in a 1-0 triumph over Czechoslovakia during the 1958 World Cup). Dougan was in Bill McGarry's side that beat Manchester City 2-1 in the League Cup Final to secure the Wanderers's first trophy in 14 years.

Whilst the much-travelled marksman might not have had a wealth of silverware to show for all his years of service, he was a player who always added colour to the game. It was often dark. With his abrasive nature and fierce temper, Dougan landed in more than one spot of bother with officialdom; there were irreparable fall-outs with teammates (John Richards being one) and numerous other high-profile football figures. But wherever he played supporters always got their money's worth. Nicknamed the 'Clown Prince of Football' during his Molineux days, Dougan sometimes seemed to take a rather amused attitude on the pitch but was deadly serious about his role as an entertainer. He was a born crowd-pleaser and, above all, a very fine performer. Dougan's retirement after 123 goals in 323 appearances was a loss Wolves failed to effectively overcome; the team began to lose its edge. Just two seasons after he quit, the club dropped down to the Second Division once more.

At the commencement of the 1970s, the prediction amongst the game's experts was that, as one put it, 'with more young players than ever before running out to rising fame and top honours,' the decade would be the age of youth in top-class football. 'If you're good enough, you're old enough' was a Sir Matt Busby motto. Yet an increasing emphasis on the untried and untested or not, most football clubs still put a high value on experience, the ones who'd been there, done that and had the T-shirt (plus a few swapped international jerseys) to prove it.

Warhorses who'd survived numerous battles over the years, they weren't necessarily the most skilful players, but what they knew about the game – a hard-won wisdom – was priceless. Clough was one of those managers. Though never shying away from pitching in a youngster if he believed he was ready, he always placed great trust in the seasoned campaigners. After all, the man he named as number 12 for his own Old Crocks United would have liked nothing better than to have become one himself.

6–12 April 1974

It's the big match: football versus television. How much soccer should be shown and how much should TV pay? Brian Clough gives some of the answers …

THE GUILTY MEN OF TV SOCCER

BOB Lord, chairman of Burnley, banned television cameras from his sixth-round Football Associate Cup tie against Wrexham recently and Queen's Park Rangers manager Gordon Jago kept the cameras away from the exciting replay against Coventry a few weeks earlier. As I made clear when I started this column, I write not as a television commentator but as a football manager, and as such I say both clubs were right.

That is no criticism of television. The fault lies with the football authorities who negotiate the television deals. I think they are guilty of two things: they don't provide enough money for the clubs taking part in televised games, and the contracts they make are inflexible to the point of stupidity.

Lord complained that his club would receive a ridiculously low fee for allowing cameras inside Burnley's ground, and that is a fair point. When I was at Derby I once banned television cameras because I was offered the scandalous sum of £87.50 for the screening of a cup match against Notts County. I made my position quite clear at the time – I could earn more than £87.50 selling programmes on the corner. I did have other reasons for the ban as well. I felt that Notts County – not a glamorous club and unused to the attention of television cameras – would raise the standard of their game against Derby *because* they were on television. Even if I was wrong about that, I didn't want to take the chance and lose the match. But the money angle remained a firm motive. League and cup matches are negotiated separately and there is much discussion going on about the total fee.

Whatever final deal is settled, my main point is that the bodies which govern football must distribute more of the money they get to the clubs who actually sell the game on TV.

My second point is that the contracts negotiated are far too rigid, which brings me to something I think could bang a few thousand-pound notes into the game 'at a stroke', as the gentleman once said.

When contracts are discussed again I would like to see machinery set up by which a television company could bid to screen any match, live if possible, at any time. Supposing this season, for instance, the match which would decide the First Division Championship was due to be played on a Tuesday night along with several others. The clever thing to do would be for the League to switch the match to a day on which no others were being played, negotiate a massive sum from the television companies and let them show it live. Everyone would benefit. Soccer would be richer – I reckon £30,000 would be a fair fee. The television company that won the contract would corner 15 million viewers that night, and our national game would receive the best possible advertisement.

It makes my blood boil to see chances like that missed, and when I talk about £30,000 I'm not talking in telephone numbers. Tom Jones can command a fee of £450,000 for a five-week stint at Caesar's Palace in Las Vegas. If somebody is prepared to pay it, good for Tom Jones, I say. But soccer, which is watched by far larger audiences, has its price, too.

Football has a market value on television, but nothing should be allowed to interfere with the game's essence – the close relationship between a cheering, jeering crowd and the players on the pitch. Some people in the business have suggested over and over that television exposure reduces gates. I don't accept this. I rather think television stimulates interest and when I conducted a survey in *TVTimes* last year, 80 per cent of the fans said they didn't think there was too much soccer on television.

There is a way to settle this argument once and for all … ban television soccer for six months. The figures would then be there for all to see and we would know conclusively whether or not TV affected attendances. I am pretty sure what the answer would be – it doesn't.

The TV companies have already said that if soccer was banned from the screens they would hook up with continental television and show European matches live. I think this would be a dead loss. Who wants to watch Heynckes of Borussia Mönchengladbach kicking Grabowski of Eintracht Frankfurt? I don't. I think the fans have to identify with their own players and clubs, and showing foreign soccer wouldn't keep one supporter away from a ground.

The nub of the argument is that we must bring some simple common sense into our attitude towards television and soccer. There must be a balance between saturation coverage, which makes soccer look stale in the long run, and no televised soccer at all. Football authorities must sell their game much better. Television has almost convinced the public that they get a better deal watching at home, but the time has come for the FA and the League to give their side of the story.

They should tell people that they only experience a fraction of soccer's pageant on TV. Viewers don't taste the sawdust, or see the whole canvas of the pitch in front of them.

Football is like a beautiful flower. Seeing it close up on television is fine. But it must be smelt and seen in its setting to be enjoyed completely.

13–19 April 1974

There's Don Revie in a tracksuit ... training with his players. There's Don Revie in pyjamas ... reading in his bed. The documentary next week, *The Don of Elland Road*, tells the story of a week in the life of Leeds United's remarkable manager. Here, Brian Clough assesses Revie's success ...

DON REVIE ...
MY MAN FOR ALL SEASONS

PERFECTIONIST, teacher, iron man, thinker ... the words come easily when the subject is Don Revie. I have been the first to criticise him in the past. I got into hot water at the beginning of the season when I said Leeds should have been slung into the Second Division because of their bad disciplinary record.

But I like to think I can be the first man to praise him as well. I have no hesitation in calling him the best manager in football today and undoubtedly the man of the season despite Leeds's slump and that recent 4-1 thrashing at the hands of Burnley.

In terms of sheer football-management ability I honestly think that myself and Peter Taylor run Don Revie a close second: we've had our share of success in the past and in time we'll taste it again, but this year is Don Revie's year. In a documentary next week you will get a glimpse of what he's all about. What is he like on matchday? How far does he get involved with his players? How does he unwind at home?

Revie tackles the game like a high-powered business, where Saturday night is what he calls 'the end of the working week'. To an outsider, the game might look like 22 blokes banging a bit of leather and wind around a piece of grass for an hour and a half a week. To a man like Revie, it could be ICI or English Electric. He has the sort of brain which could easily put him in the chairman's seat of any international company.

He works out his players' diets. He sends three men separately to watch every opponent, a few weeks before Leeds are due to play them. He works out a different strategy, in bed, every Friday night. He employs a retired headmaster to look after his juniors.

I think that one thing Revie did when he started as manager of Leeds says much about his eventual success. He had been transferred to Leeds as a player in 1958, for £12,000 from Sunderland, and when he was asked to take over the hotseat as manager in 1961 they were bottom of the Second Division and looked as if they were going to drop into the Third. He managed, though, to keep them up and three years later he took them into the First Division. And even while they were struggling in the Second he made the players believe in themselves. He made them know that they were the club's biggest asset. And the players responded with results.

Revie's record after ten years in the First Division speaks for itself. For the last nine years Leeds haven't been out of the top four places in the league. They have won the First Division championship once, the UEFA Cup twice, the League Cup once, the FA Cup once, and this year they'll be taking another league championship trophy, the key to Don Revie's biggest dream, to win the European Cup. Before long, Revie will have more cups to clean than a washer-up in Joe Lyons.

Revie commands respect among all football managers. Bill McGarry of Wolves, who, with Revie, used to play in the England team during the 50s, could talk about him for days.

'Early on, he spotted young lads like Bremner, Hunter and Reaney and he drummed good footballing habits into them,' says McGarry. 'In doing this he bred players who could repeat brilliant performances week after week.

'I think that you can foresee how good a manager is going to be by the way he played.

'I remember Don as a player of great skill who, at the same time, was not afraid to open his mouth and give the others the stick if he didn't like what they were doing. He took this attitude into management. His greatest asset is self-confidence.'

One of the younger managers in the game, Coventry's Gordon Milne, agrees: 'He does everything so professionally. There's no guesswork, no risks. I can't think of a single mistake Revie has made. In the early days everybody said Leeds played boring, defensive football. So they did. But that's because Revie wanted to establish good foundations in the First Division.

'He is a man who believes in the evolution of a team, the slow, correct building which takes years. Now Leeds are still solid, but much more adventurous. They've reached a peak and they'll stay there for years.'

Sid Waddell, producer of the documentary, says that Revie has an amazing presence. 'He's a hot gospeller. Sometimes like the Godfather. Sometimes a nursemaid. Between 11am and 12 on a Saturday he starts to brief his team. No one is allowed into the room.

'He tells them just how he wants them to play, and he generates in his team fantastic belief that they are the greatest in the world before they go out on the pitch.

'Before a match,' says Waddell, 'he personally massages some of the players. Afterwards, if they've won, he embraces them like a schoolboy.

'Revie is a £20,000-a-year man but he still works in his overalls. He gets to the ground at 8.30 every morning and by 8.40 he's in a tracksuit ready to go out with the players. Later, I've seen him in his office behind a bank of telephones and an intercom, still in his tracksuit, telling a 15-year-old junior that he's sorry to hear about his grandma.

'I think Revie gets the greatest pleasure of all out of taking lads under his wing and grooming them into the first team. I know that the worst job he knows in the world is having to tell a youngster he's not good enough for Leeds.'

About a year ago there was a strong rumour in football that Revie was going to move from Leeds to Everton for a gigantic salary – and he was tempted. It came to a head after Leeds lost 1-0 in the

European Cup Winners' Cup Final against Inter Milan in Greece. I think Don felt he'd done all he could for Leeds. It was time for a change. He said then, 'I told the boys that it was 95 per cent certain I was leaving. Then I looked at their faces. It's terrible seeing tears in the eyes of hard, young men.'

I had the same experience at Derby, leaving behind a family of bright, brilliant lads, every one of them close to my heart. In my particular circumstances I felt I had no choice but to resign. But Revie stayed at Leeds. He couldn't do anything else because he realised that you can't weigh great players against pound notes.

I believe he will stay there forever now – unless he takes over the England job, which he would do brilliantly. And Leeds look all set to become the Real Madrid of the 70s.

* * * *

Clough, in fact, had long been a big admirer of Revie's but, as he described it in *Cloughie: Walking on Water*, 'had serious reservations about the way the "family", as he [Revie] called it, sometimes went about their business'. What Clough 'despised' (the word he used in his book) about the West Yorkshire club under Revie was 'what they stood for'. For Clough that meant an all-too-often cynical approach to the game, a desire to succeed at any cost that led to ill-discipline and negated whatever was good about their football. Leeds players were, Clough felt, guilty of a long list of crimes that included 'systematically putting referees under pressure, both physical and verbal, their overreactions, and the unsavoury spectacle of Bremner running alongside the referee constantly yelling in his ear'. Any side took its lead from the manager, so Clough laid the blame squarely at the feet of Revie.

Most managers had had some Clough stick at one time or another – and as a consequence tended to be a little acid about him – but Revie was chief among the targets. Famously in his sensational *Sunday Express* article of 5 August 1973, Clough had criticised the FA's decision to fine Leeds £3,000 for their bad disciplinary record and suspend the punishment – 'The men who run soccer have missed the most marvellous chance of cleaning

WHERE HAVE ALL THE GOALSCORERS GONE?

Back in the 1927-28 season, Dixie Dean, an Everton player, scored 82 goals. The year before, George Camsell of Middlesbrough struck in 75.

Today, if a player scores half that number we regard him as a goal machine, a genius.

British football these days is suffering a chronic shortage of that magic commodity, natural goalscorers—men who are born, not taught, to be prolific scorers.

I thought Ted MacDougall had that magic when he scored 46 goals for Bournemouth in the 1971-72 season, but since he moved to Manchester United and West Ham, he hasn't shown that innate ability. Last season John Richards of Wolves almost convinced me he had it. He was England's top goalscorer with 36 goals in all competitions (27 in League games) a remarkable feat. But this season he has managed only a handful of goals.

MacDougall and Richards are the sum total of possible natural goalscorers in the League today, apart from one man who should have been wearing an England shirt against Poland in October—Newcastle's Malcolm MacDonald. He's my last hope.

He's chunky, arrogant and attacks goal like a bull;

some say he's bigheaded. But he's resilient and skilful, he tackles ferociously and behaves like a thoroughbred who's prepared to do the donkey work. He's a master of the art of shielding the ball, which is a brave and thankless thing for a centre-forward to do. While he has his body between an opponent and the ball, he knows he's going to get clobbered. But MacDougall sticks it out, and seems to have the uncanny talent for scoring.

He scored 31 in the 1971-72 season, 28 in 1972-73, and he's well up to that standard this year. I would say, and only time will really tell, that Mac has the knack.

I really believe people like MacDonald are born to score goals. I think it's the same in any creative field. Like great writers, painters and musicians, they must have the seed sown early on. You can either score a goal or you can't.

As a player I scored 251 goals in 271 matches, a scoring record that still stands. If football continues to be the tight, give-nothing-away affair it is today, that record will stand for 1,000 years. Goals were like a drug to me, and I'm sure it was the same with players like MacDonald, Dixie Dean, Arthur Rowley (the all-time highest scorer, with 434 Football League

goals) and Jimmy Greaves (357 in his League career.)

I sometimes ask myself how I did it, how I scored my goals. But I can honestly say I don't know. I concentrated so hard on scoring I shut everything else out of my mind. I was unaware of people around me, ignorant of what defenders could do to me, unafraid of what the crowd might say if I missed. At the precise moment of scoring, I thought only of putting the ball away. There are few moments in life when you are so engrossed in what you are doing that everything else is shut out. If you work in a factory or an office you do your job, but you are conscious of things going on around you. For me, scoring

was like stopping breathing. In another world. The goal went in and my heart was pumping away, and suddenly I realised somebody was clapping, putting their arm round me, we were one up. It was an extraordinary feeling of detachment.

When Walter Winterbottom was England team manager 11 years ago, he took great interest in researching the physical qualities of goalscorers. "There has been a wealth of work done on the subject of why certain people make better sportsmen than others," he says. "But the one thing on which everyone agrees is that some skills are inborn. Research has shown that there are two vital factors. The first is anticipation—the ability to read a situation quickly and so gain time to carry out a job on the field. This can be learned by experience. The other factor is built-in at birth, and that is the speed of muscle reaction.

"Scientists have found that players from warm countries like South America, Italy and Spain have faster muscle reactions than those from colder

countries. This is why so many South American players appear faster than North Europeans. But there are exceptions—brilliant ones like Puskas, Finney and Greaves. They had the magic combination of anticipation (which put them in the right place at the right time) and fast muscle reactions (which enabled them to strike the ball so fast that they didn't allow the goalkeeper the luxury of knowing which way they were going to shoot)."

You might think it's curious that my partner, Peter Taylor, who was a goalkeeper in his playing days, is a better judge of a centre-forward, or a goalscorer, than I am. It's probably because he spent so much time trying to anticipate which way a forward was going to put the ball past him, and so much time fishing it out of the back of the net afterwards, that he knows instinctively whether or not a player has a special scoring gift. As a goalscorer myself (I never went more than four games without scoring), I'm a better judge of goalkeepers, because I spent so much time trying to bang the ball past them. A great goalscorer gets to know a keeper's flaws very quickly—and then exploits them.

But there isn't much of this talent about in British football today. It could be that we are not recognising the natural

Today, Brian Clough is ren off; 10 years ago he was Malcolm MacDonald (right

---

WE'LL SUCCEED BECAUSE WE'RE THE BEST

Whether you are running a brewery, a vast multi-national company, a whelk-stall factory or a Football League club, the essence of successful management is the same. There are three ingredients for successful management wherever you are: the ability to communicate, the gift of decision-making, and wholehearted involvement.

The combination of myself and Peter Taylor is the best football management team in the country. There is only one other manager to compare with us in our thorough approach to the job, Don Revie at Leeds. He earns laurels from me. Leeds haven't been out of the top four places in the First Division for nine years and in that time they have won the F.A. Cup, been beaten in two finals, won the U.E.F.A. Cup twice, and narrowly lost the Cup Winners' Cup Final last year. In 1974 they'll win the League as surely as the sun comes up tomorrow.

We all have our own ways of doing things and unlike me, Revie keeps very quiet about his job. But I am sure that those three qualities which I have spotlighted would come top of his list, too. Take communication with his players. Revie knows them inside out. He knows every shade of their ability. This two-way flow of understanding with them means that his will is literally transferred to the pitch. It's as if 11 Don Revies were out there playing.

You have to bear in mind that your ability to manage depends on the commodity you're dealing with. A manager in business would have his work cut out if he was trying to sell sub-standard goods, and in football it is harder to manage a club with indifferent players than one with star players. Bad players need good management more than good players, but the biggest secret is how to extract the very best from any player.

Wherever Peter Taylor and I have worked we have applied this rule: look at a player, then decide what things he is good at and what things he is bad at. Then develop, encourage and perfect his good points. Too many managers make the mistake of concentrating on improving a player's weaknesses. But that same player may have instincts for other aspects of the game which aren't worth exploiting.

The ability to make decisions is a rare quality. There are only a handful of people in any field you care to name who can make decisions. I know of one manager who used to ask other managers their opinion of a player before he had the courage to put his money where his mouth was and make an offer.

We rely on our judgment, and that includes the judgment to know when you've made a mistake. If I spent £200,000 on a player who did not live up to expectation, I would have no hesitation in dropping him—quickly. Many managers turn their backs when it comes to this sort

of decision and these are the people who never find success. If you are not a man of decision, you might as well go and sweep the streets as be a football manager.

I often envy the business manager—he can go to a board meeting and tell his directors that at another nine months they'll be 10 per cent up on sales. But we in football are not dealing with crates of machine tools—but with human nature, and we have to sit on a touchline 50 or more times a season, watching our decisions succeed or fail in front of thousands of people.

I can best illustrate the third quality—having total involvement—by talking about my days at Derby. We built up one of the greatest sides of all time, and when it established itself, there was not a bit more we could tell them. They knew what we wanted and they went out and put it into practice. And that's when we made the mistake of being complacent. A surgeon might remove so many tonsils that he could probably take them out blindfold. But the day he thinks he can is the day he makes a mess of it.

Three or four times at Derby I thought I could relax before a game, have a big lunch and a few beers and leave the players to themselves, and curiously, on those occasions we lost the game. We knew we were playing inferior sides, we knew we could beat them with our eyes shut, but this attitude had a strange way of rebounding.

At about this time the captain, Roy McFarland, accused me of not spending enough time with the players and I accepted what he said—but I made sure he never had the chance to say it again. On match days we got to the ground at 10 a.m., and made sure everything was perfect. We ate with the players, breathed the air they breathed right up to the kick-off. We even did up their boots.

I apply the same philosophy at Brighton. I walked out of the Goldstone Road for a beer and a sandwich for lunch and I saw two of my apprentices walking into the ground. One of them had his hands in his pockets and I said, "O.K. get 'em out, lad." Now if I hadn't been there, on the job, watching, I wouldn't have seen that. What will putting his hands in his pockets do to that boy's footballing skills? I'm not sure it makes any difference at all. But it could be that putting your hands in your pockets reflects a lazy state of mind which could show on the pitch, and I'm not going to take that risk.

No manager can find lasting success without the three qualities I have outlined. There are 92 managerial jobs in the Football League, and, for various reasons, 800 managers have changed or quit their jobs (me and Peter included) since World War Two. Quite a turnover isn't it? But there is a gift in management—it's not something you can just play at. And I think we've got it. Watch Brighton and you'll see what I mean.

23

CLOUGH SOUNDS OFF

The World Cup pace is hotting up. On Saturday, Scotland play their vital game against Yugoslavia, and on Sunday ITV bring you exclusive live coverage of the match between Poland—who put England out of the competition—and highly-fancied Italy. Wednesday sees the start of the final round matches, two of them live on ITV. Brian Clough thinks the game of the week could be Poland v. Italy—a battle between goalkeepers

THE CLOWN V THE GENIUS

Poland's Jan Tomaszewski. Will his luck beat the skilful Italians?   **Italy's Dino Zoff. His brilliance will be tested by Lato and Gadocha.**

I CALLED one of them a clown. The other is a genius. And Sunday's match between Poland and Italy could give us final proof; it's an intriguing confrontation which could turn out to be The Tale of Two Goalkeepers.

On one hand – provided he has recovered from a recent injury – is Jan Tomaszewski of Poland, towering, brave and incredibly lucky. On the other, Italy's Dino Zoff, cat-like, instinctive, brilliant.

I came in for a lot of stick and criticism last October when England drew 1-1 with Poland and went sailing out of the World Cup. I labelled Tomaszewski a clown when all around me were saying he was the greatest thing since shin pads. But I stick by what I said. For 90min. that night Mr. Tomaszewski had a guardian angel standing on the line behind him, and although Allan Clarke managed to squeeze in a penalty, our lads could have played till midnight and they wouldn't have scored again. Tomaszewski brought off a string of saves that night which weren't as good as they looked. Technically he was a poor keeper, but he had the good fortune to keep out shots he didn't even see arriving. Spurs goalkeeper Pat Jennings said the next day that he had never seen a man make so many mistakes and get away with it.

I hope Tomaszewski will be playing on Sunday because, sooner or later, a man's luck runs out and he is punished for the errors he has made in the past. Every fan in England will

want to see how he performs. We'll watch this match because we still can't believe what happened at Wembley. Were the Poles that good? Personally, I thought them a sound, reliable, if uninspiring, side. They were blessed with a couple of world-class wingers in Lato and Gadocha, men who could make a few dents in the factory finish of the Italian defence.

If they do penetrate the first layers of that brilliantly disciplined stone-wall rearguard, they then have to contend with Dino Zoff, the most costly, and arguably the best goalkeeper in the world.

I know about Zoff to my cost. He played two fine games for Juventus against Derby in the semi-finals of the European Cup two years ago. When his club paid Napoli £196,000 for him in 1971—a world record for a goalkeeper—it wasn't a lira too much. The man's temperament is supreme.

P LAYING in front of a packed defence, Zoff might have to spend most of a match waiting for the occasional shot to come his way—perhaps a rocket from 25 yards, perhaps a speculative thump deflected through a mass of legs. But he is always equal to it. Somehow he can key himself up for the whole game at the peak of alertness, ready for that vital moment when he's needed.

Against Poland last year, Peter Shilton was a spectator until Domarski fired in a goal after 57min. I think

that if he had been busier beforehand Shilton would have picked up that shot in his teeth.

That's the sort of situation Zoff finds himself in most of the time, but his consistency is remarkable. He holds the Italian league record for not conceding a goal—903min. before he was beaten by a penalty.

Latin countries have never been noted for their great goalkeepers. But in a land where short tempers and hot-headedness on the pitch are almost an accepted part of the game, 32-year-old Zoff is an exception. He is cool as ice, safe, agile and unspectacular. And with the Italians reported to be in £20,000 a man to win the World Cup, it's a coolness which is vital this week.

I think that the Italians have so much all-round ability that they will win this game and go on to do well in the final stages of the World Cup. But I have mixed feelings about whether this is a good thing for the game.

I admire the Italians' skill and the meticulous way they defend, and I reckon that a convict has a better chance of escaping from the maximum security wing of Parkhurst than the Poles have of prising open the Italian barricades. But in the last 10 or 15 years the Italians have not emerged as a world footballing power. They should have done; they have the players, the crowds and the money, but they have stifled themselves with negative tactics.

Defending is only an art if it is used as a springboard for attack. If you

drink champagne until it comes out of your ears it loses its magic. In the same way, defensive football, good as it can be, becomes poison when it's dished up excessively.

I think that the Italians' tactics are built so much on defence that they have forgotten how to attack. This is why the few attackers who have been allowed to develop in Italy are so good. Players such as Riva and Rivera might create only one scoring chance in a match and they take it gratefully.

L AST season Riva's club, Cagliari, scored 23 goals in the league. That's less than half the average total for a middle-of-the-table English or Scottish First Division side. But of those 23 goals, Riva scored 14, an incredible feat.

Given a hint of fresh air between the Polish defenders on Sunday, the Italian attackers will bite with the glee of a child eating a choc ice.

It all adds up to the most interesting match of the week. You never know, those Italians might flick so many shots past Mr. Tomaszewski that they'll get the taste for goals again. And the winner will be football.

The World Cup becomes decisive next week and by Wednesday evening the finalists will be known. Watch ITV for all the action leading up to the great game—plus expert comment from Brian Clough and the panellists.

14

CLOUGH SOUNDS OFF

1973—a year of turmoil in British football, and in the thick of it has been our own columnist Brian Clough. Here he examines the shape of soccer to come, and throws in his own wish for a much happier New Year

LET'S MAKE '74 CHAMPAGNE YEAR

W HAT will football be like on New Year's Eve, 1983? Well, apart from the odd certainty—like Brighton riding high in the First Division —and one or two imponderables (will Alf Ramsey still be trying to get the England team to find the net as he works up to the 1986 World Cup on the Moon?) I believe that the game itself will be vastly different in many ways.

The biggest and best change in football will be that it will become a young man's game, from the boardroom to the pitch. The average age of a First Division football manager today is 45. Not long ago they were on till they were 65 but I think this figure will fall below the 40-mark in the next 10 years. This summer, for the first time, the Professional Footballers' Association held a Management course at the St. Helens College of Technology, in Lancashire, with young, intelligent men like Paddy Crerand, Ian St. John, and Bobby Charlton, sitting behind a desk as pupil-managers.

Young management means young men at boardroom level, too—and I can see us clearing out the dead wood of the men who treat football like a game of tiddlywinks.

There has been a contemporary trend for players to think that they are over the hill by the time they reach 30. But I predict a reversal of this. If we have younger managers, people who know how to get the best out of a player and how to use his particular abilities, it will mean that players will last longer. We will go more for brains and less for brawn, and mature players of 33, 34, and 35 will be giving the game greater composure and grace.

What about football itself in Britain? We've seen fear creeping into it—the chronic fear of losing, and this has created boring, methodical football, reflected at its worst at international level. The influx of young, creative people at all levels of the game will do more for it than any artificial stimulants, like giving points for goals and changing the rules.

I think we'll close the gap in ball skill between ourselves and the continentals. We will encourage, develop and demand skill from our players because, if it comes to a choice, people would rather see skill than goals. The Italian League is the only one in Europe which showed an increase in attendances last season, and they have the most defensive football in the world. But, as we saw at Wembley in October, they have an abundance of skill.

We'll get the players—we might even get round to importing a few continental ones—and we'll have the people to watch them, in comfort. One day, certainly before 1984, one rich First Division club is going to announce that their

ground will be converted to seated, covered stands all round the pitch. Once one team does it, the rest will follow.

It will certainly cost more for the average fan—a pound or two, admission for each match—but I think he'll be prepared to pay for more comfort and better facilities.

Youth, skill, facilities: it sounds good and I really think that it can happen in the next few years.

This last year may have been one of self-examination for English soccer—but it's been a hell of a year for me, personally. I started it leading Derby in the European Cup. I signed for ITV in August, and ended up in the Third Division with Brighton in November.

We had a lot of Christmasses at Derby, and they didn't always come at the end of the year. The champagne flowed in the dressing-room and I built up my own stock of the stuff—the best I could get—at home. And I'd earned it.

Now I'm going to get it coming through the taps at Brighton, despite the hammering we took last month. Which brings me, at this festive time, to ponder over what to send Sam Longson, the Chairman at Derby, for Christmas. I could think of a few well chosen words written on them—but I'll be nice, and offer him the present he might least like to receive—Brighton's success.

To Sam, with love: two points from sunny Brighton. Merry Christmas, and a Happy New Year.

In a season when the newspapers have been packed with tales of football hooliganism, Brian Clough turns his attention to a more pleasant aspect of watching football, the scarves, pennants and stickers which add colour to the game—the souvenir boom, which is bounding ahead

THE POWER OF THE NAUGHTY NIGHTIES

John and Mary Crow are so fanatical in their support for Arsenal that they have decorated their Ilford, Essex, home from top to bottom in red and white, the Gunners' colours, and every wall hangs heavily with fan paraphernalia.

On Saturday at Hampden Park, Glasgow, Scotland play their last international—against the "auld enemy" England—before next month's World Cup finals. Viewers can see the match, live, plus comment from the famous ITV panel, in *World of Sport*. Here Brian Clough takes a look at the big match, and talks to panellist Paddy Crerand about Scotland's World Cup prospects . . .

NEVER MIND MUNICH, IT'S HAGGIS AND HAMPDEN THAT COUNT

Ken Dalglish (left) and Joe Jordan in action when Scotland lost to Brazil last year

NEXT WEEK: Clough looks at England's game against E. Germany, and talks to Derek Dougan.

21

It's the big match: Football v. Television. How much soccer should be shown and how much should TV pay? Brian Clough gives some of the answers

THE GUILTY MEN OF TV SOCCER

BOB LORD, Chairman of Burnley, banned television cameras from his sixth round Football Association Cup tie against Wrexham recently and Queen's Park Rangers manager Gordon Jago kept the cameras away from the exciting replay against Coventry a few weeks earlier. As I made clear when I started this column, I write not as a television commentator but as a football manager, and as such I say both clubs were right.

That is no criticism of television. The fault lies with the football authorities who negotiate the television deals. I think they are guilty of two things: they don't provide enough money for the clubs taking part in televised games, and the contracts they make are inflexible to the point of stupidity.

Lord complained that his club would receive a ridiculously low fee for allowing cameras inside Burnley's ground, and that is a fair point. When I was at Derby I once banned television cameras because I was offended the scandalous sum of £87.50 for the screening of a Cup match against Notts. County. I made my position quite clear at the time—I could earn more than £87.50 selling programmes on the corner. I did have other reasons for the ban as well. I felt that Notts County—not a glamorous club and unused to the attention of television cameras—would raise the standard of their game against Derby because they were on television. Even if I was wrong about that, I didn't want to take the chance and lose the match.

But the money angle remained a firm motive. League and cup matches are negotiated separately and there is much discussion going on about the total fee.

Whatever final deal is settled, my main point is that the bodies which govern football must distribute more of the money they get to the clubs who actually sell the game on TV.

My second point is that the contracts negotiated are far too rigid, which brings me to something I think could bring a few thousand pound notes into the game "at a stroke", as the gentleman once said.

When contracts are discussed again I would like to see machinery set up by which a television company could bid to screen any match, live if possible, at any time. Supposing this season, for instance, the match which would decide the First Division Championship was due to be played on a Tuesday night along with several others. The clever thing to do would be for the League to switch the match to a day on which no others were being played, negotiate a massive sum from the television companies and let them show it live.

Everyone would benefit. Soccer would be richer—I reckon £30,000 would be a fair fee. The television company which won the contract would corner 15 million viewers that night, and our national game would receive the best possible advertisement.

It makes my blood boil to see chances like that missed, and when I talk about £30,000 I'm not talking in telephone numbers. Tom Jones can command a fee of £450,000 for a five-week stint at Caesar's Palace in Las Vegas. If somebody is prepared to pay it, good for Tom Jones, I say. But soccer, which is watched by far larger audiences, has its price, too.

Football has a market value on television, but nothing should be allowed to interfere with the game's essence —the close relationship between a cheering, jeering crowd and the players on the pitch. Some people in the business have sniggered over and over that television exposure reduces gates. I don't accept this. I rather think television stimulates interest and when I conducted a survey at 7½'7 two last year, 80 per cent of the fans said they didn't think there was too much soccer on television.

There is a way to settle this argument once and for all . . . ban televised soccer for six months. The figures would then be there for all to see and we would know conclusively whether or not TV affected attendances. I am pretty sure what the answer would be—it doesn't.

The TV companies have already said that if soccer was banned from the screens they would hook up with continental television and show European matches live. I think this would be a dead loss. Who wants to watch Bayerns of Berunsie Moenchengladbach kicking Grabowski of Eintracht Frankfurt? I don't think the fans have to identify with their own players and clubs, and showing foreign soccer wouldn't keep one supporter away from a ground.

The nub of the argument is that we must bring some simple common sense into our attitude towards television and soccer. There must be a balance between saturation coverage, which makes soccer look stale in the long run, and no televised soccer at all. Football authorities must sell their game much better. Television has almost convinced the public that they get a better deal watching at home, but the time has come for the F.A. and the League to give their side of the story.

They should tell people that they only experience a fraction of soccer's pageant on TV. Viewers don't taste the sawdust, or see the whole canvas of the pitch in front of them.

Football is like a beautiful flower. Seeing it close up on television is fine. But it must be smelt and seen in its setting to be enjoyed completely.

DRIVE

Television cameramen record football matches for millions of viewers. How much money should TV pay to screen them?

Who is the best footballer in England: the best young player: the best team? These questions will all be answered on Sunday night when the results will be announced of a members' ballot of the Professional Footballers' Association. Meanwhile, Brian Clough makes his choice

MIGHTY MICK
MY PLAYER OF THE YEAR

IT IS MY HOPE that when the Professional Footballers' Association declares the winner of their first Player of the Year award on Sunday, the man who picks up the trophy won't be one of the great international stars such as Bobby Moore, Martin Peters, or Colin Bell.

The players themselves will choose somebody who doesn't steal the headlines, a grafter who slogs away practically unnoticed for 60 games, an unsung one-hundred-per-center. A player's player.

There are quite a few blokes around who could fit the bill. I had a couple at Derby—John McGovern and Henry Newton, and there's always that man I raved about in this column the other week, Newcastle's Malcolm Macdonald. But my choice—a man who could be the managers' player as well as the players' player—is someone who has never won an England senior shirt, whose talents are often ignored in contrast to the glittering names playing around him: Mick Jones of Leeds United.

Jones is playing in the most difficult position in football—centre forward. He gets his fair share of goals, but he shirks nothing, he takes an incredible number of knocks, and he's always suffering injuries. This can mean two things in football. Either a man is injury prone—and this is a real problem for some players—or, like Jones, he is suicidal in his determination to get into the thick of it. Jones puts his foot where a less courageous player would pull it out. Jones puts his head into a goal-mouth where another man wouldn't even go into the penalty area.

I often think that soccer should take a lesson from ice hockey—and football clubs like Chelsea—and, instead of simply noting the players who score the goals, should recognise "assists" as well. That way, the man who laid on the goal gets some of the credit—officially. Mick Jones plays in the enormously talented shadow of Allan Clarke, who gets the goals and pinches the limelight at Elland Road. But I would like to know how many "assists" Jones has chalked up in his career. I would guess that if Leeds scored 70 goals in a season, and Jones scored 10 of them, you could credit him with 30 or 40 "assists", and some important ones, too.

Remember the 1972 F.A. Cup Final? We ripped past the Arsenal defence with that snoring, loping run, pulled the ball back from the goal line and put over a beautiful centre for Allan Clarke to head the winning goal? It was Jones. And at the end of the match, who had his face screwed up in agony after dislocating his elbow in another of those Kamikaze leaps into the penalty area. It was Jones.

Managers warm to these types of players. They never cause you a discipline problem, and when it comes to making out the team sheet, the name writes itself automatically, it flows from your pen. Sometimes players like Jones are paid a terrible injustice because the manager doesn't realise just how much he puts into a game.

On a wet Saturday night when you're sitting at home after losing a match in the afternoon, when you're feeling depressed and you're going over the game in your head, that's the time when you suddenly think: "God, that poor devil went through fire and water for me today." That's when you get it into perspective.

I have often heard Don Revie talk about his greatest team—his Madeleys and his Coopers and his Charltons—but I doubt whether penny for penny he has ever spent a better £100,000 than when he forked it out to buy Mick Jones from Sheffield United in 1967.

In the Young Player section the choice is more difficult. There haven't been that many outstanding young players rising to the surface in the last year. A few names spring

Winning the F.A. Cup in 1972 cost Leeds striker Mick Jones a dislocated elbow. Having helped Allan Clarke score the goal which beat Arsenal, he left in the last seconds of the game and was helped off by Dr. I. D. Adams, the Leeds doctor.

to mind, Trevor Francis and Bob Latchford of Birmingham City, Gerry Francis of Queen's Park Rangers, Leighton James of Burnley.

But I can't see further than one youngster who made 22 first-team appearances at Derby last season, who played in the European Cup, and all at the age of 17. Young Steve Powell would get my vote because, in addition to his undoubted skills, he has matured to such an extent in 1973 that it is a certainty that he'll become one of the great footballing names of the future. If we're looking forward to the World Cup in 1978 we should be grooming players like Powell now.

My First Division team (on 1973 form) is: P. Shilton (Leicester City); C. Todd, R. McFarland (Derby County), E. Hughes (Liverpool), D. Nish (Derby), B. Bremner (Leeds United, captain), T. Brooking (West Ham), P. Osgood (Chelsea), A. Clarke, M. Jones (Leeds), M. Macdonald (Newcastle United). If the usual five "international" substitutes were allowed, they would be: P. Jennings (Tottenham Hotspur); B. Moncur (Newcastle), M. Dobson (Burnley), R. Marsh (Manchester City), M. Channon (Southampton).

Whoever wins the awards on Sunday night, the most pleasing thing about the whole affair is that, for the first time, players are asserting themselves as a unit. Once, anyone who played football for a living was considered thick and stupid, unable to put two intelligible words together. It is slowly dawning on people that many footballers are educated, talented men.

That's what I mean when I say: I'm pleased that the players are now beginning to behave like a professional body, and the more we hear the voice of the players the better. Because players are football.

Steve Powell: best young player of 1973, claims Clough

Clough shoots for goal during Sunderland's 2-1 Second Division home win over Leeds, 9 September 1961. 'I sometimes ask myself how I did it, how I scored my goals. But I can honestly say I don't know.'

A 31-year-old Clough in his Derby County office with assistant Peter Taylor, 11 October 1967. 'The combination of myself and Peter Taylor is the best football management team in the country.'

Clough in rehearsals for an appearance on **The Big Match**, *23 August 1973. 'People are afraid to get down to business. They talk round a subject, as if it were a bad germ; they never get into it and say exactly what they feel.'*

Clough preparing for punditry duties alongside Brian Moore. 'I've been working regularly for ITV now for three months and apart from the tedious journeys up and down the motorway every week, and having my face powdered once every ten minutes, I'm enjoying it immensely.'

Clough with his Derby players Colin Todd and Roy McFarland before England's World Cup qualifier at Wembley versus Poland, 17 October 1973. 'I buy Colin Todd because I see a graceful athlete. I buy Roy McFarland because I see balance and pure skill.'

Polish goalkeeper Jan Tomaszewski during the 1-1 draw at Wembley that saw England fail to qualify for the World Cup finals in West Germany. 'I labelled Tomaszewski a clown when all around me were saying he was the greatest thing since shin pads. But I stick by what I said.'

Clough and Taylor watch Brighton play York City, 3 November 1973. 'It is my job, and my belief, that Brighton won't be in the Third Division for very long...'

*Clough instructs his Brighton players during the goalless FA Cup tie at Walton &
Hersham, 24 November 1973. '...when we slithered to a 4-0 defeat in the replay, it
ranks as the worst 90 minutes I have ever spent on a touchline.'*

*Leicester City goalkeepers Gordon Banks and Peter Shilton during training at the
club's Filbert Street ground, 1965. 'Peter Shilton, in my opinion, is even better
than Banks.'*

Stoke City's manager Tony Waddington – 'the sort of bloke who has made an art out of keeping a low profile' – with World Cup hero Geoff Hurst, preparing for an FA disciplinary meeting, 13 October 1972.

Leeds's Mick Jones, 'his face screwed up in agony' after dislocating his elbow at the end of the FA Cup Final versus Arsenal, 6 May 1972.

Billy Bremner – 'The perfect and unique combination of grit and the refined skills of ball control' – scores for Leeds against Leicester City, 16 September 1972.

Goalscorer Martin Peters with Scottish keeper Ally Hunter during England's 1-0 win at Wembley, 19 May 1973. 'Any time Scotland play England, there isn't a ticket to spare.'

Kevin Keegan gets Liverpool's third (and his second) against Newcastle United in the FA Cup Final, 4 May 1974. 'I still think he has something to learn about slowing down, looking around him and dictating the game. But he'll probably be the first to prove me wrong.'

The Middlesbrough Motormouth meets the Louisville Lip, Madison Square Garden, January 1974. 'Ali has made as many fans with his mouth as he has with his fists. I think he is a very underestimated man in this respect, and this applies to everybody who talks a lot.'

A grim faced Sir Alf Ramsey, after England's failure versus Poland. 'I actually admired Sir Alf. You've got to hand it to a bloke who can stand by his guns with an almost serene stubbornness.'

Denis Law in action versus Zaire in Dortmund, 14 June 1974, his last Scottish international. '...with Yugoslavia and Brazil in their group, they [Scotland] only have to make one slip to be wiped out.'

Scotland striker Joe Jordan clashes with Brazilian defender Luís Pereira in Frankfurt, 18 June 1974. '...they should respect Brazil but not fear them...'

West Germany's Gerd Müller mobbed by teammates after scoring the World Cup Final winner against Holland in Munich, 7 July 1974. '... if we can keep this a clean World Cup, it will be a great competition. I don't care who wins so long as they win it worthily and skilfully.'

Don Revie prepares to say goodbye at Elland Road on 5 July 1974 following his appointment as England boss. 'I believe he will stay there [at Leeds] forever now – unless he takes over the England job, which he would do brilliantly.'

Mick Channon lifts the FA Cup aloft on Southampton's victory parade, 2 May 1976. 'There's a story going around that when Channon takes off his Southampton shirt after a match, he's still painted in red-and-white stripes underneath.'

Malcolm Macdonald scores his second during Newcastle United's 2-0 FA Cup semi-final win v Burnley at Hillsborough, 30 March 1974. 'I really believe people like Macdonald are born to score goals.'

up the game in one swoop,' he raged – and even gone so far as to state that Revie should be fined for encouraging his players in their unsporting behaviour and Leeds be relegated to the Second Division.

Clough claimed that his 1972 title winners weren't a physical side. Though, in late December during that campaign, had actually unleashed an attack on his Derby players for lacking toughness. 'We are not big enough and strong enough to dish it out when it needs to be dished out,' he moaned to reporters, shortly after watching his side get soundly beaten 3-0 at Elland Road. Revie took Clough's words with a pinch of salt. It was all 'part of Clough's bluff,' he told *Radio Times* at the start of the following campaign. 'I find it surprising that he should appear to be so indignant about teams going in hard for the ball,' Revie said. 'No matter what he might say to the contrary, you can take it from me that Derby are as physically intimidating as anyone when the need arises.'

Never one to back down from a verbal battle, Revie would defend his Leeds players to the death, but was reluctant to enter a war of words when asked by *TV Times* a year later what he thought of Clough's attacks on both him and his team. 'All I'll say on the subject of Clough['s] outside football activities is that if all managers and players acted like him, knocking each other all the time, there very soon wouldn't be any game left.'

The two men, born just a few streets apart from one another in Middlesbrough, had crossed paths and swords many times over the years, both as players and managers. But for a rejection on Revie's part, the pair might well have been teammates. In September 1958, backing their drive for promotion from the Second Division, Middlesbrough, where Clough was grabbing goals as if they were going out of fashion, put in a £15,000 bid for Revie, then at Sunderland. But Revie, a creative midfielder, rejected the move, joining Leeds just two months later.

Clough's last two goals in league football were actually against Leeds, both scored when Clough himself was wearing the colours of the Roker Park club where, he said later, he 'got so much pleasure from playing the game, it's untrue'. On 22 December 1962, four days before he suffered the injury that effectively ended his career in the clash with Bury, Clough notched one of the goals in Sunderland's 2-1 home win over United. Revie was player-manager at Elland Road by then. Then, at the beginning of 1964/65, in one of three appearances he made to fulfil his ambition to play First Division football before medical advisors and common sense told him to quit, Clough got one of Sunderland's three goals on 5 September 1964 as they finished level with United at Roker Park.

There's a case for saying that Clough's goal in that 3-3 draw ultimately helped deprive Leeds of the title that season. On 61 points at its end, the same as Manchester United, the West Yorkshire club, with Revie now concentrated fully on management duties, lost out on goal ratio, the two sides separated according to goal average (goals scored divided by goals conceded). Leeds had got so close but not close enough. It became a recurring story over the next few years.

By the start of 1973/74, Leeds, under Revie's stewardship, had not finished out of the top four since their return to the top flight in 1964. Yet cynics said they had faltered at the final hurdle too many times to be considered as one of the truly greats. They'd ended as cup runners-up or in second place an amazing ten times. For all their successes, there was a sense of unfulfilled potential hanging over the team.

After their disastrous defeat to Sunderland in the 1973 FA Cup Final, a side in which many players had grown older together was written off as 'over the hill'. But it was a side for whom labels were nothing new. Ever since the early years of Revie's management when, match after match, his homespun team battled tigerishly, relying a little too much on enthusiasm and spirit than on skill, Leeds were roundly accused of overstepping the mark in terms of professionalism. Revie's emphasis on graft over craft gave his sides an air of impregnability but spawned a style of football in which sinew was frequently far more in evidence than finesse, their play at times bordering on the x-rated. Moreover, Leeds were chastised for beating opponents with their bullying tactics rather than their footballing abilities.

A particularly ill-tempered contest at Goodison Park on 7 November 1964 – the referee forced to take both teams off the pitch to cool down for ten minutes when tempers frayed and ferocious challenges flew in from the opening seconds – brought castigation from the press and the condemnation of the FA. While Everton were disciplined for having a player, Sandy Brown, sent off and the behaviour of their fans who pelted missiles at the visitors' players, Revie's side escaped punishment. But the tag of 'Dirty Leeds' was born that day. Shaking it off would prove more or less impossible.

Arguably it worked in their favour sometimes: some teams almost felt beaten by Leeds before they'd even faced them. Yet it was a blanket and blinkered view that time and again failed to recognise the immense talent present throughout the Elland Road outfit, and what the *Yorkshire Post's* Terry Brindle saw as 'the extraordinary aura of class' they possessed. Revie's commitment to clinging on to leads rather than go all-out attack and kill off matches was strong, but when he let his side off the leash they often ran riot. Leeds won their first-ever league title in 1969 – with a record number of points (67) and only two defeats – and for the next few years, playing an expansive brand of near-Total Football, they became a team to compare with Europe's very best.

Yet even when they really turned on the style – a 7-0 home hammering of Southampton on 4 March 1972, for example, when, by the end, Leeds's toying with the opposition was, in Barry Davies's words, 'almost cruel' – whatever praise they received was, by and large, grudging and quickly countered by certain sections of the press opting to focus more on the odd on-field scrap, the occasional recklessness and loss of control.

In 1972 Revie was the first to push for an outlawing of the tackle from behind, as one answer to the increasingly jaded players and joyless football of the time. 'It's spoiling our game by suffocating players' skills,' he said. Freed from the fear of having their legs swept from under them, forwards 'would be able to develop the kind of goal-making and scoring skills we are now losing'. The previous season's clampdown by refs had done a lot of good to begin with, but too much pressure from all sides meant the campaign lost its impetus halfway through the season. The clean-up, in Revie's view, needed to be intensified. 'I think the new disciplinary system which is to be tried this [1972/73] season – with bookings leading to automatic suspension – will help a lot.'

As it was, Leeds's record was poor throughout the season – hence Clough's calls for their penalising. Before they entered into the 1973/74 campaign, Revie told his squad he wanted them to keep their noses clean. More than anything else, though, he yearned to win a second title – and to do so, if possible, without a single slip-up during the 42-game marathon. Fed up with the perception of Leeds, despite being among the top two or three of the First Division's leading scorers for the past few years, as 'a methodical, well-drilled, hard side,' Revie urged his players pre-season to 'get out there and show everyone what a great team you are.'

They won their first seven games. By Christmas, they were unbeaten in 21 outings and seven points clear at the top of the table, ahead of reigning champions Liverpool. When they went to Birmingham on the last Saturday of 1973 and drew 1-1, it made 23 without defeat, and Leeds had overhauled Sheffield United's 74-year-old record of 22 matches unbeaten since the start of a season in First Division football. They were even in serious danger of winning over a few new admirers.

The Times's Geoffrey Green penned a glowing tribute: 'Within the past decade, Leeds, by their achievements, have grown to be the aristocrats of the English game. But more importantly this season ... they have made a conscious effort to change their former image of being a hard, greedy, ruthless side up to every act of gamesmanship in the professional book where the Corinthian ethos of old has scarcely survived. They have succeeded so far in taking a duster to the slate with the happy result that they are now not only a better side, but have also achieved a new stature that is attracting the attention of a selective public.'

Six league games later, however, on the back of a shock FA Cup exit at home to Second Division Bristol City, that unblemished run was ended at Stoke and, beset by a spate of injuries and a seeming crisis of confidence, Leeds began to stutter. The players, now more anxious, were no longer stroking the ball about with the confidence of batsmen who'd passed their century but ones who feared bagging a pair. The tension was telling and the tests of temperament they'd passed so comfortably earlier in the season were regularly being failed.

The Don of Elland Road documentary, showing Revie over a couple of weeks in March 1974, captured his side at a time when they were still in a trough. The two matches highlighted in the film both ended in defeat: away against their nearest challenger, Liverpool, on 16 March 1974 – the 13th anniversary of Revie's appointment as manager – when 56,003 were at Anfield to witness Steve Heighway get a closely fought game's only goal on 82 minutes, followed by a demoralising 4-1 beating at home by Burnley. The Saturday after that Leeds lost again, 3-1 at West Ham, and suddenly everyone began to wonder whether they would run out of steam once more.

They didn't. A 2-0 win at Sheffield United in mid-April and a home success against Ipswich Town restored a five-point lead for Revie's side, who had one game to play, at QPR. Liverpool had three games remaining, all against London clubs. When Bill Shankly's side lost the first of those, 1-0 at home to Arsenal, it ended their double hopes and handed the title to Leeds. On 27 April Allan Clarke's goal sealed a 1-0 victory at Loftus Road and cemented Leeds's status as worthy champions.

Appointed player-manager in the final weeks of 1960/61, Revie took over a side for whom relegation from the Second Division seemed imminent and, as one writer put it, 'the future at Elland Road looked about as bright as that of a box of matches soaked in water'. Revie transformed the club. A team of nonentities were elevated to a position where they were, if not always one of the most esteemed, definitely the most feared side in the land. Whilst over the years they'd experienced more than their fair share of misfortune and near-misses, whatever hardships they suffered, they suffered as a nigh on unbreakable unit. Marching on together. Side before self every time.

It was Clough's belief that only one job had enough magnetic pull to wrench Revie away from the family of which he was head.

On 1 May 1974, just a week after Leeds had secured their second title under his leadership, that job became available. Had it been two years earlier, Clough himself, as the manager of the newly crowned league champions, might have been in with a shout of it. Not now.

Now he was languishing in the Third Division with a club to whom he was devoting less and less time and from whom he was itching to escape. Little did he realise but, because of that England vacancy and the 'man for all seasons' about to fill it, the chance to make a break would soon be forthcoming. A few weeks later, when, as Clough later recounted it, 'the big offer came along', it was one he would jump at. It was also one, in hindsight, he really should have looked at more closely before he leapt.

A Leeds United Football Club triumvirate of strength: Les Cocker, trainer; Don Revie, manager; and defender Roy Ellam.

20–26 April 1974

The league season draws to a climax, and by the time clubs start operating again each will be coaching a new intake of apprentices: young hopefuls who may one day be thrilling the big crowds. But Brian Clough says our system isn't good enough. We must start treating our junior players like heroes instead of idiots who boot footballs because they can't do anything else …

LET'S HAVE A SOCCER UNIVERSITY

IF this country is ever going to regain its place at the top of international football, we must put all our emphasis on building up the skills and qualities of our youngest players – an investment for the future.

What I'd like to see is a University of Soccer.

There, the best of our young players could study their sport to the full and the greatest soccer brains in the country could share their expertise with the next generation. A lad who passed his BF exam would be a Bachelor of Football.

Far-fetched? I don't think so, because sooner or later we are going to have to get a grip on our methods of finding, training, and encouraging young boys who want to play football for a living.

The Americans and Russians have the right idea. As soon as a young American shows promise in sport, whether it's swimming, athletics or football, they can win places at well-equipped universities where the gifts they have can be brought out and perfected, ready for the next Olympics or a prominent local team. The sporting student is respected on a par with the academically minded. In Russia, they make sure ability is encouraged by sticking useful-looking athletes into the Red Army. People like Olympic sprinter Valeriy Borzov are made colonels and spend most of their time on the running track instead of the parade ground.

What is the difference between a man who uses his considerable brainpower to churn out formulae in the field of nuclear science, and a man who uses his brain and his body on the football field to give people immense pleasure?

They are both essential to the community, but we sell the young footballer tragically short in terms of facilities, opportunities and status.

The situation now is that scouts all over the country are looking for promising lads aged about 13 and 14. At 14 a boy can join a club as an 'associated schoolboy', which means he can train at the club and play for their junior sides. At 16, when he can leave school, the club has first choice of signing him as an apprentice professional. League clubs are allowed to employ only 30 apprentices at any one time, and frankly I think those lads would be lucky if even one eventually made it into the first team. My assistant Peter Taylor and I make that absolutely clear to any boy who joins us at Brighton.

That is why I always insist my lads continue to study for another job while they are with us. At Derby, Steve Powell, one of the few juniors who was certain to be a star, had the qualifications to go to university after he passed his A-levels while he was with the club. If he had to pack up his career now, he could walk into a top job.

Powell is not an exception, but the young footballer today is still regarded by society as an idiot – a lad who boots a ball around for a living because he cannot do anything else. It is time people realised that football is an art form.

Most schools stream pupils according to their abilities in certain subjects. If they are good at mathematics and chemistry, they are given the opportunity to concentrate on those subjects. If a child shows exceptional ability at playing the piano or violin, he can win a scholarship to the Royal College of Music.

But if a boy can perform magic with a football, what help does he get? None. At 14, the cream of our soccer talent could be sent to a special soccer college, where they could continue their academic studies, but put the accent on their physical skills.

This cream wouldn't be hard to find. Like every league club, Brighton have a scouting network throughout the nation to rival the KGB. Our contacts tip us off if they think they have seen an able young player and Peter Taylor, in my view the best judge of talent in the business, goes to see for himself. Often he sees nothing. Sometimes he sees potential – now and again, a star. A great player is never discovered. If any scout said he'd discovered George Best or Peter Shilton or Johan Cruyff, I'd tell him he was talking out of the back of his head. Players like that stand out like diamonds in a bed of broken glass.

The important thing about young players is that the earlier they are coached correctly, the better they become. I like to get a player under my wing as soon as possible, when he can be conditioned to my methods and my way of thinking. Sometimes you get somebody who comes into the game too late, and it's always more difficult to stamp your personality on a player like that.

At Derby, centre-forward Roger Davies came to us when he was 21 from non-league Ilkeston Town. For us that was four years too late. You can never make up the ground in terms of imprinting a way of life upon a young man, because I pay attention to everything in the youngster's life, from the way he kicks the ball on the pitch, to the things he eats at home, to his girlfriend.

Of course, we have made mistakes. In our early days at Derby we weighed up the chances of a young lad on the playing staff and we decided there was no place for him. We let him go to York City for a small fee. In January, six years later, Norwich wrote out a cheque for £145,000 to buy the same lad, Phil Boyer, from Bournemouth.

You can't win them all, but I would say very few quality players slip anyone's net. The main thing is not just to catch them and let them get on with it, but to educate them – to make them feel proud of being artists and entertainers. Perhaps the day when we see a centre-forward with a first-class degree in football is not too far away.

27 April–3 May 1974

For every full-scale match a club plays, they get through ten games of five-a-side in training. On Wednesday, you can see the *London Evening Standard* five-a-side tournament with some great names of football pounding the boards of the Empire Pool, Wembley. Here, Brian Clough turns the spotlight on five-a-side, and names his own Big Five ...

FIVE-A-SIDE ... A NATURAL BREAK FROM THE MOST INSANE SEASON IN THE WORLD

BEHIND every great team performance on the football field is a week of grafting, bending, running, stretching, sweating, liniment-rubbing on the treatment table, tactical talks in the dressing room – and the mind-sharpening exercise of five-a-side football.

At this time of the season, unless you happen to be lined up in a World Cup squad or cup final team, five-a-side tournaments are a light relaxation after a gruelling nine-month season – the longest, most intense and most insanely demanding season in the world.

But throughout that week-by-week winter slog, every club relies to a large extent on five-a-side football, or variations of it, for the essential honing of ball skills and for quickening players' reactions.

At Brighton, as at Derby, we split our first-team squad into two teams of six or seven players and play a variation of five-a-side called two-touch. The game is the basis of our footballing philosophy. The rules are simple: you are allowed to kick the ball only twice each time you receive it, in other words, trap it and pass it on. The goals are low benches and you can only score within a six-yard radius.

Apart from being a test of stamina, the game develops quickness of mind and movement, and it looks good because the best football is that in which the ball never stops, but flows all the time.

Nobody over-elaborates in five-a-side or two-touch. You can't afford to waste time playing fancy tricks, drawing pretty patterns on the turf. There is also a hell of a lot of pressure on the players. They must get the ball and, in a split second, know what they're going to do with it, and play it.

I think this has been the foundation of the method used by the greatest teams in recent history – the Hungarian national side, who smashed England 6-3 at Wembley in 1953; Real Madrid at their best in the late 60s when they walked away with the European Cup year after year; Spurs when they won the double in the early 60s – they all played basically with a two-touch approach.

When you play this sort of football accurately, the opposition never get their noses near enough to smell the ball. Our method at Derby over six years was just that: get possession, play it quickly, play it accurately. This style of soccer drains you physically. After 90 minutes you are as exhausted as a marathon runner because you do more chasing, more accelerating, more quick turning than in any other method of football.

Everything you do in football stems from the brain, and five-a-side demands quickness of thought and action, teaching the players also to play the ball in a confined space. There are more than 5,000 square yards on the average football field and that's 230 square yards for each player to graze on. But go down to touchline level next time you watch a league match, and see how little space and time a player has.

Being able to play creative five-a-side football in a confined space is the hallmark of a great player. It's where the Third Division and First Division seem light-years apart. In the First you find a high number of gifted players who can worm their way out of an impossible situation. In the Third, the game gets bogged down because less-gifted players are unable to do this.

In five-a-side, too, the goalkeeper has to be lightning-sharp, especially with indoor five-a-side where the ball, difficult enough to control on the springy wooden boards, can skid past you like a meteorite.

The good players for five-a-side are the Roy McFarland-type players who are all-round footballers, not specialist attackers or defenders, blockers or wingers, the sort of players I would like 11 of in any side of mine if I could find them.

Which brings me to my own nominations for a British five-a-side team: the Clough Quintet.

Having to choose 11 players to form a cohesive unit is difficult enough. Choosing five is nearly impossible. But here goes:

1. Roy McFarland: Derby. Quick with his delivery, brilliant with his ball control – the thinking man's footballer.
2. Billy Bremner: Leeds. The perfect and unique combination of grit and the refined skills of ball control.
3. Alan Hudson: Stoke. A natural grafter, what I call a short build-up man, able to construct moves intelligently.
4. Denis Law: Manchester City. Superbly arrogant, sure of his own ability, a player who always seems to say, 'Give me the ball.'
5. Ray Clemence: Liverpool, goalkeeper. Inferior to Peter Shilton as an all-round keeper but perhaps the sharpest reflex goalkeeper around.

So there you are. A famous five to warm the heart and put a few holes in the net. I'd pay a few bob to see them in action.

* * * *

There's a famous story from Bill Shankly's early days at Liverpool about a five-a-side game (or in Bob Paisley's version, a seven-a-side) which, depending who's telling it, either took place at the club's Melwood training ground between some senior players and the coaching staff or in the car park behind the main stand at Anfield with a team of apprentice professionals taking on Shankly and his fellow Boot Room boys. The super-competitive Shankly was renowned for treating training sessions as a serious business and, especially, these typically hard-fought matches which were never over until the Liverpool boss got the result he wanted – a win.

On this particular occasion, one of the usual participants, Chris Lawler, was sitting it out, having suffered a rare injury when teammate Tommy Smith 'did' him in another five-a-side match. Appointed as referee, Lawler, a player of so few words his teammates christened him 'Silent Knight', was watching from the sidelines when Shankly claimed a goal with a rising shot from long range, which the opposition insisted had gone over the 'bar'. There were no proper goalposts, only shoes, on this day, so it was up to Lawler to adjudicate. 'You are in the perfect position, son,' Shankly shouted over. 'Was that a goal?' 'No,' came the quiet man's terse reply. 'Good God, Chris,' Shankly said in his raw Scottish voice, 'this is the first time I've heard you speak to me and you tell me a bloody lie!'

On 7 November 1973 Derby, Clough-less for just over three weeks, took a team to the *Daily Express* national five-a-side championship at the Empire Pool, Wembley, and won it – 3-1 in the final against Celtic (the first Scottish club to make the last two). Both the *Express*-sponsored competition and the *London Evening Standard* tournament, also at the Empire Pool (though, first held at Empress Hall, Earls Court, before a year later transferring to the Harringay Arena, it didn't find a home in the north London suburb until 1959), weren't perhaps entered into as fiercely as many training-ground encounters acted out on a weekly basis at clubs up and down the country. Nevertheless, while there was certainly less physical contact and flying tackles than in your average league clash, these mini-format challenges were extremely keenly contested; no team who accepted an invitation to take part went in to them seeking anything other than outright success.

Of the two annual events, while the *Standard*-backed contest, having begun in 1954, had longevity on its side, it was undoubtedly the *Express* version which the nation of football fans took to its collective heart, with the BBC making it a popular one-off fixture in the television schedule, broadcasting the best of the evening's action on their midweek *Sportsnight* programme. Normally played on a Wednesday in early November, the competition was launched in 1968, attracting many top clubs from the outset, with Charlton Athletic, victorious in the first *London Evening Standard* finals 14 years earlier, having the honour of being the inaugural winners.

The Beeb, sensing that this novel knockout football could attract a large audience eager to see (five-man) teams in an unusual setting and adapting to a whole new set of rules – no passing back to the goalkeeper and the ball can't go above shoulder height being the two chief ones the players had to lodge in their footballing brains – were equally as enthusiastic about selling it. 'The fastest and most thrilling indoor football in the world,' was the *Radio Times*'s billing on 6 November 1969, with David Coleman – hosting 'Britain's biggest-ever indoor football evening' – giving 'live commentaries on the semi-finals and final of this three-and-a-half-hour soccer spectacular'.

In truth, the soccer wasn't always that stunning, but the relative simplicity of the limited laws, together with the confined space (often forcing referees to adopt unusual spur-of-the-moment positions to keep out of the way of the action) in which the games were fought, meant that it was swift-paced and almost continuously moving. Considered approach play definitely took the night off. 'It's a quick game with a lot of first-time passing,' Manchester City's Alan Oakes told *Radio Times* in 1970, though added, 'but you do get your [Peter] Osgoods who'll take a man on and dribble.'

Clubs used to five-a-side in training knew what was required: speed over a short distance and manoeuvrability rather than strength. Above all, non-stop effort. This was Total Football on a very miniature, intimate scale and, while games might have been short – averaging around five minutes each half – with players involved virtually from kick-off to final whistle there was no room for any slackers. They tended to choose their squads accordingly.

In 1969 it had been City, beating League Cup holders Swindon Town 2-1 in the final, who'd emerged as overall winners. The Manchester club had taken a squad of eight including Oakes, Colin Bell, Glyn Pardoe and Neil Young, all of whom had been part of their winning FA Cup side in May, keen to add further silverware to the trophy cabinet. Though, as Colin Bell confessed in his autobiography *Reluctant Hero*, the incentive to do so did substantially increase once the City coach on the night, Dave Ewing, revealed to the players they would be rewarded financially with cash payments for progressing further; something of which they were previously unaware. Very generously, they shared the money with the rest of their teammates on returning to Manchester the following day.

Generally, although some clubs grabbed the opportunity to blood younger talent against more senior footballers, while others were reluctant to send important players if they had a European game that week or a vital match forthcoming, most managers respected the tournament's prestige by sending down a squad comprising established first-teamers. Customarily, it was also the case that those clubs fielding a strong line-up reaped the rewards. In 1970, as City's neighbours United triumphed, beating Spurs 2-1 in the final, their side featured four top players from their 1968 European Cup win: Alex Stepney, David Sadler, Bobby Charlton and George Best. It was probably wise that they did; United didn't win another trophy until the FA Cup seven years later.

Stepney was still at Old Trafford in 1977; Best by that time had long gone, though, walking out on the club for one last time six weeks after appearing in United's 1973 five-a-side team. Even then, he still managed to do one of his famous disappearing acts, failing to show for a meeting with some executives from a Japanese clothing company in the reception of the London hotel where the United squad was staying.

The following year, when Tommy Docherty's side had what would be just a one-season stay in the Second Division, they opened their league campaign with a 2-0 away win at Orient's Brisbane Road. Less than three months later it was the Londoners who claimed the *Daily Express* prize, Spurs again the beaten finalists. Unlikely champions? Not really. If nothing else, the competition was a genuine leveller. Less fashionable and unfancied sides always had a chance.

Second Division Sunderland, scoring ten goals in four games, took the coveted trophy back to Wearside in 1979, and a youthful Celtic, the one Scottish team to win it, hauled it even further north in 1981, overcoming an experienced Southampton quintet containing World Cup winner Alan Ball and twice European Footballer of the Year Kevin Keegan 1-0 in the final. Nine years before, on 15 November 1972, as Keegan (along with then Liverpool teammate Ray Clemence) made his international debut in a World Cup group-five qualifier at Ninian Park, won 1-0 by England, on the same night Spurs were all-conquering at the Empire Pool. With the international highlights on ITV immediately following the five-a-sides (shown on the Beeb in the first half of a two-part *Sportsnight*), it was a rare double dose of football on the box for those armchair supporters who fancied it – plus were happy to get up and flick over channels in those pre-remote control days. Between its 1968 origin and 1983, the last year the competition was televised, only Wolves achieved back-to-back victories (in 1975 and 1976), while Southampton were the one other club to register two successes (albeit 12 years apart). Ipswich Town, Crystal Palace (beating Chelsea on spot kicks after a 2-2 draw in the 1978 final), Aston Villa and Arsenal all enjoyed the spoils of victory, too.

Advertising the 1974 tournament, Orient, according to *Radio Times*, were just one of '16 top British teams whose supporters always make this one of the noisiest nights of the year at Wembley's Empire Pool.' With a full house usually guaranteed – very much on the side of the London teams – a special atmosphere was created. And while much of the supporters' noise echoing under the arena roof was fairly shrill (the sell-out attendances largely consisting of pre-adolescents), added to the thud of the wooden boards surrounding the playing surface as one-twos were played off them, the squeak of training shoes on the hard floor, and the familiar-to-Saturday cries of 'man on', 'square ball' and 'give and go', it all made for a soundtrack unique to this particular evening in the calendar of 'high-speed football excitement'.

Inevitably, when the BBC decided to stop its coverage, the *Daily Express* competition's appeal withered and eventually died.

A new Atari-sponsored Soccer Sixes competition held at the NEC in Birmingham didn't help. Watford, Oxford United and Norwich City (thrashing Manchester City 5-0 in the final) were the last three winners.

For viewers watching on television, the enticements had been many: the possibility of getting a first glimpse at a previously unheard-of youngster, an up-and-coming talent worth making note of for the future; the refreshing sight of big names and star players chasing a giant tennis ball around in an incongruous setting, playing a game that they themselves had enjoyed in the school playground or at the local sports centre. There were frustrations: you might not see your own team at all, only being told by the *Sportsnight* host that they'd exited at the first round (especially galling if it had been via a penalty shoot-out; all drawn matches being quickly resolved in this manner); or, perhaps worse, your hopes would be raised by watching your heroes give a masterful display in the early stages only to then be fairly perfunctorily informed that they'd been dispatched in their next outing.

But all in all, the plusses far outweighed the drawbacks, and given the general paucity of soccer on the small screen during those years, no one was really complaining. After all, when you could witness, as *Radio Times* hailed it in their preview of Wednesday, 3 November 1976, 'Ball-playing skills and spectacular shooting thrills from football's fastest competitive action of the season', truly, what was there to moan about?

4–10 May 1974

Saturday is Cup Final day. At Wembley, Newcastle United take on Liverpool and *World of Sport* cameras will be there to bring you the build-up to the big match, plus live coverage of the game – and the famous ITV panel's no-holds-barred assessment of who will win. Brian Clough surveys the match and offers his predictions …

IT'S LIVERPOOL FOR THE CUP

WHOEVER wins Saturday's Football Association Cup Final, it's going to be a cracking game. British football will be getting a free 90-minute commercial, because Newcastle United and Liverpool are two sides who can't get stuck in a rut. They bring their skills into the open, they play flowing, attacking football; tight at the back, killers up front. You couldn't ask for anything more.

But it's a hell of a difficult match to forecast, and after Sunderland's win over Leeds last year, and Poland's win which knocked England out of the World Cup, this forecasting is becoming a dicey business. A few more bad predictions and I'll be out of a job as a pundit.

But let's look at the match. Liverpool may be one of football's cream sides, but the First Division is so evenly matched these days that there is little between the top and bottom in terms of ability. In a cup final, when league form doesn't count and both teams are playing away, you might as well spin a coin to find the winner.

The cup final at Wembley stands on its own. There is nothing to compare with it. Wembley can put jelly into the tough knees of the most consistent defenders. On the other hand, it can bring out latent brilliance, inspiration and guts from players who have never been stars.

But there are some things you can count on. Both teams include players tested and proved under all sorts of conditions.

Newcastle have John Tudor, rejected by Coventry City, transferred to Sheffield United, then resurrected at St James' Park to become one of the most intelligent and spirited players in the game – a scorer of vital goals and a skilful man who will find the Wembley surface to his liking. They have the surging, fighting talent of Bobby Moncur, who will say to himself before the game: 'This is going to be my last chance for a winner's medal, and I'm not going to let it go.' Then they have the incomparable Malcolm Macdonald.

Some readers may be forgiven if they think I am becoming Macdonald's unpaid public relations officer, but I will never stop talking about the bloke. You won't shut me up. He is not blessed with the finest of ball skills and he does not perform like a ballet dancer. You are more likely to find a bloke like Macdonald on a building site than at the Bolshoi. But Macdonald is lethal. Put the ball in front of him within 25 yards of goal and he'll give any defender a coronary, especially if the ball is put on his left foot. When Alf Ramsey put the number nine on Macdonald's back in England's match against Portugal last month, it was his best bit of selection for years.

If anybody is going to break Liverpool's defence, generally accepted as the strongest in the business, it will be Macdonald, because he has the physical power and the willpower to take advantage of a single chance.

Newcastle's failing this season is that they have been so inconsistent. They have lost silly matches, especially on their own ground in front of their own crowd, but they have occasionally shown glimmers of greatness, like the day, earlier this year, when they smashed Coventry 5-1. Against Liverpool, they haven't had a lot of luck. They drew 0-0 at home, and lost 2-1 away, both typical Liverpool results. Trying to beat their defence is like trying to open a can of beans with your teeth.

But Liverpool don't score many goals. They seem to have the infuriating capacity to win every other match 1-0 or 2-1.

Like Tudor, Moncur and Macdonald, Liverpool have their hard core of brilliant players with big match temperament. Emlyn Hughes is a truly great defender always ready to forage upfield and have a go. His face nearly always betrays his feelings for the game; he wears an expression of anguish for 90 minutes, summing up his tension and determination.

Hughes is a typical Bill Shankly player, burning and ferocious – but for my money, the man who can swing the match is Ian Callaghan.

Callaghan is a footballer's footballer. Quiet, clean, and without a rival as a competitor. He has been around for many years now and, though he never won regular international honours, I doubt whether Shankly can measure in cash the value this man has been to his side.

Callaghan combines midfield generalship – being able to control a game, cool the pace – with the rare sting of a genuine winger. Callaghan can tear down the touchline, beat his man, and cross the ball beautifully. You can count the number of players who can do that in English football on one hand.

Kevin Keegan is another matter. He has the same brave involvement of the rest of the Liverpool team, but I will be looking for evidence on Saturday that he is a complete player. I still think he has something to learn about slowing down, looking around him and dictating the game. But he'll probably be the first to prove me wrong.

Of the 100,000 crowd at Wembley, I think there will be more genuine football supporters than in any previous final.

Right, you're waiting for a prediction. Quite honestly, I'd like to duck out of this one, because it's full of imponderables, quite apart from the fact that I'm a north-easterner myself and my heart craves for a Newcastle win. But one word has made up my mind. Shankly. Shankly is the key. His will to win must give them the edge. He will win for Liverpool.

It doesn't matter how many games they play in a season, the enthusiasm of this man is unquenchable and it seeps through to every member of his team; 24 hours a day, seven days a week, 52 weeks a year. He will instil this excitement into his players this week.

There won't be many goals in it, but for me it must be Liverpool – by a whisker.

* * * *

Despite Clough's optimism, 'cracking' was not a superlative any journalist used to describe the 1974 FA Cup Final in their match report. At least not the part played in it by the team from the North East. 'Newcastle's frail, fumbling challenge hardly amounted to a challenge at all,' wrote David Lacey in *The Guardian*, while in the verdict of the *Daily Mirror*'s Frank McGhee, '[United deserved to be] prosecuted under the Trades Description Act for masquerading as a first-class football side'. They were harsh but accurate assessments. The two competing clubs may, the month before the match, have asked the FA to allow extra time in the final were there a deadlock after 90 minutes, but, in truth, on the day that eventuality was never going to happen.

Liverpool, beaten just twice in 27 games since Boxing Day, had, in their semi-final replay versus Leicester City at Villa Park on 3 April, turned on a commanding display of collectiveness, their trademark pass-and-move football, with every player helping out each of the others, seeing them to a superb 3-1 victory. On 4 May, if anything, they were even better.

Settling swiftly into their rhythm, they did all the early attacking, having much the better of the opening exchanges. Yet despite causing one or two anxious moments, Shankly's men couldn't convert the few ripe opportunities they created and, after a largely uneventful first half hour in which both sides cancelled each other out in midfield, Newcastle, albeit with far less of the ball, were still in the game. If it took Liverpool that long to fully realise they had the upper hand, however, once they did so their grip on proceedings grew tighter and tighter.

Nil-nil at half-time, they were unlucky not to lead six minutes after the break when an Alec Lindsay strike from a tight angle was erroneously ruled out for offside. On 57 minutes, though, thei pressure was rewarded. Increasingly pressed back and surrendering possession, 'Newcastle at the moment, [were] looking just a little disorganised,' commentated ITV's Brian Moore. It was the precise time at which Tommy Smith's cross-field ball evaded the ducking Brian Hall and found its way to Kevin Keegan on the edge of the opposition box. 'And now a chance for Keegan – and that's it,' said Moore, 'Kevin Keegan has scored for Liverpool.' It hardly had the flourish of David Coleman's 'Goals pay the rent; Keegan does his share!' over on the BBC, but the fact of the matter remained the same: Keegan had flicked up the ball, volleyed it sublimely past keeper Iam McFaul, and Liverpool at last had the advantage their dominance deserved.

In the 74th minute, Heighway, latching on to Toshack's back header before dispatching the ball low past McFaul's right hand from just inside the 'D', added a second, and from thereon the game became almost completely lopsided. With Shankly, arms motioning side to side, conducting from the bench, the Liverpool orchestra was in full swing. Confident and in control, they put on an enthralling show, moving the ball about almost arrogantly, finding spaces at will, with an outclassed Newcastle side simply unable to match them. The Total Football TV viewers the world over were soon to witness at the World Cup finals, delivered by the Dutch in their brilliant orange, Liverpool, in their vivid red, were now serving up on a drizzly afternoon in London. Two minutes from time, they scored a third that perfectly exemplified their style, Keegan touching the ball home from four yards after an 11-pass movement, involving the England international and six teammates, had scissored apart their opponents' back line.

At 3-0 at the end, the winning margin was the largest in an FA Cup final since 1960. For Newcastle, appearing in a then record 11th final, and having won the cup on each of their five visits to Wembley, ⸍as a first-ever defeat in the competition at the Empire Stadium. ⸍lso became the first team to lose at Wembley wearing stripes. ⸍me had been on the cup, it was only ever pencilled in. ⸍might have been on Newcastle's side, but Liverpool had ⸍irs. Voted man of the match and, in David Lacey's view, 'no more obvious an executioner had he worn a black mask', the impish number seven had enjoyed the fortunes that his England teammate Malcolm Macdonald had brazenly claimed pre-match would be his. Exactly three years earlier, the Londoner, after two seasons at Kenilworth Road during which he'd snapped up 49 league goals, had signed off at Luton Town with a hat-trick in a 3-0 win versus Cardiff, his last game before heading north in a £180,000 move. On Tyneside, Macdonald had become a folk hero, adored for his goalscoring exploits. But his public declarations about the damage he intended to do to opposing defences could be just as abundant.

Selected for England's friendly match on a wet evening in Lisbon, on the same night that Liverpool were beating Leicester in Birmingham, the striker had boasted to teammate Stan Bowles there was only one way he [Macdonald] was going to be carried off the rain-sodden pitch that evening 'and that's shoulder-high'. But as England played out a goalless draw with the Portuguese, Macdonald's left foot, which usually struck, sports reporter Colin Malam once wrote, 'with the sizzling power of forked lightning', continually let him down and the powerfully built Londoner was withdrawn on 75 minutes, replaced with Arsenal's Alan Ball. (It was, as it transpired, one of Sir Alf Ramsey's last acts as England manager – three weeks later, Ramsey was relieved of his role.)

In the run-up to the final, Macdonald was at it again. 'I guarantee a goal at Wembley,' he told reporters. Yet both his self-confidence and Clough's faith in the dynamic Newcastle number nine proved much misguided. 'Supermac strikes more than the miners' proclaimed one humorous homemade banner among the Geordie faithful; it wasn't exactly a portent of things to come. Unable to shake off the shackles of Smith, Lindsay, Thompson and Hughes, Macdonald barely got a sniff all afternoon and 'the photographers flanking the goal posts were in greater danger' than keeper Clemence, sneered Frank McGhee. Bruce Forsyth had displayed deadlier finishing when planting the ball in the back of an empty net at the Liverpool end in the pre-match build-up. At the full-time whistle, Macdonald, as predicted by *TV Times* astrologe

Roger Elliot, struck a 'terribly depressed' figure and was, again as forecast, 'recounting his troubles'. 'Let's face it,' the centre-forward told interviewer Gerald Sinstadt, 'Liverpool were the tops today. They were out of this world and we just couldn't get started.'

For Liverpool, after bettering Leeds nine years earlier, it was their second FA Cup triumph. More importantly, perhaps, the performance epitomised the way Bill Shankly and his coaching staff wanted to play; the fluid football they'd toiled so tirelessly at their Melwood training ground to perfect. It signposted the direction the club would take over the next 15 years, as they established themselves as the dominant force in both British and European football. But it was a future with a new driver at the steering wheel for much of the way. Clough may have been wrong in thinking it would be a close contest, but he picked the right winners. A selection based ultimately on Shankly. Yet what Clough, Roger Elliot, nor anyone for that matter, could have foreseen was that the final would be the Lanarkshire-born manager's very last game in charge of the Merseyside club.

On 12 July 1974 came the almost inconceivable news that Shankly was retiring from his post. The enthusiasm might have remained but, after nearly 15 years of rule at Anfield, in which he'd taken the club into the First Division then to three league titles, two FA Cup wins, and a UEFA Cup success, the 58-year-old was starting to feel the strain. 'The pressures have built up so much during my 40 years in the game,' he explained, 'that I felt it was time to have a rest.' Taking his family into consideration, Shankly had made the decision to leave five weeks earlier, but the club's directors had been trying to persuade him to stay. They'd failed.

Shankly, succeeded by assistant Bob Paisley, would lead out Liverpool side one more time – again at Wembley, for the FA ~rity Shield showdown with league champions Leeds United ~hat afternoon in May had been his real farewell. And even at the home of English football, synonymous with the ~ment in the national side's history, the Scot could not ~r a more impressive send-off.

18–24 May 1974

On Saturday at Hampden Park, Glasgow, Scotland play their last international – against 'the Auld Enemy' England – before next month's World Cup. Viewers can see the match, live, plus comment from the famous ITV panel, in *World of Sport*. Here, Brian Clough takes a look at the big match and talks to panellist Paddy Crerand about Scotland's World Cup prospects …

NEVER MIND MUNICH, IT'S HAGGIS AND HAMPDEN THAT COUNT

IT wouldn't matter if World War Three had broken out. Any time Scotland play England, there isn't a ticket to spare. In football folklore, it is a match out on its own. It creates an atmosphere of magic, and this season there is an added ingredient – the World Cup.

It's the last time Scotland play at home before the competition starts on 13 June, and there couldn't be a better test for their preparations. Even though England are not going to Munich, I still regard them as one of the strongest teams in the world. The best thing that could happen to Scotland is for them to give England a hiding at Hampden. If that happened, and if I was Scotland manager Willie Ormond, I'd send the team home and tell them n to bother to turn up again until World Cup time. There could be a bigger morale booster: it would be worth two weeks of tac and training.

But I can't see it happening. I think England's all-i strength will tell against the Scottish team, which can be b one day and pathetic the next. I take England to win.

I know that every Scot in Christendom will be after my saying that, and one of them is my fellow TV soccer anal

Crerand. He was a superb midfield player for Manchester United and Scotland until he quit to join United's training staff a few years ago. He has never thought twice about choosing his words when he has appeared on ITV, and at times he has been an outspoken critic of the Scottish team.

I dare say Crerand and I will be having some rare battles on TV in the next few weeks, when we line up with Derek Dougan, Malcolm Allison, Jackie Charlton and Bobby Moncur on the ITV panel.

The squabbles are starting with the Scotland-England match: Paddy predicts a Scottish win.

'They will win because they've got so much riding on this one,' he says. 'They'll be fighting to win as if this was a World Cup Final. There will be a tense atmosphere at Hampden, too, which will help the Scots. England will be playing a strong and skilful side in this game. Sir Alf Ramsey had started to experiment with younger players and proper footballers. This was changing the character of the England team. It will be an experimental side on Saturday, and rightly so because they are out of the World Cup and looking 1978 now. The only thing they stand to lose in this match is 'r pride.

ς for the Scots, I sometimes wince at their ineptitude. Manager Ⴢrmond has been quoted as saying he won't necessarily ᴧ his best World Cup side against England. If this is so, nonsense. His main aim this week should be to get a ᴼr Munich.

orrying problem is Scotland's lack of goalscoring ᴧet that, before these Home Internationals began, ᴧwo of their last eight internationals.

ᴧer in that period was George Graham of ᴧ he won't be in the side this week. The two for goals are Dalglish and Jordan, who I ᴧin strikers in Germany.

ᴧ is one of the most accomplished ᴧ would be of more use in midfield ᴧd when Scotland lost 2-1 to West

Germany in March that he can take his chances well. He banged in Scotland's only chance in the whole match.

'I regard Joe Jordan of Leeds as more of a natural striker than Dalglish, and Ormond will be praying for more goals from him like the powerful header he scored against Czechoslovakia last year to put Scotland through to the finals. But will Jordan's season with Leeds United leave him exhausted and stale? Along with Bremner, Lorimer, Harvey and McQueen, he will need some motivation from the manager if he is to be fresh for more action.

'There are three more vital men who can help Scotland,' says Crerand. 'They are Willie Morgan, Tommy Hutchison and Denis Law. Scotland must play Hutchison as a winger. He can penetrate a packed defence, and that is the most sought-after quality in modern football. Willie Morgan, captain of Manchester United, could be the revelation of the World Cup for Scotland. If he is used in a positive role he could put the power in attack which Scotland needs.

'Finally, I hope Ormond plays Denis Law on Saturday. Law runs five miles an hour faster when he puts on a Scottish shirt, and his presence in the team acts as a stimulant to the others.'

How does Crerand think Scotland will fare in the Cup?

'Well, they are in group two with Zaire, Yugoslavia, and Brazil. I think we can rule out Zaire and hand one of the two places in the next round to Brazil. This could mean the crunch game will be Scotland's last one in group two against Yugoslavia. The team which wins that will go through. I would be happier about Scotland's chances if they had a settled team right now, so I only rate their chances of making it to the quarter-finals at 50-50.

'On the competition in general, West Germany are my favourites, with Italy close behind and Holland the dark horses – for the simple reason that any team with Johan Cruyff in it can set them alight.'

That is how Paddy Crerand sees the big competition. But it is a month away and from Scotland's viewpoint, I hope they are not dreaming of Sachertorte and sauerkraut just yet. They would do better to concentrate on haggis and Hampden, because Saturday's game against England will be more than a full dress rehearsal for

. June pageant. It should show once and for all whether Scotland .ave it in them to carry the football flag for Britain.

* * * *

In 1973 there was a feeling that the British Championship (or the Home Internationals as they were commonly known) wasn't working.

Previously spread throughout the season, the six games had, from 1969, been concentrated into one eight-day springtime period once the domestic campaign was over but the tournament, inaugurated in 1884, had lost much of its former glamour and, despite the television companies and most of the press battling hopefully to inject some enthusiasm, the view that it was little more than a nuisance, a tired anti-climax to the footballing calendar, was becoming increasingly widespread. To many minds, it had developed into a 'something tagged on to the tail-end' affair, and it would be better to revert to the old system. Or maybe ought to be scrapped altogether.

There were concerns about an attitude change in players; that the view that to represent your country was the greatest achievement in the game had been lost. Prior to that year's matches, Jimmy Hill contended that the competition, coming at the end of an exhaustive nine or so months in which some players would have completed at least 50 games – and, with the closing stages of European competitions and the postponement of vital league fixtures, might still have pressing engagements – needed an adrenalin shot of sponsorship, with financial incentives for the footballers involved.

Hill acknowledged that it was an honour for a player to be selected for his country – to be recognised as having reached the peak of his profession – but implied that those who stated they'd pull on an international shirt for nothing were lying. 'A player who stands to win £500 for winning a Home International,' Hill said, 'is going to put in more effort than one dragging his tired legs round the pitch in an end-of-the-season game for less than he would collect for playing at club level.'

As it stood, £60 appearance money was given to each international player, but there was no win or draw bonus. Hill suggested that inviting sponsorship – 'and there must be plenty of big firms willing to jump on the bandwagon' – would mean big money for the players, plus extra cash in the form of man of the match awards. Incentivised footballers would then produce better entertainment for supporters. It was a win-win scenario.

Exhausted limbs or not, no player from either side of the border needed any additional enticement when a slice of Anglo-Scottish civil war was fought out. For crowd appeal and partisanship, there was still nothing to beat it. Most of the other games in the championship just didn't have the supporter drawing power – they could often be devoid of any international flavour, class or atmosphere – but this was one everyone wanted to see; the only result the rest of the world regarded with anything more than a passing interest. Some 149,547 had crammed into Hampden Park for the 1937 contest. An England-Scotland international might not have been the most played (that honour belonged to Argentina versus Uruguay), but it was definitely football's oldest rivalry and, the traditional climax to the British Championship, was easily the most emotional match of the six-game series.

Few other fixtures stirred such fierce pride and passion. Ancient hatreds were renewed. The battles of Bannockburn and Culloden remembered. Old wounds slashed open. The 1972 encounter in Glasgow had been particularly vicious, the referee Sergio Gonella of Italy calling captains Bobby Moore and Billy McNeill together and ordering them to tell their players to calm things down after 46 free kicks had been awarded in the first 30 minutes. For long spells players seemed more intent on kicking each other rather than the ball and, afterwards, Scottish FA President Hugh Nelson made no secret of the fact that he thought England had started it with their retaliate-first approach. The clash brought out the bad blood in both. Ahead of the 1970 game, journalist Ian Wooldridge quoted one Scottish newspaper advocating the Scotland team 'should grind England into the dust', an editorial comment, Wooldridge opined, which made 'Chairman Mao sound like a zany old liberal'.

'This rivalry [with England] is, for the Scots, intensely real,' wrote Brian Glanville, 'and you sometimes feel that their continuing existence as a separate footballing nation stands also for their proud independence as a distinctive country.' Did the game matter more to the men from the north? Arguably. 'You could virtually pick any 11 players with a Scottish birth certificate and they'd run themselves ragged against the Auld Enemy,' observed Jack Charlton in *TVTimes* before the 1972 encounter. 'I know – I've played against them and rarely see greater fervour anywhere in the world.'

Charlton, in a later *TVTimes*, would recall how the attitude of his Scottish teammates at Leeds changed drastically towards the English players as the big match loomed. Suddenly they were enemies – 'and if they won we didn't hear the end of it for a year'. According to Bruce Rioch, a Scot born in England, who would score from the spot at Wembley in only his fourth Scotland international as Willie Ormond's side suffered a humiliating 5-1 beating in May 1975, 'Depending how the Home Internationals had gone, the first game back at your club was always interesting. If England had won their players would merely smile. If we'd won we were unbearable.' But, of course, the English were desperate to triumph, too. Jack's brother, Bobby, who'd won his first England cap and notched up his first international goal with a cracking volley in the 4-0 victory over Scotland at Hampden in April 1958, often talked about how much success in the meeting meant to him.

Sir Alf Ramsey was certainly one Englishman for whom the mere thought of coming out second best against Scotland was unthinkable. Normal team talks became far more demonstrative when the opposition was in dark blue. Allan Clarke, in his book *Sniffer*, recorded that all the England manager would say to his players before the game was, 'You know who we're playing today, get them beat; if you don't, we'll not live it down till next season.' Roy McFarland remembered Ramsey sending out a team with a more abrupt battle cry: 'Come on boys,' he told them, 'let's get into these Scots fuckers.'

In his early years as England boss, Ramsey hadn't enjoyed the best record against Scotland – just one win in the first six encounters – but there'd been four successive victories since 1971. In 1973 England had even triumphed twice: a 5-0 St Valentine's Day massacre at Hampden Park in a friendly to celebrate the centenary of the Scottish Football Association, followed just over three months later by a 1-0 Home Internationals success when Martin Peters's 54th-minute header at Wembley earned Ramsey the gloating rights once more.

But Ramsey's revels ended there. He never got the chance to put one over those 'Scots fuckers' again. Although his position as England manager was confirmed in October 1962, for Ramsey's first three games he was part of an International Select Committee before he formally took charge on 1 May 1963. And it was exactly 11 years later that the expiration date on his role had arrived, as the FA announced his dismissal.

Ramsey must surely have known it was coming. Ever since he'd taken over, neither he nor his policies were consistently popular. Even after England's glory on 30 July 1966, lose and the old moans against Ramsey's style were soon renewed. The manager, Brian Glanville observed in *TVTimes*, May 1970, 'had weathered everything from bitter criticism to hero worship with the coolness of an iceberg' and, despite being a man easily wounded, it didn't make a note of difference to his approach 'for he is as single-minded and as inner-directed as a Cromwellian Puritan'. That approach, however, had progressively failed to yield the right results in the matches that mattered.

A 0-0 draw in West Berlin in a European Championship quarter-final second leg on 13 May 1972 had drawn especially vociferous Fleet Street disapproval. Needing to claw back a 3-1 deficit, England, with Arsenal's Peter Storey and Leeds's Norman Hunter, not the two most creative footballers, occupying midfield roles, had produced a foul-littered display that left Ramsey proud of his team's performance but his German counterpart Helmut Schön complaining about England's 'brutal methods'. Man of the match Franz Beckenbauer told the German press, 'The English had no idea how to deal with our two-goal advantage. They confused the jungle with a football pitch.'

quite some time, his tactics pigeonholed as being far too
ve, his teams earning a reputation for austere, stereotypical
ball, the back-page pressmen had been determinedly after
msey's scalp. As well as prickly relations with the press – he
egarded them mostly as annoying interlopers; they saw him as
being Sphinx-like, overly guarded, haughty and aloof – Ramsey's
failure to get on well with the mandarins at the FA, in particular the
imperious fellow knight Sir Harold Thompson, had never helped.
Clough's bear-baiting hadn't done him many favours, either. Some
of Clough's most vitriolic remarks had been directed at Ramsey.
Clough saw himself and the England manager as sitting in
completely opposite camps. One of his most damaging comments
had come the previous autumn: 'The split is between managers like
myself who believe in exciting football and managers like Sir Alf
Ramsey who want to play like the Russians – clockwork football,
without rhapsody, music or rhythm,' Clough said. 'Until someone
told me he's from Dagenham, I thought he *was* a Russian.'

Ramsey was, according to Glanville, 'A man who broods and
smoulders, neither forgets nor forgives easily, though he has a
touching, basic humility and can bravely admit he has been wrong.'
In Clough's view there'd been little evidence of the England boss
owning up to any mistakes. In one article in a Sunday newspaper,
Clough, audacious as ever, even offered to swap jobs with Ramsey
– he and his associates could take over Derby, and Clough and
his colleagues would run England. Understandably, Ramsey was
reluctant to enter into any verbal jousting, though felt compelled
to reply (via *TVTimes*) to the slurs levelled at him. 'I think the first
thing we should get straight about Mr Clough is that he doesn't
mean all he says. I have no set views on how the game should be
played ... there's room for different styles. However, I'll admit that
there's a vast gap between us in terms of our attitude to publicity.
Mr Clough would seem to be a man who needs to be in the public
eye. If someone's made that way, he's made that way.'

All Ramsey had to say in response to the idea of Clough in
charge of England was to point out that during 1971/72 two Derby
players had failed to report for international duty when they were

due to take on West Germany at Wembley. Ramsey understood that they were unfit, only to find they both played in a league match two days later. 'That is just to illustrate,' Ramsey added dryly, 'that, as I said, not everything Clough says is worth listening to.'

At Lancaster Gate, though, Ramsey had an even more vindictive foe. The professorial Thompson, with a long-held vendetta against the manager – essentially for standing up to him – had been waging a personal campaign to have him expelled. The knives had been out and sharpened for some while; England's absence for the first time from a World Cup finals tournament that they had deigned to enter had given Thompson the perfect excuse to plunge them in.

'Have I failed? I wouldn't say that,' Ramsey had reacted sniffily in a post-match interview after the Poland game. 'Remember that England had never won a World Cup until 1966.' True, but the setback wasn't just a blow to national pride; it had financial implications, too. England's reduced world standing meant that they couldn't guarantee future lucrative friendlies and, consequently, the FA would be denied the fees for their coffers. All the same, his sacking right or not, Ramsey was treated extremely harshly, especially at the hands of the malevolent FA chief. Few publicly mourned the manager's removal but many believed he merited a more sympathetic send-off.

Ironically, after frequent accusations that he remained too loyal to certain individuals considered well past their sell-by date, in what was Ramsey's final match in charge, a 0-0 friendly draw with Portugal in Lisbon on 3 April 1974, no less than six players – Phil Parkes, Mike Pejic, Martin Dobson, Dave Watson, Stan Bowles and Trevor Brooking – had all been handed first caps. New sheets on an old bed perhaps, but now, with Ramsey's axing, a genuine opportunity appeared to have presented itself for the next man in line to rearrange the décor altogether.

With a flurry of international fixtures ahead, it was decided that a caretaker should be appointed to hold the fort. With the approval of Coventry City, where he was general manager, Joe Mercer agreed to undertake the task. Twelve years earlier, Mercer, then moulding a talented young side at Aston Villa, had been in the frame to succeed Walter Winterbottom before Ramsey got the nod. Now, though jumping at the opportunity to return to the dugout, the 59-year-old made it clear straightaway he had no wish to be considered for a full-time role once his interim duties were done. Sky Blues's team boss Gordon Milne was one of those under consideration to take over on a permanent basis.

Mercer's stated mission was to have his players – a 20-strong squad selected by Ramsey 12 days before his sacking – expressing themselves naturally, with a definite emphasis on attacking football. It started well enough; QPR's Stan Bowles, brought in for his second cap, and Kevin Keegan, playing only his third international since his debut in November 1972, both scored their first for their country as Wales were beaten 2-0 at Cardiff's Ninian Park.

The England back line for the game had a refreshingly green look about it: between them, David Nish of Derby County, Stoke's Mike Pejic, and Colin Todd, partnering his Baseball Ground teammate Roy McFarland, had played just eight internationals. Up front, Leicester's Keith Weller made his debut. While with Liverpool's Emlyn Hughes taking over the captain's armband from Martin Peters, the chain with the 1966 World Cup team was broken, for now at least.

Against Northern Ireland the following Wednesday, Weller's 73rd-minute header at Wembley gave Mercer two wins out of two. On the night, Frank Worthington, Weller's Filbert Street cohort, was another introduced to the international stage. Worthington had come on after 55 minutes for Bowles, Mercer feeling the need for a slightly more orthodox centre-forward when Irish keeper Pat Jennings easily dealt with too many centres into the box. Bowles, later claiming that Mercer at half-time had told trainer Harold Shepherdson to bring off the player after ten minutes of the second period, was so annoyed by it – 'Now in that ten minutes I could have scored twice. As it happens, I didn't. But I might have done,' Bowles later protested – he absconded afterwards from the team's Welwyn hotel and headed straight to the dog track. Despite an apology, there was to be no way back for the Rangers man under Mercer's management.

And so to Hampden. On a sodden pitch that Saturday, a strong Scotland line-up didn't inflict the 'hiding' Clough believed would have been so invaluable, but they were worthy winners. Aside from the injured McQueen, all the Leeds players started, and there was no sign of weariness. Lorimer and Jordan in attack were particularly outstanding, as England flailed against a dark-blue tide. In the fifth minute it was Jordan's shot, deflected by Pejic, that gave the Scots the lead. On 31 minutes another England defender made it two, Colin Todd diverting a harmless-looking cross past Peter Shilton. Scotland's players definitely still had haggis on their minds and the scent of English blood in their nostrils. It remained 2-0, yet while most of the Scotsmen and women in the 94,487 crowd went home joyous, concerns about a lack of firepower were still legitimate, which two own goals had done little to alleviate.

Scotland came into the England game on the back of a 1-0 loss to Northern Ireland and a 2-0 victory over Wales. Before the World Cup finals commenced, they would play two warm-ups, a 2-1 defeat in Bruges and a 2-1 win over Norway in Oslo. With such a mixed bag of results, it was difficult to assess their chances in Munich. An incident in the Norwegian capital – Billy Bremner and Jimmy Johnstone breaking a curfew to join a group of journalists drinking in a student bar – had provoked much criticism from the press when the team returned home, especially in light of some reports of excessive drinking in Belgium, too. Scottish skipper Bremner, in particular, took exception to the media's treatment, feeling that the side was being disregarded before they'd even had the chance to test themselves. As the first game in West Germany approached, he and his teammates knew they had a point to prove and were even more determined to do so.

25–31 May 1974

England play East Germany on Wednesday (coverage from Leipzig the same night on ITV), Bulgaria on 1 June and Yugoslavia on 5 June. How England fare, after Sir Alf, is a vital pointer to their future World Cup hopes – and to Scotland's chances in Munich, declares Brian Clough ...

ALF HAD A GOOD INNINGS – NOW LET'S GET ON WITH WINNING IN '78

SO it's the end of the road for Alf. And when England begin their close-season tour with games against three East European countries, it will be the start of a new era in our game.

I have always believed that the national team is the guiding light, the North Star for the way football is played at club level, so we can now look out for a new style, new ideas and a completely fresh outlook throughout our game.

Alf Ramsey had a good innings and his stepping-down from the England manager's job has been well timed. It gives the new boss almost four years to put over his ideas on how the game should be played, and to mould and blend a winning World Cup squad.

I know that over the last couple of years I have given Alf Ramsey more stick than a Victorian schoolmaster. But I maintain that anyone in his position – or mine, for that matter – has to carry the can and take criticism when things aren't going well.

I actually admired Sir Alf. You've got to hand it to a bloke who can stand by his guns with an almost serene stubbornness. To be stubborn is an essential quality of the football manager – if he hasn't the strength of nerve to stick by his ideas and his decisions, he will never win the respect of his players. He won't win many matches, either. Yet where I believed Alf went wrong was that he didn't temper this steel resolve with flexibility, the ability to put his head on the block and say, 'I was wrong'.

The pity is that during Alf's last stand he was showing a willingness to change, and the 20-man squad he picked for next week's tour was – except for the omission of Derby's David Nish (since called up by Joe Mercer) – a well-balanced collection of players, young enough to be reaching maturity by 1978 and the World Cup in Argentina.

Now the interesting question about Sir Alf is – assuming he takes a football management job – can he survive the hellhouse of 60 or 70 games a season in the toughest league in the world? Ipswich, 1962, is a long way from Leeds, 1974. Going back into league management will be like asking a country stationmaster to do a rush-hour shift at King's Cross, London. But I wish him well.

Meanwhile the circus goes on. England's game against East Germany – see it on ITV on Wednesday – is a game against the World Cup's mystery team. I think most pundits know more about Kakoko, Mwamba and Kidumu, the cream of the team from Zaire, than they do about these 'other' Germans. But there are two things we – and Scotland, in particular – should remember. First, in the World Cup the East Germans will be playing practically at home. And second, in the Munich Olympics of 1972, the East Germans smashed the America-Russia monopoly of medals by seizing 20 golds, 23 silvers and 23 bronzes (including one in the football event). They are the most rapidly emerging nation in every sporting field.

The West Germans have flair and skill, but behind it all they have a ruthless regard to detail and strength in all positions on the field. The East Germans possess the same national characteristics: they can be relied upon to be solid, absolutely thorough and efficient, perhaps only a little less exciting and inventive than their counterparts in the west.

It'll be a hard match for England to win, especially as the Germans will desperately want a good result so soon before they start their World Cup campaign in group one with West Germany,

Australia, and Chile. Likewise, England can expect tough opposition from Yugoslavia on 5 June. This could be a valuable pointer for the Scots, for Yugoslavia loom menacingly across their Munich path.

If I was in the England manager's shoes next week, I would regard this tour as anything but a friendly jaunt around Eastern Europe. In my opinion there is no such thing as a 'friendly' match, and England need every opportunity to get their squad into shape before this autumn's European Championship. This is the team I would pick: Shilton, Nish, Pejic, McFarland, Hunter, Todd, Hughes, Brooking, Keegan, Macdonald, Channon; with Peters as substitute.

One man who has had first-hand experience of the East Germans this season is my fellow ITV panellist Derek Dougan, who played two UEFA Cup games against one of their top sides, Lokomotive Leipzig. He says they were an immensely strong team with attacking ideas. 'I particularly liked the look of their tall striker, Matoul, who should be in the East German side next week, and another international, Gröbner, a defender. The East Germans are definitely on the upsurge and they could be one of the surprise teams in Munich.

'I think England's new-look team will have an especially difficult game in Leipzig,' continues Dougan. 'This is a time when they should be throwing everything into forming a good squad for 1978, and we can expect to see a lot of new blood tried out, and some failures. It's a strange thing about international football that some players who perform brilliantly for their clubs can't seem to make it for their country. Kevin Keegan is a good example. Absolutely brilliant for Liverpool, but in the two games he has played for England you wouldn't have known he was on the field. It's people like Keegan, Macdonald, Bowles and McKenzie who have to prove they have the temperament for international matches. This tour could sort out a lot of those answers.'

About the World Cup, Dougan agrees with Paddy Crerand, who said recently that European sides would do well in the competition. 'I fancy Italy,' he says. 'I've liked the way they played in recent games. They play so tight they don't give away an inch of ground, and that's what football seems to be about these days. The Italians defend with true skill, and they are capable of quick and lethal raids upfield. They're my favourites.

'After them, I would name Yugoslavia, Poland, and Brazil as likely contenders. A lot of people blamed England for what happened when the Poles fought that draw at Wembley last year, but nobody really noticed that the Poles were an extremely talented side. Yugoslavia looked good in their World Cup play-off against Spain – we'll know just *how* good when England play them in Belgrade on 5 June – and you can't leave out the Brazilians, whose preparations for the World Cup are more professional and complete than that of any other nation.

'Scotland? I hope Billy Bremner and the rest of the Leeds squad can get some rest before the World Cup starts,' says Dougan. 'They need two weeks to forget about football to be in good mental shape for the competition. To me, Scotland have lacked a reliable goalkeeper, and if David Harvey of Leeds can relax after the pressure of the league season, he'll bring confidence to the defence. I see Scotland putting up as good a show as they can, but with only two teams in their group going through to the quarter-finals their chances must be regarded as moderate.

The main thing is the game. With teams like Zaire and Australia in the competition, it truly is a *World* Cup and so long as we keep it clean – and that means strict refereeing – we are in for a feast of football. I can't wait for it to start.'

* * * *

Clough wasn't exactly correct: Ramsey hadn't stepped down from his England post – he'd been handed a hefty shove over the edge, and his fall had demonstrated the one glaring truth of football management; as Jack Charlton reflected in *TV Times* in August 1977: 'Every manager knows that, in the end, he is playing a game he can't win.' The usual managerial price for failure had been exacted and, after a less-than-golden handshake – a settling of his £7,200-a-year contract, a lump sum of £8,000 plus an annual pension of £1,200 granted – the man who masterminded success in the world's most pre-eminent football competition went off to do some gardening.

Failure or not, another job offer wasn't long in coming – though from a most unexpected direction. On 18 May 1974, less that three weeks after Ramsey's unceremonious dumping by the FA, Athletic Bilbao inquired if the 54-year-old wanted to coach in Spain. He didn't. There were rumours, too, of interest from Second Division Aston Villa, their hotseat vacant after Vic Crowe's removal. Yet far from seeking a return to the 'hellhouse' of English football or La Liga, Ramsey yearned for a period of complete rest.

When he eventually did resume employment in 'the toughest league in the world' it wasn't until three years later in September 1977 when Ramsey, already on the club's board of directors since January 1976, took up temporary charge of First Division basement side Birmingham City, following the resignation of Willie Bell. 'The longer I have stayed out of it, the more I have missed it,' he told the press upon assuming the position. 'But I haven't missed *you*.'

Initially a stop-gap while a long-term replacement was found, after enjoying a happy honeymoon period when City's results elevated them to 11th in the table, Ramsey quit the board and accepted the full-time manager's role. (Ramsey disliked the words 'boss' or 'gaffer' – 'It smacks of the factory floor, and Alf is far too familiar,' he told the players when introducing himself at St Andrew's. 'If you call me Sir Alf then I think we should get along famously.') But if Ipswich, 1962 was, to quote Clough, 'a long way from Leeds, 1974' it was even further from Birmingham, 1977. For Cliff Richard & The Shadows' 'The Young Ones' now read the Sex Pistols' 'Never Mind the Bollocks'.

With England, Ramsey had inspired in his players immense, reciprocal loyalty. But the individual who, in sportswriter Geoffrey Green's words, 'succeeded in cementing a team spirit, equivalent to that of a successful club side, which has never existed at a national level' failed to find the same rapport at the Midlands outfit. Ramsey got on far from famously with the Blues's one-time 'Superboy' Trevor Francis and, amidst ongoing acrimonious relations, results took a downward turn. When, after first agreeing to Francis's transfer request (with Ramsey recommending the club's star striker be allowed to leave), the City board then changed their minds, Ramsey resigned, ostensibly for health reasons, after barely six months in charge. There were, he insisted, 'no regrets'. And for England's yesterday's man there would be no more tomorrows in English football, too.

For Joe Mercer in the spring of 1974, whilst urging the England players to stake a claim for the Argentina 1978 squad, tomorrow meant not the World Cup finals four years away but, more immediately, a friendly match at Wembley. On the Wednesday night following the defeat at Hampden Park, England had Argentina's national side in their sights.

The visitors were making a first return to the stadium since the infamous afternoon of 1966 when, despite the hosts committing 33 fouls against 19, Ramsey dismissed Juan Carlos Lorenzo's players as 'animals', the image of Antonio Rattin's refusal to leave the pitch was imprinted on the British psyche and the stereotype of the South Americans as 'dirty' was born. Eight years later, Argentina came to London with a side that included the speedy-off-the-mark and equally quick-tempered Atlético Madrid forward Ruben Ayala, who'd missed the European Cup Final the week before through suspension, and one of the current pin-ups of Argentine football, Miguel Ángel Brindisi. But it was young striker Mario Kempes who left the deepest impression.

Watched by a crowd of 68,000, Mercer's men had played with pace and rhythm on the night, their pressing rewarded by two superbly taken goals from Mick Channon and Frank Worthington either side of half-time. But with the game threatening to get out of control as personal feuds developed between the two sets of players, the South Americans recovered to level. And it was Kempes, who exactly a month earlier had grabbed his first senior international goal, the decider in a 2-1 friendly win against Romania, that got both, the second a last-minute penalty converted after the number nine himself had been upended in the box by England captain Emlyn Hughes and taken a theatrical tumble which convinced the referee, Kempes's fellow countryman Arturo Ithurralde, to point to the spot.

That the subsequent tour of Eastern Europe had, in Brian Glanville's description, 'a holiday atmosphere about it' was more to do with Genial Joe's relaxed approach off the field than his charges' attitude on it. For the England players it was anything but the 'friendly jaunt' that Clough feared. In Leipzig, before 95,000 at the Zentralstadion, another Channon strike, direct from a free kick just 90 seconds after Joachim Streich's 67th-minute opener against the run of play, earned England a 1-1 draw. Liverpool full-back Alec Lindsay, blooded against Argentina, and Burnley's Martin Dobson made their second full appearances. For Lindsay's club teammate Ray Clemence and West Ham midfielder Trevor Brooking it was only a third cap each. Against the World Cup's 'mystery team', one who had won all of their last 12 matches, the real mystery was how the visitors didn't win; England carved out numerous chances and hit the woodwork on four occasions – 'more times than a team of lumberjacks,' Mercer lamented afterwards.

They didn't have to wait long for a deserved victory. Watched by 60,000 in Sofia's Vasil Levski Stadium, England, with Keegan, Worthington and Channon disorientating the Bulgarian back four with their marauding runs, were worthy winners, though only had Worthington's calm finish on 44 minutes, beating the offside trap and then the home keeper in a one-on-one, to show for it.

It was in the third match of the tour behind the Iron Curtain that England's players faced their most formidable opposition. On arriving for the game, at Belgrade airport, they'd also encountered a rather over-zealous and heavy-handed Yugoslavian border police force, an unsavoury sequence of events and misunderstandings seeing Kevin Keegan carted off, beaten up, falsely accused of assault and disturbing the peace, before being released 'under surveillance', in tears, bloodied and badly shaken. Some England players protested that they should go straight home, but were persuaded to stay and play the match.

It said much for the young Liverpool striker's resilience that, when he took to the field in the Red Star Stadium, Keegan capped an impressive performance with a goal. The previous meeting between the two sides had ended in a 1-1 draw at Wembley in

October 1972, a game in which Sir Alf Ramsey had handed debuts to full-backs Mick Mills of Ipswich Town and West Ham's Frank Lampard, as well as Mick Channon. And it was the Southampton man, now playing his 19th international, who scored, along with Keegan, as the two countries finished level again. After the hosts, taking time to get into their stride, had replied to Channon's seventh international goal on six minutes with some inventive, intelligent football, netting twice just after half-time through Petković (heading in a byline pull-back on 23 minutes) and Oblak's thunderous 30-yarder (a left-foot screamer that struck the stanchion at the back of Clemence's net before the keeper had even moved), it was Keegan's diving header from a ball by substitute Malcolm Macdonald 15 minutes from time that made the score 2-2. Dougan's negative assessment of Keegan's abilities at the highest level were more than a little premature, to say the least. Had Macdonald not missed an opportunity he would normally have dispatched without any trouble, England could well have won.

In his caretaking capacity, Mercer's plan was to get the team playing together as a unit. They'd done just that. Against the three Eastern bloc countries, he'd named the same starting line-up every time and the side's cohesion grew with each game. Of the XI Clough would have picked, Shilton, Nish, Pejic, McFarland (victim of a serious Achilles injury during the Home Internationals), Hunter and Peters didn't feature at all. The 30-year-old Peters, in fact, would never pull on an England jersey again, the loss in Glasgow being the last of his 67 international appearances.

Originally scheduled as a programme of matches to prepare for the World Cup, with England eliminated, the tour served no real purpose, especially as the incoming permanent manager might have completely different ideas to Mercer, who himself was working with players selected by Ramsey. Even so, unbeaten on their travels and playing with a vitality and vigour that boded well for the future, England, the warm-up act for those going to 'The Greatest Soccer Show on Earth', had, if nothing else, given a welcome reminder that they were still more than capable of performing on the main bill themselves.

1–7 June 1974

This Saturday in *World of Sport* you can see, live from Wembley Stadium, the second half of the schoolboys international football match between England and West Germany. Are the 16-year-olds taking part stars of the future, or one-game wonders? How many will make the 1978 World Cup? Brian Clough has an answer ...

WHAT *DOES* HAPPEN TO THE LIKELY LADS OF FOOTBALL?

ON Saturday, 13 schoolboys (two substitutes) will put on white England shirts in the Wembley dressing room, ready to do their bit against the West Germans. But how many of those teenage hopefuls will be wearing their country's shirt in the World Cups of 1978, 1982, and 1986? I'd bet that 11 or 12 of those lads never win full international caps. So whatever happens to our likely lads?

I think it is impossible to judge the potential of a footballer at 15 or 16. He is at a crucial point in his development. Nobody knows how he will develop physically or emotionally. Has he reached the limit of his ability, or will his skill improve? Would he be better at accountancy? You just can't say.

One reason why so few of these boy-wonders filter through to full international level is that they are not necessarily the most skilful players. Inevitably the stronger, larger types are chosen for schoolboys internationals because you can't send 11 brilliant ball-playing four-stone-weaklings to face a West German side which will have its complement of thick-thighed sons of Bavarian farmers, endowed with muscles as well as skill.

Most of the boys playing this week will be attached to league clubs as associated schoolboys, which means they can train at the club with a view to joining as an apprentice when they leave school. But in many cases the schoolboy star fails to fulfil a club's expectations. That is why, when I take a boy on to my books, I drum it into him that his chances of first-team football, let alone international games, are practically nil.

In my nine years of football management I have only signed-on one schoolboy international, and that was young Steve Powell at Derby, who captained the [England] schoolboys side two years running. He was one of those rare people who was born to play football. But another consideration these days is that the best sportsmen at school don't necessarily choose football any more. Gone are the days when football and cricket made up the total sporting diet at school. Now there is sophisticated training in swimming, athletics, tennis, badminton and many more activities, so a youngster can take his pick.

Of those who do choose football, there is that tiny proportion who struggle through to the top. In 1950, when schoolboys internationals were first played at Wembley, a glance at the programme revealed a youngster called Johnny Haynes playing for the England side which beat Scotland 8-3. Bobby Charlton was also a schoolboy international. The great Duncan Edwards, who was killed in the Munich air disaster in 1958, was another. Nobby Stiles and Geoff Hurst, both in England's World Cup-winning side of 1966, had played for the England schoolboys side. This Wednesday, when England play Yugoslavia in Belgrade – you can see highlights on ITV – another ex-schoolboy international, Peter Shilton, will be on the field. And let's not forget the Scots. A young lad called Billy Bremner was first seen at schoolboys international level. Not to mention the man whose cannonball shots might make all the difference between survival and extinction for the Scots at Munich – Peter Lorimer.

There was another 15-year-old who played for Aberdeen schoolboys in the late 50s. He turned up for a Scottish schoolboys international wearing a pair of National Health specs with string tied across the bridge to keep them together. He carried his boots under his arm in a brown paper bag.

The boy's name was Denis Law.

Without holding out great hopes – because a lot can happen in a couple of years – there is a whisper that one of the lads playing for England on Saturday, Mark Higgins, is a footballing natural in the Duncan Edwards mould. It might be worth keeping a critical eye on him when you watch the game. But I emphasise that playing in a schoolboys international is not a passport to the top.

When I managed Hartlepools in the Fourth Division – my first job in management – I took on an apprentice called John McGovern. There was not the slimmest possibility of his being in a schoolboys international side, because he only played rugby at school. We noticed him playing football at weekends and talked to his headmaster and his parents for hours, making sure they knew the gambles involved in a football career. Then we took him on, and when we went to Derby he followed us. Now he has a Second Division championship medal, a First Division championship medal, and he has played in the semi-finals of the European Cup.

We have to get schoolboys internationals into the right perspective. You'll see some fine football at Wembley on Saturday and, with luck, you might see one or two future stars. But you won't be seeing the Junior England side in action. There are too many influences on a young man of 16 to predict how good he will be. The important thing to remember is that those boys on the pitch – and thousands like them of the same age – are our next football generation.

* * * *

On 29 May 1974, as England's senior side fought out a 1-1 draw with East Germany before 95,000 at Leipzig's Zentralstadion in the first match of a close-season tour of the Iron Curtain, among their XI that evening was Trevor Brooking who, ten years earlier, had played his one and only schoolboys international against the Germans from the west. Three days later, the England schoolboys of 1974 lined up at Wembley to face the same oppositon, West Germany, no doubt dreaming of glories to come and hoping one day to emulate the progression achieved by the West Ham midfielder.

With a crowd of 50,000 cheering schoolboys and a television audience of millions watching, they made a good impression, winning 4-0, with Manchester-born frontman Peter Coyne earning the chief plaudits after netting a hat-trick. From the squad that had beaten France 5-2 on 6 April and now the Germans, Coyne was one of five players who went on to appear in the English First Division.

He was already on the books at Old Trafford, having penned apprentice forms in October 1973. But though inevitably tagged as 'the next big thing', after making his debut for Tommy Docherty's young side, coming on as a sub for Stuart Pearson during a 2-1 defeat at Aston Villa on 21 February 1976, Coyne only pulled on a United shirt one more time, his contract cancelled the following spring.

The forward later enjoyed a decent career in the lower reaches of the football league, at Crewe Alexandra and then Swindon Town, and, while his light had quickly faded from view, it had at least shone briefly at the highest level of the English game. Far more typical were those supposedly destined for the top but whose careers never got off the floor, the hundreds who'd been in the 'one for the future' bracket for whom tomorrow didn't come. So why did so many young stars fall by the wayside?

'All sorts of things can go wrong,' said Ron Suart, who had been assistant to Docherty at Chelsea, in 1976. 'Some boys don't develop physically, gain pace or acquire new skills. Others can't cope with the pressure of playing in front of a stadium full of people. Some lack the temperament, or they develop outside interests. There are a million reasons why they fail; but there's only one why they can succeed – by working hard at the game.'

Bill McGarry, the epitome of the hard-headed, unromantic manager, had a characteristically more down-to-earth take. 'They don't fail despite being schoolboy internationals, but because of it,' he said. 'They come to us having worn the white shirt of England believing they've cracked it. That they've made the grade already. That they've arrived. If they could only get it into their heads … this is where they *start*.'

It was McGarry, when Wolves manager, who bought Martin Patching to Molineux. Patching was another of the schoolboys who'd faced West Germany. Rotherham-born, he'd started supporting the West Midlands club when the first kit he was ever bought was in old gold and, having left school in 1975 'with stickers of The Doog [Derek Dougan] plastered all over my exercise books,' a few weeks later signed a professional contract and was lining up alongside his terrace hero on the training field. 'It was a dream come true,' Patching said.

He proved a great find. After making three league appearances in 1975/76 in a side that dropped out of the top flight (costing McGarry his job after nearly eight years in command), the following season as Wolves secured an immediate return to the First Division, Patching won a regular berth. And over the years, though initially a hard-working midfielder, his versatility saw him fill virtually every position except goalkeeper in 101 appearances for the club.

One of the players Patching teamed up with for a period at Molineux, Andy Gray, believed that the schoolboys system was all wrong. Writing in his *Shoot!* column in 1981, the Scot expressed his concern that too many schoolboys were taught tactics before skills; the end result being, 'Teenagers who are dreaming of becoming professional footballers can't do the most basic acts of soccer.' According to Gray, they hit the ball with every part of the foot except the right part. Gray was saddened that 'very few have a "feel" for the ball that all kids should have'. He'd watched 10- and 11-year-olds in the park on Sundays and their focus above all else was on winning. 'At that age there should be only one reason for playing football and that's for sheer enjoyment,' Gray wrote. 'All a young boy should concentrate on is being happy while he's playing and improving his skills. Everything else will come later.'

It was Gray, then sporting Aston Villa's claret and blue, who'd notched the winner for the Midlanders on the afternoon of Peter Coyne's Manchester United debut. Like Coyne, Mark Higgins, captain of the England schoolboys side, also turned out for United – but, also like Coyne, only figured in the Old Trafford club's first team for a short stint, featuring in just six league games (plus two in the cup) after joining the Red Devils in December 1985. Before then, however, Higgins, the son of former Bolton Wanderers defender Jack, had enjoyed a long career on Merseyside with Everton.

After making his debut, aged only 18, on Tuesday, 5 October 1976 in a 2-2 draw at home to Manchester City, coming in for the injured Roger Kenyon and linking up in central defence with Toffees skipper Mick Lyons, the youngster impressed Gordon Lee so much with his potential that, by the season's end, the Goodison boss (a January 1977 replacement for the sacked Billy Bingham) was willing to sacrifice Scottish defender Ken McNaught to Aston Villa. The following campaign, Higgins established himself as a first-choice in defence, before a pelvic injury put him on the sidelines.

Injuries, sadly, were to play a prominent part throughout Higgins's Everton days, during which he either formed defensive partnerships or competed for a place with Lyons, Billy Wright, Mike Walsh and Kevin Ratcliffe, and also served as club captain for a spell. Only in 1982/83 did the Buxton-born player ever exceed the 30 league appearances mark, playing 39 games as Everton finished seventh in the top flight, 18 points behind champions Liverpool. The next season, as history repeated itself – Everton coming seventh again while their arch rivals, 18 points better off, took another title – Higgins managed just 14 starts, a more serious pelvic problem causing him to miss the League Cup and FA Cup finals against their Anfield neighbours and Watford respectively, as well as the bulk of the league fixtures.

He left Goodison Park soon after – thereby missing out on the period of domestic and European success Everton enjoyed over the next few years – but, though told by specialists he would never play football again, was determined to prove them wrong. After an 18-month battle, in which he underwent several operations, Higgins did just that; snapped up by United boss Ron Atkinson for £60,000 and making his comeback in a 2-0 FA Cup third-round home win over Rochdale on 9 January 1986. Even if he was later sold on to Bury for a paltry £10,000 by Atkinson's successor, Alex Ferguson, the 'footballing natural in the Duncan Edwards mould' fulfilled his ambition to play for the club he'd always supported as a boy.

Mick Lyons had a theory that school teams were so competitive it bred more battlers than class players; having to fight for results, youngsters couldn't relax in their play and, subsequently, defenders were easier to discover than strikers. 'If the schools copy the professional clubs in playing systems like 4-4-2,' Lyons said, 'then it stands to reason that there is less likelihood of developing talented attacking players. The modern youngsters seem to be more involved in team football at a much earlier age. When I was a kid, we played amongst ourselves on the local field. We were always out with a ball, practising our own skills, but today the lads are in teams, and consequently looking for results above all. If it's not the schools team, they'll be turning out for club sides on Saturdays and Sundays. As a result, it probably means that the lads don't have the opportunities to express themselves as goalscorers.'

Lyons's views were published in the match programme for Everton's home game with Coventry City on 10 April 1979 – a 3-3 draw in which one of the home side's goals was scored by Trevor Ross, a Greater Manchester-born midfielder who'd played eight times for the England schoolboys side but who later, with his father William originally from north of the border, opted to play for Scotland and was capped once at under-21s level.

Someone definitely expressing himself as a goalscorer was Kevin Mabbutt. That same Tuesday evening, Mabbutt, another member of the schoolboys side that had trounced the Germans five years earlier, netted one of Bristol City's three goals in a 3-1 home win over Chelsea in Division One. The previous October (21st), the skilful striker, the son of Ray Mabbutt, a Bristol Rovers hero of the 1950s and 60s, had come to national attention when he scored all three of City's goals in another 3-1 triumph – at Old Trafford, a win that elevated the south-west club to the giddy heights of ninth in the league, and had Dave Sexton, the Manchester United boss, making a substantial bid for Mabbutt's services. The player turned United down. City ended the season in a respectable 13th, but were relegated a year later, and in 1980/81, though Mabbutt received the club's player of the year award, suffered a second successive drop down the divisions. When Mabbutt left Ashton Gate for Crystal Palace in October 1981 he'd made 129 league appearances, registering 29 times on the scoresheet.

Against Bristol City, Chelsea themselves featured no less than four players – Ron Harris, Ray Wilkins, Mike Fillery and Tommy Langley (scorer of a penalty on the night) – who'd won honours for their country at schoolboys level. Long-time Blues servant Ron (or Ronald as he was listed in the match programmes of the time) Harris had earned his England caps way back in the late 50s before joining Chelsea as a 15-year-old in 1959. The rugged defender's brother, Allan, older by two years, had also represented England at schoolboys (and youth) level before he too made the grade as a pro with the London club.

Throughout the 1960s and 70s, Chelsea were renowned as one of English football's best clubs for producing young talent. By the mid-70s they claimed to watch about 800 schoolboy trialists every close season. Of those, only about 30 were invited to Stamford Bridge for evening training, with the average age of the boys being 13. By the time they were 15 probably four of them would be given the chance of an apprenticeship and of those four, two might make the league side. Two out of 800 wasn't exactly an encouraging percentage for the boys themselves. But from the club's point of view, 'screening' had to be intense … and when they found a real gem those odds were more than justified.

Generally regarded as the brightest gem of all was Ray Wilkins. Hillingdon-born, Wilkins, whose father George had been a professional with Brentford, was one of four footballing brothers – Graham, Steve and Dean the others. It was with older brother Graham and some friends that in 1969, aged 12, Ray formed a Sunday league team, Hayes Spurs. They proved almost unbeatable. 'When we were out playing we did what we liked, tried to bring out our natural ability without having someone shouting to release the ball early, or pass first time or go to the near post!' Wilkins remembered. 'There's plenty of time for coaching and tactics once you've learned the basic skills.'

By 13, he was taking things a bit more seriously; as well as joining a youth club side in Walthamstow, he'd signed schoolboy forms for Chelsea and was training at Stamford Bridge for two nights a week until he was old enough to sign professionally (on 1 October 1973). That natural ability was such that, in 1972, Wilkins appeared in the England schoolboys side that, like the one two years later, also beat West Germany 4-0 at Wembley. (Left-back John Sparrow was another in that line-up later to sign for Chelsea, making his debut for the Blues in March 1974 at just 16 years of age.)

A midfielder with an astute mind and a masterful eye for a ball, 'Butch', the nickname he was known by since childhood, clearly had true class, that extra something that set him apart. After progressing to the west Londoners' first team, making his debut at the age of 17 as a sub in a 3-0 home league win against Norwich City on 26 October 1973, his reputation as one of the country's outstanding young talents grew quickly. Wilkins's passing and control had a stamp of authority way beyond his years. By 18, he'd been handed the club captaincy, taking over from Ron Harris. At 19, he'd forced his way into the England reckoning.

Chelsea's fortunes for much of the decade, though, had been in a tailspin. In 1979 the defeat at Bristol City was just one of 27 they suffered in a miserable season that saw them gain only 20 points and plummet from the top flight. Wilkins's quality had long had the richest clubs lining up with open chequebooks. Now, with Chelsea needing to sell their prize asset to help ease mounting debts, it became obvious that club and player would part company. Despite interest from Everton and Ipswich, when Manchester United came into the equation Wilkins knew there was only one destination for him. On 1 August of that year, former Chelsea manager Dave Sexton paid out £825,000 and Wilkins, like Mark Higgins, fulfilled one of his great ambitions – to sign for the Old Trafford club.

It was as a United player that, at the 1982 World Cup finals in Spain, Wilkins started all five of the games England played in the tournament. Sporting the three lions for all but one of those games – injury meaning he missed out on the clash with Kuwait

– was another young Londoner. In his 1974 column, Clough had questioned how many of the 'teenage hopefuls [playing West Germany] will be wearing their country's shirt in the World Cups of 1978, 1982, and 1986?' Allowing for England's failure to qualify in 1978, the answer was ... one. Kenny Sansom.

Sansom emerged from the under-15s ranks to become, first with Crystal Palace (for whom he made his debut aged 16 years and 223 days) then with Arsenal, one of the finest left-backs England had ever produced. Pacy and strong-tackling, forwards seldom got the better of him. After cementing himself in the Palace side in 1976/77, playing in all 46 league games as Terry Venables's exciting outfit gained promotion from the Third Division, it quickly became obvious that Sansom, just 5ft 6in of him, was a rather special youngster, 'a kid who played with the confidence of a veteran' as one writer described him. So it was little surprise when, having starred on his England under-21s debut against Denmark in Copenhagen in the autumn of 1978, he soon progressed to the full international side, making his bow in a goalless Wembley draw with Wales in May 1979.

By 1986 Sansom was still the first-choice for his country at the World Cup in Mexico, playing in every England game until their quarter-final elimination at the hand (and feet) of Diego Maradona. (Ray Wilkins, now with AC Milan, only featured in the first two, red-carded for foolishly throwing the ball at the referee during a clash with Morocco and suspended for the next two games before being an unused sub versus Argentina.)

Four years earlier, England's exit from the competition had, if anything, been even more frustrating. Ron Greenwood's side returned from Spain unbeaten, but it was ultimately their failure to overcome the hosts in a goalless second-phase game (coming soon after drawing a blank in another stalemate with West Germany) that ended their participation. It was the manager's last game in charge of the national side. The match also marked the final international appearance of a player whom Greenwood had nurtured at West Ham after first spotting him at schoolboy level.

Clough might not have been too complimentary about Trevor Brooking – he 'floats like a butterfly – and stings like one,' was Clough's disparaging comment on the morning of the 1980 FA Cup Final (Brooking's riposte was to score the winning goal) – but few others doubted the Ilford-born midfielder's qualities. One of the most popular players to wear the claret and blue at Upton Park, he'd served both club and country magnificently. Against Spain, Brooking came on as a 63rd-minute replacement for Arsenal's Graham Rix for what would be his only-ever appearance at a World Cup finals. He might well have grabbed the vital strike England needed, too – Brooking's rasping shot forcing an excellent stop from the Spanish keeper, Luis Arconada – but it wasn't to be. England went out, and the man who had taken to the field in Leipzig for his third cap in 1974 didn't feature again for his country.

The stated main aim of the Schoolboys Association was 'the mental, moral and physical development and improvement of these boys through the medium of Association Football.' Finally, though, the hope was that it would produce, as *TVTimes* classed them, 'future soccer superstars'. Clough had been spot-on in his estimate that probably only one of the England schoolboys that year (1974) would go on to become a full international. Given that statistics showed that less than half of the boys who'd gained schoolboys honours made professional footballers – and comparatively few of those in the First Division – perhaps one full international really wasn't such a poor ratio.

Representing the England schoolboys in the annual international match on what *TVTimes* called 'the most hallowed playing field in the land' was a giant leap from having a kickabout with friends on the local rec. To be among the cream of junior footballers, enjoying 'a taste of the big time', proudly displaying their incipient gifts was, as the magazine often billed it, 'the day that's every schoolboy's dream'.

However, the jump from being the 'promising youngsters of today' to 'the international stars of tomorrow', performing for their country in a tournament amongst the world's elite was, at the end of the day, maybe even more colossal. As well as determination, character, enthusiasm and talent, plus a healthy helping of luck, it required much bigger dreams. Yet, despite the disappointing end result on the night, with their presence on the pitch that Monday evening of 5 July 1982 in Real Madrid's Bernabéu Stadium, Messrs Sansom, Wilkins and Brooking proved that the leap could be made, and that sometimes even the biggest dreams of all really did come true.

8–14 June 1974

In Germany next Thursday, 16 teams begin their assault on football's biggest prize, the World Cup. Here, Brian Clough guides you through ITV's coverage of the big competition and offers his views ...

JOIN ITV FOR THE BIG
FOOTBALL LOCK-IN

PACK those cans of beer into the fridge. Get that TV picture perfect. Draw the curtains. Keep your *TVTimes* at the ready and put your feet up. This week the 1974 World Cup gets under way in Munich and millions of armchair fans will be locking themselves in for ITV's football fiesta – 73 hours of the very best in world football.

Brian Moore, Derek Dougan, Malcolm Allison, Paddy Crerand, Bobby Moncur, Jackie Charlton and myself will be booked into a hotel a few hundred yards from the ITV World Cup Operations Centre at London Weekend Television's South Bank studios. We're in for a three-week marathon next to the goggle box, watching all the matches as they are fed through to the studios from Germany, assessing what we see and giving our views daily about the World Cup scene.

In Germany, ITV's 30-strong team of commentators and technicians will be helping to make our coverage of the big competition the most thorough and informative possible.

The technological miracle is a triumph in itself. For instance, there aren't enough landlines to transmit four matches simultaneously from Germany to Britain, and pictures of some games will be bounced off a satellite 25,000 miles out in space in order to get them to London.

We will kick off on Thursday with Brazil's opening match against Yugoslavia, and I expect the Brazilians to show all their traditional skill.

Then, on Friday, there's the match we've all got to cheer for – Scotland's first game, against Zaire, in Dortmund, West Germany.

I have heard some people say that the Africans might provide the shock of the World Cup, but they have no experience playing against the best teams in Europe and South America. It will be a surprise to me if they do well in this competition.

But a word of warning to the Scots. Everybody is talking about how they are going to tackle Brazil next week. I only hope that Willie Ormond is at this moment concentrating all his team's thought on one question: 'How are we going to beat Zaire?'

The word 'Brazil' shouldn't pass the Scottish players' lips until the moment they have *left* the pitch after Friday's match against Zaire.

I have my reservations about Scotland's overall chances because I don't think they have an efficient, sound squad of players to survive a competition as demanding as the World Cup. But this first-round draw has given them a good chance of proving me and everybody else wrong. A big win against Zaire would be a tremendous confidence-boost. But if they don't thrash them, they might as well catch the first plane back, because with Yugoslavia and Brazil in their group, they only have to make one slip to be wiped out.

Apart from following Scotland and casting an eye on the new Brazil, what are the other big matches you can see on ITV in the first week?

I recommend that you take a look at West Germany versus Chile. It'll give important clues as to how well the Germans, who are highly fancied, can play against a typically tight South American defence. I name West Germany as my favourites because I think they have the best-balanced side in the competition. Only an idiot would discount Brazil, but I wouldn't be surprised to see Uruguay or Argentina causing some problems and getting into the last stages, although I definitely think a European side will take the trophy.

I say this, not just because they are playing in their own conditions, but because I believe European football has progressed so much in the last four years that it now matches the South American game in almost every department. And when I say European, I don't count British football, because I think this World Cup will show just how far our own game has lagged behind the rest of the continent in ideas, skills and tactics.

One man who knows what it's like to take home a World Cup winners' medal is my mate on the ITV panel, Jackie Charlton. Jack also picks the West Germans and Brazilians to do well, although, like Malcolm Allison, he fancies the Yugoslavians to cause a few upsets. But I agree with Jack that the Italians might prove to be the most consistent team of all.

'They have mastered the art of defence,' says Jack. 'They can win 1-0 six times in a row and everybody thinks they're lucky, but that is their method. They give nothing away.'

This World Cup ought to be the shop window of football throughout the globe, and I desperately hope it won't be a violent competition. Yet I fear it could be, unless FIFA, football's governing body, gets stuck in and makes one thing clear before a ball is kicked on Thursday.

In England, in 1966, there were flashes of violence bordering on thuggery, and Brazil, the most skilful of all footballing nations, were kicked out of the competition by some ruthless tackling. But in Mexico, in 1970, from the very first day, referees clamped down on any rough play.

The biggest service that Sir Stanley Rous, president of FIFA, could render to football would be to call together all the referees and impress upon them the need to be strong in their interpretation of the laws of the game. If they don't do that, then we could have a situation which makes Celtic versus Atlético Madrid* look like Mary Poppins on ice.

Football is a man's game: if we can keep this a clean World Cup, it will be a great competition. I don't care who wins so long as they win it worthily and skilfully.

* On 10 April 1974, in a scandalous European Cup semi-final first-leg encounter at Parkhead, Atlético Madrid had three players – Ayala, Diaz and substitute Quique – sent off in the second half by Turkish referee Doğan Babacan, as they, quite literally, fought their way to a 0-0 draw with Jock Stein's Celtic. The Spaniards, managed by Juan Carlos Lorenzo (the man in charge of the Argentina side during the 1966 World Cup famously branded as 'animals' by Alf Ramsey), resorted to outright violence almost from the kick-off – Celtic's Jimmy Johnstone a particular target for vicious attacks – conceded 50 free kicks on the night and, in total, had seven booked, including their keeper, whilst two of the Glasgow club's players received cautions for retaliation. There was even fisticuffs after the final whistle as the home team were assaulted on their way back to the dressing room. The shameful display left *The Times*'s football correspondent Geoffrey Green lamenting, 'It was not football. It was Armageddon, a sick nightmare which will become an infamous scar on the game in these islands.' Atlético, with several players banned but fined only £14,000 by UEFA, won the second leg 2-0 and, then, almost the trophy itself, scoring with six minutes of extra time to play in the final in Brussels's Heysel Stadium before Bayern Munich levelled in the last minute and went on to convincingly win the replay 4-0.

* * * *

LWT's newly built World Cup studio in Bromley, Kent, on the South Bank of the Thames was decked out in silver-grey shades, but those tuning into the network's daily transmissions over the forthcoming weeks were guaranteed anything but drab and colourless proceedings. 'I'm looking forward to some scalding verbal battles and a fair share of fun working on the panel,' Clough declared ahead of the tenth staging of the tournament.

First introduced for the finals in Mexico four years earlier, the panel idea, the brainchild of ITV's executive producer John Bromley, was an instant hit. The small team of experts and extroverts had set viewers talking with their candid comments and impassioned debate. Bromley referred to it as 'pub talk'. It was often

controversial and confrontational, and wasn't without its critics –
those involved spent more time arguing amongst themselves than
delivering constructive judgement on a match, some felt – but there
was something refreshing and uninhibited about the discussions.
A new breed of individuals expressing interesting and strongly felt
views had usurped the mealy-mouthed footballers of old, always
spouting the right thing.

Derek Dougan, one of them, believed that Jimmy Hill and
Brian Moore, the men behind the commercial coverage, had sensed
exactly what approach appealed most to viewers, whether those
viewers were committed to the game or knew little about it. 'They
humanised it,' the Irishman said shortly after his TV appearances.
'Their approach made the technicalities more vivid, colourful,
dramatic.' Crucial to the experiment's success had been the
chemistry of widely contrasting personalities: aside from Dougan
himself with his almost impenetrable Irish accent, there was the
flamboyant, Cuban cigar-puffing Manchester City coach Malcolm
Allison ('He often leads with his chin – but it isn't made of glass,'
Dougan said. 'It wasn't a screen image. It's the way he is: sincere,
forthright, provocative'), Glaswegian Paddy Crerand, the former
hard-tackling Celtic and Manchester United midfielder (passionate
for the game, 'which he prefers played in a romantic, individualistic
manner. If Paddy had a magic wand, every game would end in a 9-9
draw or a 7-6 win, and Pelé would be in every team') and the quiet
one of the bunch, Arsenal's full-back Bob McNab (whose 'boyish
twinkle conceals a shrewd awareness').

Dougan, an often volatile figure on the field, expected 'to
explode like a firecracker, shout my mouth off, and embarrass
everyone – the trouble-maker-in chief', had surprised a few people
with what one Sunday newspaper termed 'a calm, moderate,
intelligent, articulate influence' off it. Instead, it was Crerand, with
his frenzied outbursts about the match he'd just seen, who'd proved
the most abrasive, whilst Allison, from accusing England midfielder
Alan Mullery of being unfit for international duties to suggesting
that the Russians and Romanians were all peasants, had practically
had the ITV switchboard jammed with protests on occasions.

If the characters' sartorial choices – from Dougan's garishly mismatched blazer and shirt combos to Allison's kipper ties and wide collars – were loud and brash, their opinions, at times outrageous, insulting, even bigoted, were even louder, but it all made for innovative television almost as enthralling as the football itself. For the first – and thus far, only – time, ITV's viewing figures for a World Cup tournament bettered those of the BBC. The panel, Dougan said, 'had helped to make the game a mass entertainment on television, not something just for the specialists and pundits, the devotees and the armchair terrace fans.'

Now, four years later, he, Allison and Crerand were back for more, but this time there was not just Jack Charlton and Bobby Moncur as well, but Clough as an added ingredient. The ties were still big but the mouths were, if anything, even bigger.

In 1970, Dougan & co. had, the Northern Irishman said, 'proved that people – ordinary people – enjoy hearing professionals talking about other professionals in a manner which isn't condescending.' Clough anticipated his own role in 1974 being much the same. 'As I have said before, when I say something on television, I am hoping, like the rest of the panel, that I'm saying what the ordinary turnstile-clicking football fan is really thinking. I believe that's what the panel is about.' And if the ordinary turnstile-clicking football fan wasn't really on the same wavelength as Clough, he/ she could voice an opinion, too; during some of the early evening programmes there would be a phone-in when viewers could challenge the experts. 'So if you think Brazil's Rivelino is the greatest and Brian Clough talks a load of rubbish,' Clough assured *TVTimes* readers, 'this will be your chance to say so.'

Clough could also talk a good deal of sense, of course. He fully recognised that against the relatively unfancied and definitely unknown Zaire, the biggest danger Scotland faced, aside from overcoming complacency, was failing to register as many goals as possible. The Central African minnows, though superbly skilled, were unlikely to have the sort of impact made by the little North Koreans in 1966 or Peru, who reached the quarter-finals in Mexico, and were considered the one easy touch in the group. In a real

David versus Goliath clash, Willie Ormond's side couldn't afford to make any mistakes.

'You can't please everyone,' reflected Billy Bremner later. 'If we had scored a hatful against Zaire we would have been branded as bullies. If we didn't we would be branded as inadequate.' As it was, Scotland's first-ever victory in a World Cup finals was secured by a two-goal margin. In a pre-tournament ITV preview, Clough, talking about Zaire, had told Brian Moore: 'They'll need somebody to run down Joe Jordan like somebody caught that zebra, because I think he [Jordan] will cause the problems.' The 'somebody' in question was winger Kakoko, the country's leading scorer in the qualifiers who, so a film from the team's headquarters had informed Clough, was said to have once 'run down' one of the black-and-white striped quadrupeds.

Indeed, Jordan it was who did cause problems. On 24 minutes his nod back to Peter Lorimer from a David Hay cross resulted in his Leeds teammate volleying Scotland's opener. Then it was Jordan himself who got the second, his header from Bremner's 33rd-minute free kick slipping embarrassingly through keeper Mwamba and into the net. But the hoped-for deluge never came. Jordan missed an open goal on 70 minutes; Lorimer saw another shot hit the woodwork; in the dying stages Law had a shot clawed behind for a corner. After seeing his effort saved, the Manchester City forward sat on the turf for a few seconds almost sensing that his last chance of a World Cup finals goal had gone. It had. Law was sporting a Scotland jersey for the 55th and final time.

According to Bremner, he and his teammates had 'sat back with the notion that we still had our toughest two games to come and we didn't want injuries or suspensions spoiling our chances'. The team received the usual criticism for their performance, but 'to gain your first World Cup win, with something left in reserve, was good enough for us,' the Scottish skipper said.

Soon after half-time in the Westfalenstadion, the floodlights had failed, prompting ITV commentator Hugh Johns to ask Sir Alf Ramsey for his thoughts on the problem. (It can only have been an act of some mischief-making to put the renowned Scottish-hater in the box as Johns's sidekick for the evening.) 'I am not an electrician,' came Ramsey's curt reply. The players remained on the pitch and after a four-minute hold-up, the action resumed.

But the Scots who had, effectively, gone into the game in the dark were no more enlightened once it was over. In the unfortunate position of opening their campaign against the least-known-about team in group two, gauging what would constitute a satisfactory scoreline should goal difference come into play was practically impossible. Had they got it right? Were two goals enough? Or would those too-tentative steps taken on a Friday night in Dortmund mean that the lights were soon to go out on their World Cup dreams altogether?

15–21 June 1974

Billy Bremner's game is football, and his determination to win renowned. It's a determination which could provide shocks as he leads Scotland against Brazil in Tuesday's World Cup match (ITV, 7pm). Brian Clough looks at the man and at his formidable opponents ...

DID YOU SAY IT'S ONLY A GAME?

FROM the Gorbals in Glasgow to the neatly trimmed lawns of Godalming in Surrey; from the suburbs of Belfast to the pubs of Cardiff ... next Tuesday is the day we wear our kilts and shout with one voice, for Scotland. That's the day when Billy Bremner's men play their second World Cup match, against the pirouetting geniuses of Brazil. The champions.

It will be Scotland's most difficult, heart-stretching, vital clash since Bonnie Prince Charlie took on the English. I'll be watching the game from ITV's World Cup studio in London, and cheering them on as loudly as the next man, and though my heart is praying for a form upset on Tuesday, I can't for the life of me see the Scots doing it.

But there is one man who, on his day, is worth more than any Clodoaldo, Rivelino or Jairzinho – one whose inspiration could cause the biggest upset in football since Poland knocked England out of the World Cup: Billy Bremner. Any team he plays in depends upon him. Even Sir Alf Ramsey once said that he wished he was in his team, and recently 50 top British players voted him the captain they would most like to play under.

I don't blame them. Bremner has a rare combination of a staunch refusal to accept defeat at any time, and a need to win that is almost warlike. If he could put this into a bottle and market it, he could make a million.

When I played for Middlesbrough and Sunderland, people used to ask me: 'What contribution do you make to the side?' And I used to say: 'I score goals, and when I put one away, the rest of the team grow ten inches.' Bremner is like that. When he brings off a great tackle, or makes one of his long runs down field like a runaway armoured car, Bremner inspires the Scots in the same way.

Johan Cruyff, who knows a bit about football himself, and who you'll be seeing in action for Holland this week, sums Bremner up when he says: 'He has natural leadership. He can score goals, make goals, and stop goals. The Scots tend to run and run when sometimes it would be better to slow the pace, ask where they are running and why. Bremner is the man who can cool them.'

The player himself, who is not a man of many words (off the pitch), said everything about this incredible determination when he said: 'I have this feeling that it's just me against the rest. I'm involved in every moment of the match. Every tackle. Every kick and every move. It's as though I feel them all. When the ball goes into our net, I hurt as if I've been stabbed. It's that awful feeling that you can't change anything; the ball is in the net forever. That's why I feel you must force effort out of the others all the time.'

Bremner's presence in the Scottish side might mean that I'll be eating my words on Tuesday, but one glance at the intensive preparations for the World Cup made by Brazil shows up the fantastic difference between the sides.

Just look at some of the lengths they have gone to. *Two years ago* they asked their UK football delegate Peter Pullen, who works in the Brazilian Trade Mission in London, to submit every detail about Germany's cup venues, hotels, stadiums, food and weather to the football authorities back home.

The sort of detail Pullen went into in his report is mind-boggling. In scores of possible hotels, he tested the mattresses on the beds to make sure they would be firm enough for the Brazilian stars to sleep on. He measured the height of the steps on each staircase in all hotels, and eliminated those establishments where deep steps might cause the players to stretch and pull muscles. He made note of the position of the sun at kick-off time at every World Cup venue. He inspected dressing rooms and noted every draught creeping through a door, and any evidence of dampness. He measured the distance from each dressing room to the pitch.

'The idea is that we should know more about conditions in the World Cup than the Germans themselves,' says Pullen. 'We make it as smooth as possible for the players, so that they can concentrate on their game.'

By this week the Brazilians will have trained together for three months, and a week before they left Rio in the middle of May, their sleeping and eating habits were slowly altered. By the end of the week they were eating breakfast at five in the morning, when it was nine o'clock in Germany, and their traditional footballers' nosh – steak, chicken and salads – were cooked in German fashion. The Brazilian medical men estimate that this saved 48 hours of acclimatisation when the team arrived in Europe.

When they did get here, they spent three weeks in the Austrian ski resort of Herzogenburg, where their officials claim that the high-altitude conditions have toned up the players' systems so that when they returned to sea-level last week, they had built up resistance against fatigue.

What can the Scots do against that sort of thoroughness? So long as Brazil play their typical game, relying entirely upon their ball-playing skills, they can dance around Scotland and win this match without much trouble.

To me, there are only two question marks.

First, when Brazil toured Europe last year, they introduced a tough, uncompromising element in to their play. It ruined their rhythm, or, as someone said nicely at the time, it took the smile out of their game. I hope they don't mix skill with skulduggery this time.

Secondly, Scotland could take advantage of a chronic Brazilian weakness: bad goalkeepers. In 1970 in Mexico they played Felix in goal, and he looked as if he'd coated his hands with half a pound of lard before the match. Catch the ball? He couldn't catch a bus.

This year, their two best goalkeepers, Leão and Wendell, are both said to be suspect against the high ball.

If I was in manager Willie Ormond's shoes in the dressing room before the match, I would try to get it over to the players that they should believe in themselves and their own ability, that they should respect Brazil but not fear them, that they should try to relax and play with determination. And I would impress upon them that they should go out there and play not just for Scotland but for Britain.

There is one thing you can depend on any Scottish team to do, and that is to fight to the last drop of sweat for 90 minutes. And none more so than little Billy Bremner.

* * * *

In January 1974, when the draw for the group stages of the forthcoming World Cup was made, Scotland manager Willie Ormond attended, hoping to avoid the 'temperamental' South American teams, with one exception: Uruguay. Twenty years earlier, Ormond, an outside-left with Hibernian, had been in the Scotland side that had finished on the end of a 7-0 thrashing by the Uruguayans at the finals in Switzerland. 'Nothing could have saved us that day,' he reasoned later. Two decades on, the former Hibs forward was hoping for a rematch, not to settle old scores but because he believed his charges could better the Uruguayans now. As it was, though, Brazil were the South Americans Ormond would have to prepare his men to face.

After the final in Mexico in 1970 a new World Cup had to be minted, Brazil winning it a third time meaning that, by the rules of the competition, the solid gold Jules Rimet trophy valued at £30,000 became theirs to keep.

With their run of success – victories in 1958, 1962 and 1970 interrupted only by England in 1966 – Brazil's dominance of modern world football was unquestionable. No other country since the competition began in 1930 had won the World Cup in a foreign continent, a feat they achieved in Sweden when claiming their first triumph. It took a truly great side to play its best football regardless of a situation where pitches, crowds, climates and the whole atmosphere were so different.

The Brazilians, by their own later admission, were badly prepared for defending their trophy in England – 'We believed that we were champions already,' said Mário Zagallo, who took over as manager before the 1970 campaign – but it didn't help that a marvellous team with delicate skills was crudely kicked out of the tournament with tactics bordering on the savage. They took their bruised battalions back to Rio, having learned a vital lesson. Four years later, that lesson was well illustrated.

They were leaving nothing to chance this time. Under Zagallo's watchful eye, the meticulous preparations for Germany began in the first week of March 1974 when, together with its entourage of trainers, coaches and physicians, Brazil's 22-man squad took up full-time residence at a former priests' retreat high in the lush green mountains above Rio de Janeiro. For training sessions, the squad rode down in a fleet of minibuses to the Brazilian army's school of physical education on the shore of the Atlantic below Rio's Sugar Loaf Mountain, where they underwent rigorous routines. Holding to the belief that European football was more physical, had more speed and strength than the South American game, in which technique and skill were more important, Brazil's trainers designed exercises to match the Europeans' fitness.

But England weren't the only ones whose star was flickering. Since Mexico, Zagallo had had to rebuild, and it hadn't been a painless process. Only Jairzinho, Piazza, Paulo César, Clodoaldo and Rivelino remained from the players who won the 1970 title. To the Samba soccer that had swept aside all comers, an uncharacteristic ruthlessness had been added, and the side was now far less easy on the eye. For all the Fleet Street fawning about their flowing, cavalier, free-form style, how their players had honed their talents and passions on the back streets and beaches of Rio, the Brazilians could always handle themselves in the rough and tumble. Pelé wasn't averse to putting his foot and elbow in. Nevertheless, now more than ever, it was evident that any highly skilled Brazilian display was always backed up with a fair degree of muscle.

On a European tour in 1973, which included a 1-0 win at Hampden Park, they'd been exposed as being woefully short on class and temper. It wasn't just the retired Pelé, the architect of so many of their glories, that was missing; the flair and finesse that had floored their opponents four years earlier was virtually non-existent.

Just what was the Brazilians' 'typical' game now? The tournament's inaugural fixture provided scant indication. What, so *TVTimes* predicted, 'promises to be an opening contest of speed, skill and excitement' was a disappointing affair, not helped by the wet conditions and a very poor pitch, resulting in a goalless draw between the holders and Yugoslavia.

Ahead of the game with Scotland, the listings magazine was sticking to the stereotypes: the 'brilliant' Brazilians – 'A connoisseur's side with a style of football that is a sheer delight to watch: imaginative, smooth and exciting' – were 'out to shatter the accusation that their style is smothered against more physical European opposition'. They were, *TVTimes* eulogised, 'capable of destroying any formation with their exhilarating, devastating football'. Destruction was definitely on Mário Zagallo's mind. We'll 'skin the Scots alive,' he promised, to make amends for the scoreless opener.

'We paid them far too much respect for the first half,' Billy Bremner reminisced rather ruefully in Bernard Bale's posthumously published 1999 book, *Bremner!*, 'before realising that they were human just like we were and that they made mistakes like the rest of us.' On that June night in the Waldstadion, Frankfurt, 25 years earlier, Scotland had come so desperately close. And no one closer than their ginger-haired midfield general.

Over-cautious to begin with, Ormond's side had gradually grown in confidence and, after hearing at half-time that Yugoslavia were six goals to the good against Zaire, really went for it in the second 45 minutes, pushing forward more and more. The world champions, under a lot of pressure, resorted to far more skulduggery than skill. Ormond would later decry the Brazilians' tackling as 'unbelievably crude'. Fouls were frequent. Rivelino had a running battle with Bremner and was lucky to stay on the pitch. From one free kick, Lorimer saw his 35-yarder palmed over by Leão. After the resultant corner from the same Leeds player was messily cleared for another, from the second, a high-hanging ball across to the far post, Joe Jordan rose magnificently to power down a firm header which the less-than-impressive Brazilian keeper failed to hold, only pushing it out to the feet of the onrushing Bremner. But, with no time to react, in Bremner's own words, 'the ball came off my shins and rebounded just inches the wrong side of the post when the goalkeeper was stranded'. It was an agonising miss. An anguished Bremner was left holding his head in his hands, his pain clear for millions of TV viewers to see. *TVTimes* was a bit optimistic in their pre-match hope that the encounter 'could well turn out to be the showpiece of the tournament' but it had provided one of the finals' most memorable moments.

At 0-0 at the end, it made a Scotland win in their final game imperative. Yugoslavia had put nine past Zaire to equal Hungary's record-breaking World Cup finals win versus South Korea in 1954. Brazil would surely get a hatful against the Africans, too. In 1958 Scotland had faced Yugoslavia at the same stage at the finals in Sweden – it had finished 1-1. Then, Scotland had been little more than underdogs lacking any bite. Now, they were perhaps the most impressive team the country had ever sent on to an international field. It was all the more tragic then that when history repeated itself on 22 June, on a hot, humid evening in Frankfurt, a 90 minutes the Scots dominated but could only draw 1-1, it left them unbeaten in their three encounters but unluckily eliminated, claiming the unwanted honour of being the first team in the history of the World Cup finals to exit without losing a match.

Scotland had suffered what writer Hugh McIlvanney called 'perhaps the cruellest and least deserved blow in its history'. A side superior in the games against their two main challengers had, McIlvanney wrote, been 'removed from the World Cup by a goal scored in a stadium 150 miles away'. Brazil, 3-0 victors over Zaire in Gelsenkirchen, had ended level on points with both their chief rivals in the group but went through along with the Slavs by virtue of that extra goal against the Africans. What made it even more sickening for all those with dark-blue blood was that Brazil's crucial third, a speculative cross from the right by Valdomiro ten minutes from time which had slithered under the body of Zaire's Mwamba was, to McIlvanney, 'a shot that most goalkeepers in the park on Sunday would be expected to save'.

ITV's special pre-tournament preview programme was subtitled *Can Scotland Do It?* The answer, alas, was no. Like the World Cup song they'd released on the Polydor label, 'Easy, Easy' (which had failed to make an appearance on *Top of the Pops* having only reached number 20 in the singles chart), the Scotland squad's progress had stalled prematurely. However unjust it was, Ormond and his cohorts were boarding the plane home early, with only the small grain of comfort of a heroes' welcome awaiting them. It would be another four years before Clough got the opportunity to sport his kilt once again.

22–28 June 1974

The World Cup pace is hotting up. On Saturday, Scotland play their vital game against Yugoslavia, and on Sunday ITV brings you exclusive live coverage of the match between Poland – who put England out of the competition – and highly fancied Italy. Wednesday sees the start of the final-round matches, two of them live on TV. Brian Clough thinks the game of the week could be Poland versus Italy – a battle between goalkeepers ...

THE CLOWN v THE GENIUS

I called one of them a clown. The other is a genius. And Sunday's match between Poland and Italy could give us final proof; it's an intriguing confrontation which could turn out to be The Tale of Two Goalkeepers.

On one hand – provided he has recovered from a recent injury – is Jan Tomaszewski of Poland, towering, brave and incredibly lucky. On the other, Italy's Dino Zoff, cat-like, instinctive, brilliant.

I came in for a lot of stick and criticism last October when England drew 1-1 with Poland and went sailing out of the World Cup. I labelled Tomaszewski a clown when all around me were saying he was the greatest thing since shin pads. But I stick by what I said. For 90 minutes that night Mr Tomaszewski had a guardian angel standing on the line behind him, and although Allan Clarke managed to squeeze in a penalty, our lads could have played till midnight and they wouldn't have scored again.

Tomaszewski brought off a string of saves that night which weren't as good as they looked. Technically, he was a poor keeper, but he had the good fortune to keep out shots he didn't even see arriving. Spurs goalkeeper Pat Jennings said the next day that he had never seen a man make so many mistakes and get away with it.

I hope Tomaszewski will be playing on Sunday because, sooner or later, a man's luck runs out and he is punished for the errors he has made in the past. Every fan in England will want to see how he performs. We'll watch this match because we still can't believe what happened at Wembley. Were the Poles *that* good? Personally, I thought them a sound, reliable, if uninspiring side. They were blessed with a couple of world-class wingers in Lato and Gadocha, men who could make a few dents in the factory finish of the Italian defence.

If they do penetrate the first layers of that brilliantly disciplined stonewall rearguard, they then have to contend with Dino Zoff, the most costly, and arguably the best goalkeeper in the world.

I know about Zoff to my cost. He played two fine games for Juventus against Derby in the semi-finals of the European Cup two years ago. When his club paid Napoli £196,000 for him in 1971 – a world record for a goalkeeper – it wasn't a lire too much. The man's temperament is supreme.

Playing as he does behind a packed defence, Zoff might have to spend most of a match waiting for the occasional shot to come his way – perhaps a rocket from 25 yards, perhaps a speculative thump deflected through a mass of legs. But he is always equal to it. Somehow he can key himself up for the whole game at the peak of alertness, ready for that vital moment when he's needed.

Against Poland last year, Peter Shilton was a spectator until Domarski fired in a goal after 55 minutes. I believe that if he had been busier beforehand, Shilton would have picked up that shot in his teeth.

That's the sort of situation Zoff finds himself in most of the time, but his consistency is remarkable. He holds the Italian league record for not conceding a goal – 903 minutes before he was beaten by a penalty.

Latin countries have never been noted for their great goalkeepers. But in a land where short tempers and hot-headedness on the pitch are almost an accepted part of the game, 32-year-old Zoff is an exception. He is cool as ice, safe, agile and unspectacular.

And, with the Italians reported to be on £20,000-a-man to win the World Cup, it's a coolness which is vital this week.

I think that the Italians have so much all-round ability that they will win this game and go on to do well in the final stages of the World Cup. But I have mixed feelings about whether this is a good thing for the game.

I admire the Italians' skill and the meticulous way they defend, and I reckon that a convict has a better chance of escaping from the maximum-security wing of Parkhurst than the Poles of prising open the Italian barricades. But in the last ten or 15 years the Italians have not emerged as a world footballing power. They should have done; they have the players, the crowds and the money, but they have stifled themselves with negative tactics.

Defending is only an art if it is used as a springboard for attack. If you drink champagne until it comes out of your ears, it loses its magic. In the same way, defensive football, good as it can be, becomes poison when it's dished up excessively.

I think that the Italians' tactics are built so much on defence that they have forgotten how to attack. This is why the few attackers who have been allowed to develop in Italy are so good. Players such as Riva and Rivera might create only one scoring chance in a match and they take it gratefully.

Last season Riva's club, Cagliari, scored 23 goals in the league. That's less than half of the average total for a middle-of-the-table English or Scottish First Division side. But of those 23 goals, Riva scored 14, an incredible feat. Given a hint of fresh air between the Polish defenders on Sunday, the Italian attackers will bite with the glee of a child eating a choc ice.

It all adds up to the most interesting match of the week. You never know, those Italians might flick so many shots past Mr Tomaszewski that they'll get the taste for goals again. And the winner will be football.

* * * *

Dino Zoff went into the World Cup finals in West Germany boasting a quite astonishing record of consistency. After

Yugoslavia's Momčilo Vukotić had found the back of the Juventus keeper's net in the 73rd minute of Italy's 3-1 friendly win at Torino's Stadio Comunale on Wednesday, 20 September 1972, Fortress Zoff remained unbreached for the next 12 internationals, including two against England*. While *TVTimes* wasn't quite so bold – in Zoff, they wrote, Italy possessed 'a truly world-class goalkeeper' – pre-tournament, *Newsweek* featured Zoff on its magazine cover, beneath a headline confidently declaring him 'The world's best'.

Within 46 minutes of Italy's first group-four game against Haiti, though, played in Munich's Olympiastadion, not even the world's best, appearing between the sticks for his country for the 33rd time, could do anything when the muscular forward Emmanuel Sanon latched on to Philippe Vorbe's incisive pass through the heart of the Italian defence, escaped the attentions of Zoff's Juventus teammate Spinosi, then skipped past the keeper to give the Caribbean newcomers a shock lead. Zoff's veneer of invincibility had remained intact for an astonishing 1,142 minutes. But for all that he indicated, post-match, the relief at the ending of his 18-hour shutout – 'Now, perhaps people will stop asking me how I feel about such a record, because it is no more,' Zoff told reporters – the 22-year-old Sanon's goal had exposed a definite frailty and lack of pace in the massed Italian back line.

Against the Haitians, Italy, the heavy favourites to win the group, eventually won 3-1, but, having only managed a fortunate 1-1 draw with Argentina in their next game – the Italians gifted an equaliser through an own goal by opposition captain Perfumo – they went into the clash with Poland with progress to the second-round group stage very much on a knife edge. For the Poles, however, with maximum points from a thrilling 3-2 win over Argentina and a 7-0 sweeping aside of Haiti, qualification had already been secured.

'Should Poland get the point, or points, they need tonight, and qualify for the finals, we must congratulate them,' Brian Glanville had written in the 10p matchday programme for the clash at Wembley. 'But for all their victory there [in Germany] last year in the Olympic football tournament, it cannot be pretended that they would be anything other than remote outsiders.' Yet as one door was closing on England's Munich dream on 17 October 1973, another was opening for the Poles to enter the global football stage. When they arrived, the strength they'd drawn from their 'victory' at the Empire Stadium was evident for all to see.

With their backs-to-the-wall efforts against England, they'd proved themselves more than capable of soaking up incessant pressure; now, in Germany, the East Europeans had blossomed, producing skilful, imaginative and swift counterattacking football to equally great effect. In the absence of the powerful Lubański, up front they put their trust in Andrzej Szarmach, reinforced by the pacy wideman Grzegorz Lato and nippy winger Robert Gadocha. Between them, Lato and Szarmach had already notched up eight goals. 'Dour and aggressive they may be,' *TVTimes* wrote in the Poland-Italy match preview, 'but there are not many teams who break from defence as sweetly and efficiently.' The Dutch, with Cruyff orchestrating, might have exhilarated elsewhere in the tournament, but in playmaker Kazimierz Deyna, the Poles had their very own conductor – 'a probing midfield artist' was *TVTimes*'s description – whose tune his teammates were happy to play to.

Safe in the knowledge that a draw against Italy would see them top the group, Poland had the chance to take their foot slightly off the pedal, but were having none of it. They had momentum and were determined to keep the accelerator firmly pressed down. Coach Kazimierz Górski made no changes; he wanted his side to go out and show the world just what football they could play.

His Italian counterpart, Ferruccio Valcareggi, on the other hand, had run out of patience. Disappointed by the displays of the AC Milan inside-forward Rivera and the injury-prone Riva in the first two games, neither was selected for this decisive final group match, nor as it turned out would be picked for his country again. In 1969 the pair were voted as the top two in the ballot organised by the French weekly magazine *France Football* to determine the European Footballer of the Year, Rivera finishing four points clear to win the award. But unlike in 1970, when they'd starred, in Germany they'd failed to shine. The game with Argentina marked a last-ever appearance in the Azzurri's blue for both. In attack, Valcareggi opted instead for Pietro Anastasi and Giorgio Chinaglia, forgiven by the coach despite angrily throwing his dummy out of the pram (and then smashing eight bottles of mineral water in the dressing room) when replaced during the Haiti game.

In Stuttgart's Neckarstadion, looking livelier than they had done previously, the 1970 World Cup runners-up began well. Far from being imprisoned by a fear of defeat, the masters of defence were adventurous going forward and, with Poland on the offensive too, what *TVTimes* forecast would be 'one of the most physical encounters in the World Cup' was anything but. Still, with their deft passing making the difference, it was the Poles who proved the most explosive. Firstly, on 38 minutes, from Kasperczak's lofted ball into the box, Szarmach, scorer of a hat-trick versus Haiti, sent a powerful arcing header over the despairing Zoff and into the top-right corner of the net to give them the lead. Then, six minutes later, Kasperczak again made a telling pass from the right-hand side, this time playing a low centre along the floor and captain Deyna lashed a right-footer first time past Zoff's left hand to make it 2-0.

After the break, the Italians clawed their way back into the game but it wasn't until the 86th minute when Capello breasted down Causio's chip before firing across the face of Tomaszewski that they pulled one back. It wasn't enough. While Argentina, on the same points total as the Italians, remained alive on a better goal average after a 4-1 victory over Haiti, Valcareggi and his squad headed for home, angry fans waiting to greet them at Milan airport, though in a cunning ruse the team's plane was diverted at the last minute to Rome to avoid a repeat of the vicious egg-and-tomato welcome endured by the side eliminated by North Korea in 1966. There, they still were met with hordes of unhappy fans who, unable to get close enough to throw anything, hurled expletives at their countrymen instead, and chanted 'Buffoons, Buffoons!'

As for that 'Clown', if Clough was hoping for some *schadenfreude* at the Polish keeper's expense, he was denied. Clough still wasn't likely to join the Jan Tomaszewski fan club, but there was little question that, as nonconformist as he was, the huge-framed number two (his shirt number allocated for the finals) was a remarkably effective last line of defence who, as journalist David Miller put it, 'continued to save shots with both ends of his body, often unwittingly, with an improbability which had its own special charm – if you were not on the other side'.

Poland finished as the only nation to take maximum points from the first-phase matches and, such was the deep mark they'd made, they were now being tipped by many to meet the Netherlands in the final. A 1-0 win over Sweden in their opening phase-two game, Lato's header just before half-time settling a hard-fought clash, only encouraged even more backers. Against the Swedes, once again Tomaszewski had earned his corn, fingertipping away Tapper's spot kick on 64 minutes after the penalty was harshly awarded when Polish defender Gorgoń appeared to have cleanly robbed Torstensson.

In their next clash, with Yugoslavia, it was the Poles who benefitted from a penalty decision themselves, a hawk-eyed Rudi Glöckner, referee for the 1970 final, catching Karasi clearly kicking out at Szarmach in the area off the ball in the 24th minute. After Deyna had dispatched from 12 yards, the villain Karasi, scorer of the goal versus Scotland, then turned hero, equalising on 43 minutes, but it was perhaps inevitably left to little Lato, a 23-year-old whose thinning hair gave him a much older appearance, to come up with the match-winner – he did so, flicking home a header from a 63rd-minute corner.

And so to their third and last Group B game. When Poland faced West Germany in Frankfurt on 3 July, results and fixtures had worked out to effectively make the match a semi-final, though the hosts, with a favourable goal difference, knew a draw would be good enough to send them through. The Poles were not only up against a strong German unit and an expectant home crowd but appalling weather conditions, too. Heavy downpours had left large pools of rainwater lying on the surface of the Waldstadion pitch. When the game kicked off, half an hour later than scheduled, it was obvious that there was little hope of Górski's side replicating the free-flowing, fast-paced football for which they'd become noted.

They took the initiative, but when they weren't halted by the muddy quagmire, the fine form of German keeper Sepp Maier kept them at bay. In the second half, with the Germans more to the fore, Tomaszewski's 53rd-minute penalty stop – Uli Hoeneß's weak effort easily dealt with – gained him a place in the history books as the first keeper to save two spot kicks in two different matches in a World Cup finals. But 14 minutes from the end even he was powerless to stop the game's only goal: when Rainer Bonhof broke into the Polish penalty area, Szymanowski's tackle only diverted the ball into the path of Gerd Müller and, with the time to pick his spot, the diminutive Bayern forward didn't miss.

Arguably, the Poles had been beaten by the German weather as much as by their footballers. 'Under normal circumstances we probably wouldn't have stood a chance,' admitted the German captain Franz Beckenbauer afterwards. Three days later, Lato's goal in a 1-0 win over Brazil earned him the Golden Boot as the tournament's top scorer and his side third place overall, their highest-ever World Cup finish. It was no more than Poland deserved, though there were many, some German players included, who believed that they were not only a real force but definitely the best team in the competition.

Poland, wrote David Miller, 'shone a rainbow across the World Cup while others were more concerned with the crock of gold at its end'. With a little share of the vast fortune of luck they'd enjoyed at Wembley and but for a sodden surface in Frankfurt they might well have claimed football's most glittering prize as well.

* Prior to their 1-0 friendly win at Wembley in November 1973, Italy had also beaten Sir Alf Ramsey's side 2-0 on Thursday, 14 June 1973 in another friendly, to mark 75 years of Italy's Football Federation (FIGC). The match, in Turin, was the 150th Italy had played at home, their 100th win at home, but their very first victory against England in nine encounters spread over 40 years. Bobby Moore, captaining England, set a new appearances record, earning his 107th cap for his country, overtaking Bobby Charlton's tally of 106.

6–12 July 1974

It's finals time in Munich this weekend, when the winners of the *TVTimes* World Cup competition* will be sitting in the Olympic Stadium to see the two big matches. And you can see all the thrills at home – live on ITV. On Saturday there's the third-and-fourth-place play-off game, and on Sunday the big one, the World Cup Final itself. As the 1974 competition closes, Brian Clough looks to 1978 and how England must plan for the next World Cup …

STOP THE BICKERING – THAT'S HOW TO WIN IN '78

THIS Sunday at 4pm over 400 million people all over the world will be tuned in to the big one. The World Cup Final. For myself, and the rest of the ITV panel, who have sent a few million well-chosen words over the air during the past month or so, it will be the last chance to put our money where our mouths are in the preview before the kick-off.

But whoever reaches the final, you can be sure of one thing: football in both competing countries will get a fantastic boost. Just as English football went through a wonderful, healthy spell of big gates and high confidence after the 1966 World Cup finals, the 1970 finalists, Brazil and Italy, have enjoyed four glorious years. Until now, the Brazilians have led the world in ideas, displaying skill and entertainment at its best. In Italy gates have risen steadily, while elsewhere in Europe clubs have been counting their pennies, worrying about falling attendances and blaming everything in sight from television to hooligans.

One thought should be in the minds of the four British national sides the moment the whistle blows after Sunday's game. They should be asking, 'How can we make sure that we will be at the World Cup in Argentina in 1978? And win it?'

The Scots bravely waved the flag for British football in Germany this summer. But English football will not be able to stomach another competition in which it is left out in the cold. I think we should be preparing for Argentina – now.

If I could wave a wand and set things in motion the way I would like to see them, this is what I'd do. I would prepare an international schedule to ensure that we played the best teams in the world as often as possible. I would need the full co-operation of the Football League – the continual bickering between the League and the Football Association would have to end in the common interest of putting England firmly back on the world footballing map.

Drastic action would be required to improve the organisation of our game and to ease the problems of the international team. I would shorten the leagues and reduce the number of games footballers have to play. This would give fans a keener appetite for the game. I like to see issues in black and white, and I would make no compromises.

League matches would be played twice a week during September, October and November, giving players a rest during the bad winter months, and I would make sure that the league and cup season was finished by March. Then England could train as a unit for a solid period and play three or four testing matches. I would abolish the Home Internationals tournament, which never proves anything and never will. It's nothing but a bore for players, who have had a strenuous season and want to get away to the sunshine with their families.

Players and managers need a complete break, a couple of months when they don't so much as kick a tin can down an alley.

The Brazilians would give their players a fortnight on Mars if they thought it would do them any good. It's a pity they don't treat their poorest citizens the way they treat their football team, but, truly, preparation is everything.

When I was offered the job of running the Iran national side, the authorities there were prepared to do anything to get good results. They were building an incredible £20m stadium and offered me an open ticket to Peking so that, if I became their manager, I could buzz off to see if the Chinese were playing 4-3-3 or 4-2-4 in preparation for the Asian games.

We in Britain must stop telling ourselves that we invented the game, that nobody can touch us, that we have all the raw material and only need to put it together.

There is a lot of hard work to get through before Argentina 1978. Most important of all is the need to find the types of players who will perform well together – not just the 11 most talented footballers in the country.

Everything depends on the personality and ideas of the man the FA pick as England manager. It will be a tragedy for our football if they give the job to the wrong man. (By the way, if they haven't made up their minds yet, they can still count me in the reckoning.)

An international team needs balance, blend, guidance and inspiration from the top, and it's up to the manager to provide these. The trouble is, in the heat of the domestic season, we always tend to treat the national team as a luxury instead of the vital force behind the game. We should be telling ourselves that there is nothing more important than success in the World Cup.

Once we have accepted that – as the Brazilians have – there is no problem. So let's get going now, and make sure that we'll be booting the ball around in Buenos Aires in four years' time, and not kicking our heels at home.

This year's World Cup has proved what I stressed in this column a few weeks ago – that European football is forging ahead of the South American style in ideas and thinking. We can be part of this new wave if we begin to treat our players like human beings rather than machines.

Meanwhile, I hope that FIFA's new president, the Brazilian millionaire João Havelange, can keep world football together, keep it clean, and make sure that we have a World Cup to write about in a decade's time.

* In the 11–17 May 1974 issue of *TVTimes*, Clough had invited readers to select from 11 free-kick specialists listed in the magazine and 'name three of these players who would combine most effectively in a set-piece move to give your team the best chance of scoring the winning goal'. The winner (with a companion) was to be driven to Germany in a luxurious BMW sports coupé by radio DJ and football fanatic Ed 'Stewpot' Stewart before enjoying a stay near Munich then watching the two final matches of the tournament. The verdict of Clough and a *World of Sport* panel was: Rivelino, Beckenbauer and Cruyff, with Mr Alfred Blanford from West Malling in Kent first out of the hat to agree with the choice. Mr Blanford's ten-year-old son, Gary, accompanied his father to Germany.

* * * *

As it happened, any fears Clough had that the 1974 World Cup finals might by ruined by ill-discipline or violent play and a failure of referees to clamp down on it were unfounded. The sending off by Doğan Babacan (he of the Celtic-Atlético Madrid debacle) of Chile's Carlos Caszely – the first player dismissed under the red and yellow cards system – in only the tournament's second game, a 1-0 victory for West Germany, might have given the Brighton manager cause for concern, but as in 1966, over the course of the 1974 competition, only five players – none from any European team – were sent off in total, three receiving straight reds.

The last of those was Luís Pereira of Brazil. Ironically, it was the main victims of thuggery in 1966 that were the chief culprits eight years later. Clearly not the force that they had been four years previously, Brazil, after narrowly edging out Scotland in the first round, had begun their Group A games displaying more of the natural flair and skill expected of them. One of the 1970 stars, Rivelino, whom Scottish boss Willie Ormond claimed should have been shown a red for striking Billy Bremner, struck with his feet this time, netting in both the narrow wins against East Germany (1-0) and Argentina (2-1). To top the group and go through to the final, Brazil needed to win what was effectively an unofficial semi-final against a free-flowing Dutch side that, having cruised through their opening group, had then eased to consummate victories over Argentina (4-0) and East Germany (2-0).

An ill-tempered match was, on occasion, a wince-enducing encounter that, for TV watchers, should have come with a warning about 'scenes some viewers may find upsetting'. The Dutch, for all their regal authority, possessed a physical robustness, parrying whatever weapons were used against them. Confronted with the Brazilians' spoiling tactics and often ugly attacks on their players – Cruyff was rugby tackled by Zé Maria, Neeskens elbowed in the face off the ball, Jansen floored by a blatant body-check – they needed all the grit they had. They refused to be intimidated, however, matching Zagallo's side tackle for tackle. The rain-heavy Dortmund pitch at times resembled a bloody battle zone.

Ultimately, two perfectly executed second-half strikes – the first, described by journalist David Miller as 'one of the most memorable goals of all time', when, on 50 minutes, following Cruyff's centre, a stretching Neeskens looped a shot over the keeper Leão, quickly followed by Cruyff's second, the number 14 brilliantly volleying home a Krol cross from close range – meant that skill, speed and refinement did win the day, but not before the holders had resorted to even greater brutality. Pereira's late sending-off for a waist-high assault on Neeskens followed by his foolish remonstration with members of the crowd as he left the field cast a last dark shadow over the memory of their Mexico magnificence. If, as Hugh McIlvanney wrote, the 1970 team 'may have represented the highest point of beauty and sophistication the game is destined to reach', the 1974 team signified a sad low. Brazil's cynical surrendering of their title left Sir Alf Ramsey in the ITV commentary box branding them as 'disgraceful'.

No referee was more authoritative throughout the competition than Wolverhampton's Jack Taylor, a butcher by trade, one of three British referees in West Germany along with Clive Thomas and Bobby Davidson. And it was Taylor who was handed officiating duties for the final. The second of the two nations contesting that final and, as *TVTimes* put it, 'just 90 nerve-wracking minutes away from the ultimate honour in international football' was the hosts. Though some questioned whether they'd peaked too early in winning the Nations Cup (the original title of the European Championship) in 1972, with a style described by *The Times* as 'elegance and inventiveness', before the tournament started West Germany were still clear favourites to capture soccer's most coveted prize. Clough was among those who'd tipped them.

Considering the talent available to Helmut Schön – the longest-serving national team manager in Europe – it was easy to understand why. Three Bayern Munich men – Maier in goal; Beckenbauer, their 28-year-old captain; Gerd Müller, the prolific goalscorer with 62 goals in his first 50 internationals – held the key to their possible success. But as football statistician Jack Rollin put it so alliteratively in a *Radio Times* preview, as well as a squad with players of the highest possible calibre and experience, 'they had the benefit of typical Teutonic thoroughness, but talent to go with it, too, and a proved championship-winning combination from which to draw.' The Germans were aiming to become the fourth host nation to win the trophy.

They'd struggled early on, though. A 3-0 beating of Australia followed the mediocre win over Chile, but the scoreline flattered a team jeered by their own supporters for its negative approach. When Schön's side suffered a devastating 1-0 loss in a first-ever meeting with East Germany, they were desperately in need of reinvigoration. In the majestic Beckenbauer – 'a strolling genius who never seems to work up a sweat,' according to *TVTimes*, 'yet controls the mood and tempo of a match with his cool, calculated football brain' – they had an inspirational leader, both on and off the field. Resilient and determined, the Germans gathered strength and, after seeing off Yugoslavia 2-0 and Sweden 4-2, the solitary strike from Müller, top scorer in Mexico with ten goals, settled the crucial decider with Poland to seal a date on 7 July with the most important match in the calendar of world football.

By contrast, the Dutch were easily the most exciting side the world had witnessed since Hungary's 'Magnificent Magyars' 20 years before. In Geoffrey Green's words, England, on the day they were taught a footballing lesson by Ferenc Puskás and pals in their 'cherry bright shirts' in 1953, 'found themselves strangers in a strange world, a world of flitting red spirits'. Opponents felt much the same playing these tangerine-shirted architects of Total Football, with Cruyff their magician-in-chief. A team without a central striker, the Dutch presented their foes with problems they found near impossible to solve, and instead were left spellbound, at times dumbfounded.

In the final in Munich, in little more than a minute, they were ahead. Fifteen silky passes, one devastating burst into the box by Cruyff and an Uli Hoeneß tackle later, Neeskens's penalty – a first in a World Cup Final – left 77,833 in the Olympic Stadium stunned. When Maier picked the ball from the back of his net he was the first German to touch it. It was a breathtaking opening. The victory that everyone in the game, Germans apart, predicted, and in most cases wanted, looked assured. Yet, if anything, that early goal was better for the Germans than for its scorers. As one journalist later observed, Holland went into the match with the cup already in the safe and then, when they went one up so soon after the kick-off, were conceited enough to give the Germans the key.

An unconscious reaction or not, rather than go for the kill, Holland toyed with their opponents. Slowing the rhythm of the game, Rinus Michels's men retained the ball, recycling possession almost insouciantly. But the second goal that might have demoralised the Germans didn't come. Chances went begging. And, after seemingly having the prey trapped in its mouth, the cat gifted the mouse a reprieve. Awoken to what they had to do, Schön's side acted, showing courage, character, mental tenacity. Beckenbauer et al. closed ranks, regrouped, and began to find cracks in the Dutch defence. On 25 minutes, when Holzenbein went flying over Jansen's outstretched leg, Paul Breitner, scorer of Germany's opening goal in the finals, dispatched the spot kick effortlessly.

Now on top, the Germans responded to the roar of the crowd. Yet it was the Dutch who had the best chance to regain the lead; with eight minutes of the half remaining, following another loping run, Cruyff set up Rep for a one-on-one with Maier. Eschewing the chance to go round the keeper, Rep instead struck his shot straight at Maier's body and, six minutes later, the Dutch paid the price. Two minutes before the break, the predatory Müller, reacting quickest after initially failing to control Bonhof's centre into the box, swivelled then hooked the ball wide of the statuesque Jongbloed, and Germany had the goal that was to prove the winner.

A second half almost wholly dominated by the Dutch yielded no equaliser. Under the bombardment of his goal, Maier, agile and brave, rose to the big occasion. Efforts were saved, cleared off the line, were close but not close enough. The clinical finish the Dutch sought deserted them. Even the genius of Cruyff wasn't enough to turn things around. Afterwards, the bitterly disappointed Holland captain said that he and his teammates had 'played like schoolchildren' for the last 30 minutes of the first half. That was when the match was lost. 'Holland threw away the final in 1974,' wrote David Miller, 'and with it an unchallengeable place in history because, for 20 minutes, they forgot what professionals should never forget: that being the best team is not enough. You have to prove it.' Just as they had in Switzerland in 1954, West Germany beat the favourites because they refused to let a superior footballing side get the better of them.

Three days before Franz Beckenbauer, playing in his third finals, hoisted high the newly sculpted World Cup trophy, the country he had faced in the 1966 final began their quest in earnest for qualification for the finals in Argentina four years later. On Wednesday, 3 July, Don Revie met officials at the FA and agreed a five-year deal worth £25,000 per annum to become the new England team leader. The next day, when the Leeds United board accepted his resignation, a 'delighted' Revie was confirmed as Sir Alf Ramsey's successor, declaring, 'This must be any manager's dream.' Even if some senior figures at the game's summit remained suspicious and critical of him, and had given serious thought to certain aspects of Leeds's 'tactics', Revie's appointment was never really in doubt. Clough might have been the people's choice, but his qualifications undoubtedly meant Revie was the natural one.

His remit was clear. 'The main object must be to build up for the World Cup in 1978,' Revie stated on taking up the reins. 'Four years seems a long way off, but it isn't.' The problem was that, rather than dwell in the present, he had to look ahead, yet at the same time get results, win the confidence of the fans, the players and the FA, thereby giving the lift the nation's morale needed following the Poland failure. There were many fine footballers at his command; the difficulty was moulding them together and, with important qualifying matches imminent, again he had little time to do so.

As Revie would discover, though, time wasn't the only thing he had against him. He was about to inherit many of the same predicaments faced by his predecessor: players left injured or exhausted by a too-long, tough domestic season, managers reluctant to release them for international duty, and an ongoing lack of co-operation between the Football League and the FA. And as Revie began to plot the course for English football's future, immediately flying out to Munich to watch the World Cup Final, whether he knew it or not, the snipers were already in place, their rifles' sights trained, ready for the first signs of any weakness.

17–23 August 1974

The new football season kicks off this Saturday, with ITV cameras recording highlights for Sunday afternoon viewing. It's a big day for Brian Clough the new manager of league champions Leeds United, who also teams up with Brian Moore for *On the Ball*. Here, Clough takes a typically frank look at the three new teams in the English First Division …

NEW BOYS? I'M BACKING JACKIE TO LAST

WHO are Graeme Souness, Jim Ryan and Alan Ross? No prizes if you live in Middlesbrough, Luton or Carlisle. Anyone else may not know them from the milkman. But with the new football season beginning on Saturday, these are players whose names could be flashing up on television screens during the next nine months. The three are the stars of the teams newly promoted to the English First Division.

For the first time, three clubs instead of two will be testing the hot water in the world's toughest league. Middlesbrough return to Division One after a 20-year absence, Luton are back upstairs after 14 years, and Carlisle appear for the first time.

Clubs promoted to the First Division enjoy a brief honeymoon: they are up with the big boys and luck is running their way. But when the league settles down after a few weeks, a true picture of the fledglings' form emerges. Let's take a look at the new blood.

Middlesbrough have a special place in my heart because I am a Teesider, and as a player at Ayresome Park I banged in more goals than most supporters have had hot dogs at half-time. This latest team rocketed into the First Division, winning their league impressively with a brand of football that smacked of the Leeds style – Revie-style – which Middlesbrough manager Jackie Charlton helped to create when he was at Leeds.

There were no frills about Middlesbrough, but they had the word 'win' stamped on every department of their game. They gave away nothing at the back, they dominated the middle, and with players such as Alan Foggon in attack they knew how to break away and score. Perhaps their biggest bargain, and a man who could make his mark this season, is young Graeme Souness. A couple of years ago Middlesbrough handed Spurs a measly £35,000 for him. In today's inflated transfer market that is like buying a few bars of carbolic soap for the communal bath.

Now 20, Souness is in the Scottish under-23s side, was in their World Cup squad, and is one of Middlesbrough's most consistent workers.

But any team takes its lead from the manager, and I believe Middlesbrough will do well in the top league for one reason: Jackie Charlton. He has the right qualities for the big time. He is a man of the people, regards the players as his mates, yet at the same time commands their respect and exercises authority.

My advice to Jackie is simple. He shouldn't be put off by bad results – they are bound to happen; he must stick to his guns and his beliefs until his team finds its rhythm. If he does that, Middlesbrough could do very well.

But Luton and Carlisle have bigger problems.

Manager Harry Haslam, who a few years ago was in charge of non-league Barry Town, has performed wonders at Luton, taking a team without stars into the First Division. And he did it with a brave philosophy which other managers might care to copy. When he took over the team two years ago, Haslam said, 'I don't care how many goals are scored against us so long as we get one more than they do.' Last season Luton were the runners-up in Division Two and Haslam proved his point: Luton scored 64 goals and conceded 51.

Luton must be one of the least-expensive teams ever to achieve First Division status, with players such as Jim Ryan – a £20,000 buy from Manchester United – the mainstays of the side. Like most of the team, Ryan is a worker, a man who doesn't jump through hoops to entertain the fans. But in the First Division Luton may not find it easy to continue their 'give-some-away, bang-in-more' policy. They will meet some of the best-disciplined defences in the world, and there will be no better test than the one they face on Saturday at home to Liverpool. I wish them well, but I see a tough season ahead for Luton.

It's strange to see the name Carlisle United in the First Division and when they go to Stamford Bridge to play Chelsea on Saturday, it will seem more like a plum third-round FA Cup tie for them than a First Division fixture. Unfashionable they may be, with sheep grazing in the field behind the stand, but Carlisle are in the top flight now. And no team wins promotion to the First Division by accident.

Like Luton, Carlisle is a team without stars. But manager Alan Ashman, who took West Bromwich Albion to a Wembley FA Cup Final a few years ago, is an experienced boss who believes in discipline. I think it was his determination to succeed that urged Carlisle to the top. At the end of last season a lot of people thought Carlisle didn't want to go up, that they couldn't afford to pay First Division wages. But that thought wouldn't enter the head of a man like Ashman.

So Carlisle made it, and I shall not be surprised if the player who really earns his First Division wage is goalkeeper Alan Ross. He is 31, has spent 11 years at Carlisle, and last year was the club's player of the season. I hope he has his wits about him because, on paper at least, Carlisle must be the weakest team in the division. They will do well to settle for a place above the danger zone.

Whatever happens, the first few weeks of a new season are notoriously deceptive. A team can strike form early on and lose it later when grounds become heavy.

By the beginning of the season, players have had a good three months' rest. I believe this is vitally important. When they go on holiday, I tell my players to relax and enjoy themselves, but to remember they are professional footballers and keep in good shape. The first thing I do on their return is weigh them. A player who has gained a pound must get rid of it: a man with a belly full of calamari isn't going to score goals.

After that comes the business of getting every player 100 per cent fit. But nothing is a substitute for match practice, and that's why we won't know for a month or two which teams are going to set the pace.

There are plenty of question marks surrounding the new season. How will Don Revie tackle the job of England team manager? How will Manchester United adjust to the Second Division? Will the new boys make it in the First? And I know a number of people will be interested to see how Leeds United get on with yours truly in charge.

I am making no promises: taking over the league champions, leading them into Europe, stepping into the shoes of Don Revie – it's a hell of a task. But I'll tell you what, it's good to be back at the top, and at the top I aim to stay!

* * * *

The chance to lead Leeds United into Europe never arrived. By the time they faced Switzerland's FC Zürich in the European Cup first round first-leg tie on 18 September 1974 – a game United won 4–1 at home – the short, uneasy association between Clough and club had come to an end, and the Elland Road hotseat was empty once more, with Bolton Wanderers boss Jimmy Armfield soon to be pacing the front room at his Blackpool home trying to decide whether or not he was the man to fill it.

It was around 6.15pm on Thursday, 12 September 1974 that the news was revealed nationwide: after only 44 days in charge – '44 days of trauma' the *Rothmans Football Yearbook* would later term it – Brian Clough had been sacked as Leeds United manager. Virtually from day one of Clough's tenure the talk on the back pages was of crisis at the club. Yet even after weeks of rumours of unrest, discontent and disharmony within the ranks, the story of Clough's abrupt departure still hit like a lightning bolt.

According to a *Daily Mail* report, the day before the Leeds players had given a vote of 'no-confidence' in their manager and, while club chairman Manny Cussins denied that such a meeting had taken place, when the dismissal of the man Cussins himself had considered 'an ideal manager for Leeds' a mere seven weeks earlier was announced (though only following a four-hour meeting with Clough and his solicitor before an agreement regarding compensation was reached), Cussins's terse statement left little doubt as to what, or rather who, had been the chief factor behind it. 'What has been done is for the good of the club,' Cussins explained. 'The club and the happiness of the players must come first. Nothing can be successful unless the staff is happy.'

The following day, the headlines talked about 'cowardice' and 'player-power', with David Miller fuming in the *Daily Express*: 'This disgraceful affair now more than ever raises the question, who is running professional football – the managers or the players?' That the Leeds staff weren't contented was, perhaps, no surprise. If all the underlying problems were true, it was only a matter of time before they came to the surface. The real mystery remained: exactly why did Clough, in the first place, enter into a union with a club for whom he'd habitually professed almost outright hatred rather than undying love?

At the end of the 1973/74 season, while Leeds United were peacocking proudly atop the highest perch in English football, the Seagulls on the south coast had failed miserably to take flight, Brighton and Hove Albion finishing 19th in the Third Division, just two places away from the relegation trapdoor. Despite Clough's faith in his and Peter Taylor's managerial chemistry, and a large turnover of personnel at the Goldstone, the two of them in tandem had produced no discernible reaction from their work with the East Sussex outfit. To those both inside and outside the club, it had become increasingly evident that Clough's heart wasn't really in the job; he'd left it somewhere up north.

Having touched Everest with Derby, Clough, a 'footballing Sherpa Tensing' in Bob Baldwin's description, was now at the bottom of the mountain once more and seemingly had little enthusiasm for the climb. There were regular absences from training. The travel to and from his East Midlands home was taking its toll. Clough's media commitments kept him otherwise occupied. And, with the country going to the polls in May, at one point he threw himself with more gusto into campaigning for the Labour party than managing a football club.

Above all, his frustrations with the raw materials he had to work with were difficult to hide. A stormy team meeting in early February resulted in Clough accusing his players of not only not knowing, but not even attempting to learn their own trade. In an interview with *Daily Express* journalist Steve Curry, Clough also said that the players had shirked all moral responsibilities. He was backed up by Taylor. The attack left the Brighton players angry and PFA chairman Derek Dougan responding, 'He [Clough] shouldn't criticise his players publicly, unless he allows them to answer back.' To the manager's accusation that the team was selling the club short, one player replied tartly, 'How does he know? We never see him.'

Brighton, Clough had envisaged, wouldn't be staying very long in the third tier. But he clearly saw himself moving on to better things even swifter. A lucrative contract had come with a sizeable signing-on bonus but it didn't stop Clough keeping at least one eye out for an alternative escape route. He flirted with all manner of other potential suitors.

In March 1974 an opportunity to run the Iranian national team had greatly appealed. Offered a fabulous salary, £400 a week, plus a luxurious lifestyle, by the Shah's Master of the Horse, Clough, born on the very same day that Iran changed its name from Persia, returned from the country publicly claiming that he wanted the job – Taylor wasn't interested – but Brighton were holding him to his contract, something he wasn't happy about. In reality, however, which he later admitted in his autobiography, he'd turned it down, knowing full well he'd miss the UK far too much to swap the wind and rain for the heat of the Middle East.

Clough's name was also associated with vacancies at QPR, Ajax and Aston Villa. But it went no further than that. Feelers were put out for Clough when Ron Saunders was axed at Maine Road, but the manager's recent run-in with the FA disciplinary commission had given City reservations. When Sir Alf Ramsey lost his England position, 30 per cent of readers in a *Daily Express* poll voted for Clough as the man they wanted to take it over. But it was never going to happen.

Even less likely was Clough being in the frame to fill the hotseat that became available on 4 July when Don Revie ended his 13-year reign at Elland Road, accepting the FA's offer to manage the national side. Clough, who'd flaunted his anti-Leeds attitude so willingly and so often, was surely the last man on earth the West Yorkshire club would go wooing. Wasn't he?

The Sun's John Sadler presented an interesting list of names tipped as possible replacements for Revie. Ramsey was on there. Also included were Gordon Jago, Bill McGarry, Jock Stein, Jimmy Adamson, Malcolm Allison, Gordon Milne, Jimmy Bloomfield, Freddie Goodwin and Jack Charlton. There, too, was the name of Brian Clough.

Revie's own initial recommendation to the Leeds board was Ipswich Town's Bobby Robson. But his fellow north-easterner, on an excellent contract and quite content at Portman Road, turned down Leeds's approach. If Leeds were to appoint 'in-house', Revie suggested they look no further than Johnny Giles. The quiet, affable Irishman, the Eire player-manager, was also the players' choice – someone they knew and whose know-how they respected.

Giles's interview with the Leeds board went so well the 34-year-old believed the job was his, and he told one or two teammates as such. However, when Billy Bremner caught wind of it, believing his credentials equally as compelling as Giles's, the fiery Scot made a case for himself as the best man to next occupy the manager's chair. Concerned that appointing one or the other might damage not only relations between the midfield duo but team sprit in general, Cussins opted for a safer route.

Former Liverpool forward Ian St John, the man whose goal had broken Leeds's hearts in the 1965 FA Cup Final, was his next target. The 36-year-old, managing Motherwell in his native Scotland, left a meeting with a couple of Leeds directors feeling he was in with a good chance of the role. But there was still one more man on the United shortlist.

On Sunday, 21 July, Clough broke from his holiday in Majorca to meet Leeds and Brighton directors in Hove and, in the early hours of the following day, the most unlikely marriage in footballing history was announced, with Clough accepting a five-year contract worth a reported £20,000 per annum. Once Leeds had declared their interest, Taylor had sensed the inevitability of Clough's split from the south-coast club. 'I could read Brian's ambitious mind,' he wrote in his autobiography. 'He saw himself jumping straight from the Third Division into the management of a European Cup side; he saw himself leading out Leeds United at Wembley in the following month's Charity Shield match against Liverpool.'

Leeds had very much hoped for the Clough-Taylor package, but at the last minute Taylor, out of a sense of loyalty as well as a belief that he had unfinished business at Brighton – plus, Clough indicated later, Taylor also fancied a crack at management in his own right – opted to remain by the seaside. Before Leeds had any chance to pull the plug on the deal, however, Clough announced to the press his return to the top flight. According to Taylor, his partner for 20 years, Clough had missed 'the big time'.

Understandably, the bon voyage wishes for his departing manager were in short supply from Mike Bamber. The Brighton chairman had never interfered in footballing matters, given free rein to both Clough and Taylor, provided funds for transfers, put the pair up in the best hotels, and had even laid on a new Mercedes coach for team travel. Yet while Taylor had remained faithful, not prepared to discard them even for the champions of England, Clough was deemed guilty of an act tantamount to betrayal. Bamber also accused the Leeds directors of going back on a gentleman's agreement concerning compensation for Clough's services – £75,000 was agreed, he said – and in due course would issue a writ against Clough and the West Yorkshire club claiming that Clough broke his contract and that Leeds enticed him to do so. They were allegations Manny Cussins denied, stressing that it was Clough who'd applied for the Leeds position. Whatever the truth, an astonished football world was now getting used to this new, wholly unexpected alliance. It was a relationship, though, that was effectively doomed before it had even begun.

Officially appointed on Monday, 22 July, Clough didn't actually show up at Elland Road until a wet Wednesday morning nine days later. In between, always one to place value on rest and recuperation, he'd decided to immediately fly back to Cala Millor and resume his holiday. 'I can sit here for three days and have four million thoughts about the future that I will have no time for when I get back to Leeds,' he told Barry Foster, the *Yorkshire Post's* chief football writer, who'd flown out to talk with Clough about his new job. But Clough's decision to return to the sunshine upset some Leeds players who, with the season so close at hand, regarded it as a show of contempt on their new boss's part. Clough already had some making up to do.

Getting in any good books, though, couldn't have been further from his mind. Clough didn't so much as step into Revie's shoes as arrive in West Yorkshire wearing a pair of his own heavy-duty jackboots. On taking over and a possible change of the team's playing style, Clough had said: 'Leeds have been restricted by their intense approach in the past, I feel. If a flower has nothing but water, it dies; if it has only sunshine, it withers. It has got to be a combination of both to bring it to full bloom.' But rather than arriving with a watering can or a sunny disposition, Clough went into Elland Road more intent on trampling on a well-established flowerbed.

After two days observing in near silence his new charges in training, he called the famous meeting in which, as one Leeds player put it, the manager 'committed professional suicide'. Clough prided himself on his honesty, but his targeting of individuals, criticising experienced stars for, among other things, a bad temper, a hard reputation, a propensity for diving, and a poor injury record, was woefully misguided. They were 'truths' the players didn't want to hear. Telling Eddie Gray – a footballer so balletic Revie had once said of him that he left no footprint on snow – he'd have been shot if he'd been a horse was simply insulting.

With his belittling of everything Leeds had achieved as a team, the accusation that they'd cheated their way to their medals, and a blatant desire to draw an instant line under the Revie era, Clough gave the impression that he saw the West Yorkshire club as a sick child, one for whom he offered the best remedy. Instead of the 'little bit of warmth' he wanted to incorporate in to the side, however, Clough's personality left the Leeds players completely cold. Offended, they felt no obligation to play for him. The requisite passion for the forthcoming campaign was missing. And it soon became apparent. A shabby Charity Shield clash, played at Wembley and shown live on television for the first time, proved a most uncharitable and imperfect curtain-raiser to the new season. Marred by continuous brawling between the Leeds and Liverpool players, it reached an ugly climax when Billy Bremner and Kevin Keegan traded punches and were sent off by referee Bob Matthewson. The game, won 6-5 on penalties by Liverpool after finishing 1-1 in ordinary time, was an ominous portent of things to come.

Earlier that week, Clough had signed Nottingham Forest's Duncan McKenzie for £250,000 – a record for both clubs – and the striker made his debut in the opening league game at Stoke. But Leeds lost that one and their next match, too, at home to QPR, 1-0 after a slip by keeper David Harvey, and the natives were already getting restless. Clough went back to Derby to buy John McGovern and John O'Hare in a £125,000 package, but in then leaving out players such as Scotland's World Cup centre-forward Joe Jordan and midfield man Mick Bates in favour of the two replacements from his old club, the manager again did himself no favours. Clough's viewpoint that, because of injuries and suspensions, he felt he needed to strengthen a squad which had just won the league championship, was hard for the Revie players to accept. The fortune he paid for McKenzie and the fact that he soon dropped the forward into the reserves was interpreted as another failure.

The side missed the influence of Bremner, suspended for 11 games for his bout of Wembley fisticuffs, while transfer speculation cast a confidence-destroying cloud over Elland Road. Inquiries by several clubs were made for Leeds players and, though Clough insisted, 'No one is leaving yet,' he was all set to sell England full-back Terry Cooper to Nottingham Forest. Meanwhile, Johnny Giles was strongly tipped to take over the Tottenham managership and, having had a long meeting with retiring Spurs manager Bill Nicholson, who wanted the Irishman to apply for the job, the midfielder returned to Leeds, intending to talk over his future with Clough.

On his first day at Elland Road, Clough had told reporters, 'Winning is a good habit which Leeds have, and I hope to keep that habit.' He'd been brought in to maintain, not bring, success, he'd stressed to Barry Foster. But after six league games, as Clough struggled in vain to produce a new style and tempo from a team still solidly in the Revie groove, Leeds had won only once, and sat in 19th place in the table with just four points. It was the club's worst start in 15 years.

A supporters' joke flourished that went, 'Cloughie used to claim we should have been relegated to the Second Division as a punishment. Now he's doing his best to take us there.' But no one was really laughing. After a 1-1 draw at home to Luton, the manager was roundly booed. The following game, another 1-1 draw salvaged late on in a Tuesday night League Cup tie at Huddersfield's Leeds Road – the ground Clough had brought Leeds to play a testimonial at for his first game – proved to be his last.

On returning to the Leeds ground after the match, Clough was informed that Manny Cussins wanted a word – he travelled immediately to Cussins's house. Whether Clough was told then and there that his contract was being terminated is unknown, though Clough hinted strongly at this likelihood in a TV interview with David Frost a couple of months later.

Clough described his departure as 'a very sad day for Leeds and for football'. In Johnny Giles's words, 'He never got off first base.' It was a shame. 'He would have been great for Leeds,' Giles told *The Observer* a few years later. 'I'd say he regretted that it didn't work out. I'd say we regretted it as well because it was an impossible situation.'

Was Clough's sacking another worrying example of undue influence by the employees over their bosses? The editors of the *Rothmans Football Yearbook* had no doubt. 'The irony was inescapable; whereas players had threatened strike action when Clough left Derby,' they wrote, 'it was the Leeds players whose discontented broodings provided this new downfall.'

In an official statement two days after Clough had been given the boot, the Leeds players refuted such allegations. 'We gave the same support to Mr Clough as we did to Don Revie,' it read. At any rate, the difference couldn't have been more obvious; when things went wrong under Revie, his players had complete faith in the boss's ability to put them right at half-time or from the trainers' bench. They plainly did not have the same faith in Clough.

Many saw the real culprits in the situation as the men who appointed him. Clough taking over at Leeds was, the author Don Watson put it in the book *My Favourite Year*, 'like Adolf Hitler becoming leader of the Labour Party in 1945'. In employing him and ignoring their own misgivings, as well as the advice of Revie, the Leeds board had made a gross misjudgement. Not unlike the murderous Uncle Charlie from Alfred Hitchcock's 1943 psychological thriller *Shadow of a Doubt* turning up in the town of Santa Rosa, California, and darkening the idyllic lives the residents had taken for granted for years, Clough had shattered the long-standing harmony of a close-knit family circle. But he'd hardly resorted to murder! So why such a swift change of heart from Cussins and co.? 'If Clough's behaviour lacked a sensitivity towards the feelings of his team, towards his predecessor,' *Rothmans* reflected, 'it in no way matched the callousness of the Leeds board, whose total belief in Clough turned to total disbelief in an extraordinarily short space of time.'

In 1972 Clough, in *The Sun Soccer Annual*, had written, 'You could put anybody into the manager's job there [at Elland Road] and unless he was a complete idiot, he would get results. Even with an idiot running the show, I reckon Leeds would still win a few matches before they cracked.' Clough, though clearly guilty of some foolish acts during his brief stay, was anything but an idiot.

United's directors had all but treated him like one, however. Frank McGhee of the *Daily Mirror* probably put it best in his summing up of where it all went wrong. 'Under Revie, the one thing they [the Leeds board] should have learned is that football is a fickle game that demands patience, mutual understanding – and time,' the journalist wrote. 'They didn't give Brian Clough much of any of them.'

24–30 August 1974

Tony Waddington and Brian Clough are about as different as any two men could be. But, as First Division managers, they share the same pressures and responsibilities. Last week Clough's Leeds United met Waddington's Stoke City who last season finished fifth in the league. Here, Clough looks at the masterly style of Stoke's quiet boss …

THE MAN WHO WINS BY KEEPING QUIET

THERE are some football managers (and I can hardly exclude myself) who have a habit of hitting and hogging the headlines week after week. And while I insist that my business has always been winning matches and not collecting press cuttings, there is a handful of First Division managers who move in such inconspicuous ways, you hardly know they are there at all.

Men like Tony Waddington at Stoke, manager without a mouth, the sort of bloke who has made an art out of keeping a low profile, and, ironically, my first opponent as manager of Leeds.

Waddington has been at Stoke for 22 years – 14 of them as manager – since, as a player with Crewe Alexandra, he suffered a serious cartilage injury, and he had to quit the game at the tragically young age of 26.

Slowly, unobtrusively, he has taken a shambles of a side in 1960 to fifth in the First Division last season. And next month Stoke take on Ajax of Amsterdam (the team which supplied four players in the World Cup Final) in the first round of the UEFA Cup.

Stoke is a unique club because in a game where managers lose their jobs as often as cufflinks, they have had only three men in charge since World War Two. And Waddington has kept his desk at Stoke through some of the shrewdest management moves.

When he moved from the training staff to the manager's chair, Stoke – the second-oldest club in the Football League – probably had the oldest playing staff in the league, and they were in danger of slipping headlong into the Third Division.

'I had a team who, unfortunately, had been allowed to grow old together,' says Waddington. 'They were all reaching the veteran stage at the same time. So I had to strengthen the playing staff quickly. In my first season it was a struggle just to keep up in the Second Division, and I remember it was also Don Revie's first season at Leeds and he was going through the same traumatic experience.'

Both survived to go on to greater things, but Waddington hit on a masterly stroke of management. While he encouraged a thriving football nursery at Stoke to bring on the young players, he plundered the transfer market for what an antique dealer would call real snips. If Waddington had been in business and used the same methods, he'd be a billionaire by now.

In his second season he bought Stanley Matthews, then in his late 40s, and Dennis Viollet, one of the original Busby Babes, and a year later he took Stoke into the First Division. But that wasn't the end of Waddington's forays into the bargain basement.

Eddie Clamp, Jimmy McIlroy, Peter Dobing, Roy Vernon, Maurice Setters, George Eastham, Alex Elder, Geoff Hurst – they had all been worked to the bone by other clubs and left on the shelf before Waddington picked them up for peanuts and breathed new life into them. And that's not to mention Gordon Banks, who, unbelievably, cost Waddington only £50,000 from Leicester, which was a bit like buying the Mona Lisa for your front room and knocking the Louvre down to a fiver for it.

'I didn't just buy old men; I bought thoroughbreds, players who had proved their ability. I mixed sophistication with youth,' says Waddington.

I go along with him completely, because it has always been my policy that mature players are not necessarily old players, that a

30-year-old is far from ready for the scrap heap. At Derby, when I bought Dave Mackay and Terry Hennessy, people giggled, but both men made outstanding contributions to the success of the team.

At Stoke, Tony Waddington has been a supremely cool operator, He moves in the transfer market with stealth rather than panache. And he has the football manager's number one essential quality: unflappability and faith in his own judgement.

When Gordon Banks lost the sight in one eye in a car smash two years ago, Waddington was left with a difficult decision: to rush around with a chequebook to replace the world's greatest goalkeeper, or to put his trust in reserve-team goalkeeper John Farmer, who, by being understudy to Gordon for so long, had spent most of his afternoons shivering in front of a few hundred fans in Central League [reserve-team] matches.

'I persevered with Farmer,' says Waddington. 'I knew it would be difficult for him at first. But I decided to be patient, let him grow into the position. And he has responded and made the transition magnificently. It only needed faith and patience.'

Then there was Alan Hudson. When he had a bust-up with Chelsea last season there wasn't a long queue for his signature.

Certainly, he wasn't doing much for Chelsea when he left. But Waddington moved in with the biggest cheque he's ever signed – £240,000. And he doesn't think he's ever made a better buy.

'I had no doubt about Hudson. A player doesn't suddenly lose his ability. There are ways of bringing it out again. Hudson has been a revelation at Stoke. After he arrived last season we lost only two out of the last 23 games. He dominates the middle of the field with his skill and he's rediscovered his feeling for the game.

'One of the important things is that since he joined us he has lost a stone and a half in weight through dieting and intensive training, and it's made him a shade quicker to the ball. I would be very disappointed if he didn't make the full England side this season because I consider Hudson as a Dennis Viollet, a George Eastham, a Peter Dobing and a Jimmy McIlroy rolled into one.'

Where other teams seem very remote, Stoke has the atmosphere of a family club. There's a sort of timelessness about the place. For as long as Waddington has been manager, George Mountford has been a coach, and now former players George Eastham and Gordon Banks are on the staff, Eastham as assistant manager and Gordon Banks in charge of the youth team.

'Continuity is very important,' says Waddington. 'That's not to say that we're like an old horses' home where players get put out to grass when their first-team days are over. But a certain amount of loyalty can only be a good thing.'

Stoke's big problem is how to bring about the same loyalty among the fans. I had the same trouble at Derby. With teams like Manchester United, Manchester City, Liverpool, Birmingham, Wolves and Coventry only a motorway's stretch away, it just takes a couple of bad results for a third of Stoke's potential crowd to melt away.

'We have a hard core of 15,000 to 20,000 fans,' says Waddington. 'And our average last season was 21,000. But there is a floating 10,000 on top of that who only go to watch a winning side – and you can't blame them. It's a vicious circle. As soon as we start winning, we start to siphon off fans from neighbouring clubs, and vice versa.'

One of Waddington's moves to win that support this season has been the purchase of Geoff Salmons from Sheffield United for £150,000. He doesn't spend that sort of money for nothing. 'Salmons is a rarity in the game today,' says Waddington. 'A naturally left-footed player of great skill, he's exactly what we need to speed up the middle of the field on the left-hand side.'

As a manager, it's Waddington's modest style to play down his own part in reviving a bunch of Second Division strugglers into a super side of the 70s. 'The game is about players, not managers,' he says. 'When Stanley Matthews left us to manage Port Vale, I said to him, "You won enormous respect as a player, Stan, and rightly so, but at Port Vale, nobody is going to watch the team just because you are manager. The fans pay money to watch the players."'

It's typical of him to say that.

At Stoke, they have a million pounds worth of new accommodation for the supporters, a new pitch, money in the bank, and a team on the brink of an exciting European campaign.

Never mind what the man says or doesn't say, Stoke owes a lot to Tony Waddington.

* * * *

On 26 August 1957, as Stoke City opened their Second Division campaign with a 4-1 home win over Middlesbrough, the visitors' goal that bank holiday weekend, which had given them a half-time lead, was netted in the ninth minute against the run of play by Brian Clough. Beginning a three-month stint that afternoon as Stoke's caretaker manager after a bout of illness had left City boss Frank Taylor hospitalised and unable to undertake his duties, was the former club coach and then Taylor's assistant, Tony Waddington.

Seventeen years later, when Clough went to the Victoria Ground, navigating league waters at the helm of the Good Ship Leeds United for the first time, it was Waddington, in the home dugout, who once again enjoyed a start-of-the-season victory by a three-goal margin.

That 3-0 win, secured by second-half goals from Mahoney, Greenhoff and Ritchie, was the second time in six months that a Waddington side had put three past the West Yorkshire club and wiped the smile off a United manager's face. On 23 February of that year it had been Don Revie's (not that Revie was noted for his joyful countenance), when, heading to the Potteries 29 games unbeaten since the season's start and looking to equal a run established by Burnley during the 1920/21 season, Leeds lost their spotless record in one of the most scintillating contests ever witnessed at Stoke's home ground.

At 2-0 down to a controversial 14th-minute free kick from Billy Bremner (the quick-thinking Scot, felled by Dennis Smith just outside the Stoke penalty area, dinking the ball into an unguarded net with the Stoke players mostly out of position and unprepared for the kick to be taken) and, four minutes later, Allan Clarke, the home side staged a stirring comeback.

First, Mike Pejic hammered in a left-footed free kick to reduce the arrears on 27 minutes; then Alan Hudson, latching on to a John Ritchie knock-back at the far post, coolly slotted past David

Harvey and the retreating Terry Yorath from just outside the six-yard box for his first goal in the red-and-white stripes, and parity was restored. Level at the break, after almost unyielding pressure from the home side, the game was settled 22 minutes into the second half when, following Robertson's flag kick, the last of three successive corners, Leeds failed to clear, Geoff Hurst headed on across the face of the Boothen End goalmouth and a diving Smith flung himself forward to power in the decider. It was a hard-earned but thoroughly merited triumph, one watched by a packed 39,598 crowd, including Sir Alf Ramsey among its number.

Leeds's downfall had largely been inspired by Alan Hudson, blending superbly in midfield with the tireless John Mahoney. Hudson had only been on the banks of the Trent for a few weeks but was already having a major impact, becoming an instant hero with the Boothen Enders from the day of his first Stoke appearance in a 1-1 draw with Liverpool when, at his imperious best, a virtuoso display had left them purring on the terraces and in the stands of the Victoria Ground. Former Wolverhampton Wanderers manager Stan Cullis, commentating on radio, described it as the finest debut performance he had ever seen.

Following Leeds's toppling, Hudson further endeared himself to the Stoke supporters with his after-match comments. 'It's impossible to play good football against them [Leeds] because their game is built on strength and they smother you,' he said. 'They will go on to win the league, but that shows up our game for what it's becoming because, apart from Bremner, they're a team of robots. I'd rather be lower down the league, trying to play the game than up at the top the way they're playing it.'

On the pitch, though, Hudson had been letting his educated feet do all the talking. With Hudson's skill added to the endeavour and persistence they already possessed, the balance of Stoke's side was now much improved. Third from bottom when Hudson joined them, the Staffordshire outfit rallied, rising to fifth and qualifying for the UEFA Cup by the season's end.

The move to the Potters in a £240,000 deal was a godsend for a player who needed to rebuild his career after an acrimonious falling-out with former boss Dave Sexton at Chelsea. It was a career that started with kick-about games on a bombed site in the very shadow of Stamford Bridge. Born and brought up near the King's Road, Hudson, rejected by Fulham, the club he supported as a schoolboy, had joined Chelsea as an apprentice, signing professional forms in the summer of 1968. He was soon making an impact. Youth-team captain in the 1968/69 season, after playing 21 reserve games, a series of injuries to first-teamers allowed Hudson an early chance to show what he could do; he made his senior debut on 1 February 1969 in a half-strength side walloped 5-0 by Southampton.

The result may have been disappointing for Hudson, but for Chelsea his unmistakable potential was confirmed. The following season, brimming with youthful exuberance and bewildering ball skills, Hudson rapidly came to prominence, earning rave reviews as one of the most precociously gifted players of his generation. Experts, including the England manager, were sitting up and taking notice. On a cold wintry day in 1969, Sir Alf Ramsey, telling reporters about the rich vein of young talent coming through towards full international honours, reserved a special mention for Hudson. 'There is no limit to what this boy can achieve,' he said. The 'Cockney Kid' was just 18 with only a handful of games to his name.

By the following spring, having played a huge hand as Chelsea, beaten finalists in 1967, enjoyed a triumphant run to the FA Cup Final versus Leeds, Hudson's form took him right to the brink of World Cup honours, Ramsey naming the outstanding youngster as one of 12 'reserves' in an initial 40-man pool for that summer's finals in Mexico. But Hudson was then dealt the cruellest blow: an ankle ligament injury suffered at West Brom on Easter Monday ruled him out of the Londoners' line-up for both the Wembley clash and the Old Trafford replay against Don Revie's side, the midfielder a reluctant spectator obliged to watch from the sidelines as Chelsea won the prize for the first time in the club's history.

Cup final joy – Hudson inspiring Chelsea to a European Cup Winners' Cup replay triumph against Real Madrid in Athens –

did come a year later. The season after that, there was a belated Wembley visit, too, though it yielded only a losers' medal with Hudson, scorer of the deciding goal against Spurs at White Hart Lane in the semi-final, one of the Blues side beaten 2-1 in the League Cup Final by Stoke. But, for the midfielder still regarded as one of the country's most exciting prospects – 'the best young English player I have ever seen,' Ramsey had confided – any steps towards breaking on to the international scene came to a sudden halt.

In May 1972, claiming that, with his wife expecting their first child, he wanted to remain at home to decorate his new house, Hudson refused to go on a close-season tour with the England under-23s team. He paid a high price. Lancaster Gate's reaction was swift and severe. Ramsey said that Hudson, along with Derby's Colin Todd (another who pulled out), would never play for him again. That November, out injured for several weeks after twisting an ankle at Old Trafford at the end of August, Hudson suffered another blow when the FA confirmed his two-year ban – the same punishment imposed on Todd.

Over the next year or so, with Chelsea on the slide, burdened by debt caused by the building of a new East Stand and failing to replace key players, and Hudson dogged by, in his own words, 'pretty rubbishy' form on the field, plus a reputation for frequenting the King's Road drinking dens off it, a bitter divorce from the club he'd played for all his career took place. On 3 January 1974, after another spat with the fiercely disciplined Sexton, Hudson, along with fellow star Peter Osgood, was suspended and transfer listed. After 145 league games for the Stamford Bridge club, he never played for them again.

Arriving in the Potteries with the rain pouring down and a gale blowing, as Hudson put it, it was 'not exactly picture-postcard stuff'. But he soon came to his senses; he was 'there to play football, not look at the scenery'. And what football he played. Occupying a roving midfield role that suited him far more than the out-wide-on-the-right position he'd been filling at Chelsea, Hudson flourished. As did his new club. Tony Waddington, a man who believed in playing the game the 'right way', with style and flair, craft and artistry – whilst happy to deny opponents the same privilege – allowed Hudson the freedom to go out and perform. His teammates responded in kind. Playing an entertaining, uninhibited style that Waddington described as 'the working man's ballet', Stoke became one of the finest footballing sides in the land.

First appointed as a coach in 1952 and upgraded to Frank Taylor's assistant five years later, Waddington, after assuming the manager's role on a full-time basis in the summer of 1960 after Taylor was sacked, had guided Stoke to the Second Division title in 1962/63, their centenary year, and to one League Cup Final in 1964 – beaten over two legs by Leicester City – when, in 1972, he led the club to their success over Chelsea, veteran George Eastham's winner giving City a first major honour in their 109-year history. There'd also been two consecutive FA Cup semi-finals, Stoke losing them both controversially to Arsenal after replays in 1971 and 1972, in the first of which they'd led at Hillsborough, only for the Gunners to equalise with a penalty in injury time and then win a second match at Villa Park. Now, Waddington had welded together a side that could be genuine title contenders.

The decisive 3-0 pasting of Clough's Leeds – with the 23-year-old Hudson the orchestrator-in-chief yet again – was just the opening salvo in an all-out attack on the league. On 21 November 1974, signed according to Waddington to 'give the defence that extra confidence to clinch the championship', Peter Shilton arrived from Leicester City, snatched from under the noses of Arsenal, Everton, Coventry and Derby for a massive £325,000. After a brilliant shot-stopping debut in a 2-2 draw at Wolves, which Waddington described as 'out of this world', seven days and two wins over QPR and Shilton's former employers later, Stoke hit the top of the table.

However, extremely unlucky to exit the UEFA Cup on the away goals rule to the European footballing aristocrats of Ajax (who'd actually supplied five Dutch players in the World Cup Final – Suurbier, Haan, Krol, Rep and Neeskens, though Neeskens had teamed up with Johan Cruyff at Barcelona after the finals),

Waddington's side were even more unfortunate on the injury front. On 18 March 1975, when defensive rock Dennis Smith broke his leg in a 2-1 home defeat to Ipswich, remarkably, he was the fourth Stoke player, after John Ritchie (who'd also suffered a broken leg against Ipswich, in a collision with Kevin Beattie when the two clubs had met at Portman Road in September), Jimmy Robertson and Mike Pejic, to become a fracture victim during the campaign.

Thankfully, for Waddington, Hudson was still fighting fit and arguably in the finest form of his career. The previous Wednesday, the full cap so many had been predicting for him since his initial emergence was finally Hudson's, the midfielder giving a masterclass, starring in a stylish 2-0 England victory over the reigning world champions, West Germany, in a friendly at Wembley. The dream debut earned glowing write-ups, the critics lauding Hudson's intelligence and, even, arrogance in their summaries. 'Where has England been hiding this player?' the gifted German playmaker Günter Netzer asked.

But for all the fulsome praise from Fleet Street, after the long-awaited arrival of a budding superstar, Hudson was all too swiftly being served with an eviction notice. In England's next game, a European Championship qualifier at Wembley against the far inferior opposition of Cyprus, though the home side eased to a 5-0 win, Hudson, urged constantly by Don Revie to get forward, looked completely lost, the superb choreography that had devised victory over the Germans gone. The midfield schemer produced an innocuous display, was left out of Revie's squad for the return game in Limassol then found the door on his international career was closed for good. Hudson was convinced that Revie, when in charge at Leeds, had a strong dislike for Chelsea players, or those who were ex-Chelsea, and that was a chief factor behind the midfielder's discarding from the England picture.

Meanwhile, after convincing home wins over Liverpool (2-0) and Newcastle (3-0), with three games to go, the title was still Stoke's for the taking. They failed to score in any one of them. A 2-0 defeat at Sheffield United followed by goalless draws with

Newcastle and Burnley meant that, for the second successive season, fifth place – four points behind champions Derby – was the best they could achieve. And that was as good as it ever got for Waddington, Hudson et al.

Over the weekend of 3 and 4 January 1976, disaster struck; in the worst storm of the century, while Stoke were visiting Spurs in the FA Cup, hurricane force winds battered the Victoria Ground, blowing off an uninsured section of the Butler Street Stand roof and causing considerable damage. A total of 1,182 seats were rendered out of use. In the short term, a replay with Tottenham was cancelled and a league game with Middlesbrough had to be played at nearby Vale Park. In the long term it meant rebuilding at a huge cost estimated to be around £250,000 (though, in reality, it was nearer the £2m mark), repairs which necessitated the sale of a string of star players to help foot the bill.

Thirty-year-old Jimmy Greenhoff, a firm favourite with supporters, left for Manchester United in November 1976 for £120,000, a move which Waddington admitted was 'out of my hands'; a month later Hudson, disenchanted by Greenhoff's departure, also exited, returning to London for Arsenal in a £200,000 deal. Others to leave were England full-back Pejic, Gordon Lee's first signing for Everton for £135,000, Sean Haslegrave (bought by Clough, now at Nottingham Forest) and Ian Moores to Spurs.

In March 1977, too, the tenure of the man who Clough once referred to as a 'football genius' was also over. Forced to field inexperienced players, Waddington and Stoke struggled and, on 22 March, three days after a 1-0 home defeat by Leicester left the club 14th in the table, Waddington resigned, citing mounting pressure on his family as the reason. At the time, he was the longest-serving manager in English football. Typically, it was Clough who headed the list of those tipped to take over, though the job was eventually handed to George Eastham, only the club's fourth manager since 1935. And it was under the charge of the then caretaker boss Eastham that, a couple of months later, Stoke fell through the relegation trapdoor, meaning Second Division football for the first time in 14 years.

Waddington was nothing if not a realist. He knew that Stoke were never likely to win vast crowds for their home games. But he also recognised that the way to draw more regulars to the Victoria Ground was to give them value for money. Through clever investment and careful nurturing of young talent, he did just that, producing a team that could compete with the best of them and which, for all-round enterprise and fighting spirit, couldn't be bettered. For a brief spell, Stoke, the dark horses, emerged into the light, upsetting everyone's calculations. They were, as one journalist wrote, the 'team that almost died, a few years ago, when Third Division football – and obscurity – stared the Potters in the face. The team that staged a modern soccer miracle, by finding a place in the First Division sun … and holding on to it.' Much of that was down to the quiet man in charge.

31 August–6 September 1974

Who is hitting the headlines, scoring the goals, and drawing the crowds in the football world today? Once every month, Leeds United manager Brian Clough will devote his column to his chosen Player of the Month. For September, Clough's choice is Mick Channon, and here he tells us why the strong Southampton and England striker gets his vote …

MICK CHANNON IS MY PLAYER OF THE MONTH: HE'S SKILFUL, AGGRESSIVE, COMPETITIVE – AND HIS LOYALTY IS PRICELESS

IF England are going to have a real chance of winning the World Cup in four years' time, they will need players of the calibre and character of Mick Channon.

He has skill, aggression, a tough competitive spirit, and, above all, loyalty.

When Southampton were relegated from the First Division last season, the first team to suffer from the new three-down rule, everyone expected Channon to have his transfer request on his manager's desk the next day. It looked certain that pride wouldn't allow the 25-year-old England star to exile himself from weekly contact with fellow members of the international set and that he'd soon move to one of the glamour clubs of the First Division. Had he come on to the transfer market, I can think of at least ten clubs who would have been queuing outside Southampton's ground with open chequebooks – and I'd have been one of them. Even Real Madrid were prepared to pay half a million pounds for his signature.

But it says everything about Channon that after the tension and disappointment of those last few games of the season, he went on England's close-season tour, played brilliantly, and then sat down with a cup of tea at Southampton manager Lawrie McMenemy's home and signed a new contract.

A manager can measure a player's skill, his heading ability, the power of his shot, his tackling, but loyalty like Channon's is priceless.

'Channon didn't want to go,' said McMenemy. 'All I had to do was convince him that, tragic as it was that we were relegated, we were desperate to get back. And we have the ambition and the willpower to do it. That's all he wanted to know. And as new club captain he has a vital part in getting us back into the First Division.'

Channon is almost arrogant about Southampton's promotion chances. 'After the first couple of months,' he says, 'it's going to be a procession – with the rest of the clubs falling in behind Southampton. That's how confident I am.'

What makes Channon so good? McMenemy says quickly, 'He's an attacking player who goes in where others fear to tread. Once he gets into the penalty area he knows he's going to get knocked but he takes defenders on. He also has the ability to get to the byline, which is the most difficult thing for an attacker to do today, then crosses the ball accurately.

'Channon's speed – he's a first-class sprinter – gives him that vital edge. If he has a weakness it is that he doesn't do a lot with his head, but he scored 23 goals last season so I'm not complaining. I've seen him score from anywhere, chip shots, hard shots, bending shots. The lot.

'When Channon was an England under-23s international, Sir Alf Ramsey told him that if he wanted to improve he should study the style of Gerd Müller, the man who scored the winning goal for West Germany in the World Cup Final. Channon heeded the advice: he has developed a sixth sense close to goal, he's a worrier, his reflexes are sharp, he gets to the ball before others have seen it.'

Southampton's 'Grand Old Man', Ted Bates, who moved up to general manager last year, discovered Channon ten years ago on a park pitch in Andover, when he was playing for Wiltshire schoolboys. Channon was about to sign for his local club, Swindon, until the lure of The Dell made him change his mind. He had always been a Southampton supporter so there was no contest.

At first Channon was overshadowed by Martin Chivers, but when Southampton sold Chivers to Spurs, it wasn't just for the cash: they knew Channon would be an ideal replacement. And so it proved.

I believe that players are not created on the pitch; the way they play depends on the people they are outside football. A thug at home is a thug on the pitch. Channon, modest and likeable, lives a quiet life in the country with his wife Jane and daughter Nicola (I hear there's another child on the way, too), and he's a manager's dream.

Channon, like Jimmy Greaves in his playing days, is a player who dislikes training because he finds it boring. His ideal week would be to potter around at home and play four full-scale games a week.

McMenemy adds, 'Channon is every lad's idea of the footballing hero, and I'm not going to argue with that; his attitude to the game, to himself and his club is exemplary.'

There's a story going around that when Channon takes off his Southampton shirt after a match, he's still painted in red-and-white stripes underneath. His loyalty goes that deep, and next year – his benefit season with the club – he'll find that loyalty pays with a bumper testimonial match.

I have a hunch that we haven't yet seen the best of Channon, that he's still maturing. And, quite apart from Southampton, England are going to feel the benefit of this fine, fluent player for many years to come.

* * * *

At the start of the 1974/75 season, Southampton, the club Mick Channon had joined a decade earlier as a 15-year-old apprentice straight from school, were beginning life in the Second Division again, eight years of top-flight football coming to an end when their relegation was confirmed on the season's final day the previous April despite a 3-0 away win at Everton. Channon had scored the visitors' second that afternoon. A year earlier, the striker, then reputed to be the highest-paid player in the entire league, had spoken about the club to Ed 'Stewpot' Stewart in an August 1973 issue of *Look-in*. 'Southampton gets knocked all the time,' he told the Radio One DJ, 'but we seem to surprise everyone by staying up every season. I'm hoping we're going to start winning a few cups and medals from now on.'

It was a vain hope. Despite Channon finishing as the division's top scorer with 21 goals, the Saints were unable to escape the drop and went down along with Manchester United and Norwich City. It had perhaps been coming. In the eight seasons since Channon, having already graduated to the second team before his 16th birthday (thus becoming the club's youngest-ever reserve player) made his league debut in 1965/66 as Southampton earned promotion from the Second Division, aside from seventh-place finishes in 1968/69 and 1970/71, an almost perpetual battle for survival had been fought; on three separate occasions, Saints finished 19th. In 1973/74, their Houdini act finally failed.

It was in 1968 that the Orcheston-born Channon, having signed professional forms in December 1965, really grabbed his big chance. With the £125,000 transfer of the unsettled Martin Chivers, Southampton's number-one choice, to Spurs, Channon took over Chivers's main striking role and went from strength to strength, establishing himself as a player of top quality, one with ambition and the ability to achieve international honours in the future.

If, off the pitch, the influence of manager Ted Bates had taught him the right habits, on it, the association with Welshman Ron Davies helped enormously in his development. Together they formed a sharp and powerful spearhead. Possessing tremendous pace and flair, skilful on the ground and making full use of his height in the air, the 6ft-tall Channon was a consistent scorer and quickly emerged as one of the most exciting attackers in the game.

An England call-up came in October 1972, Channon teaming up fluently with Everton's Joe Royle as Sir Alf Ramsey's side, including other debutants in Ipswich Town's Mick Mills, Frank Lampard of West Ham and Arsenal's Jeff Blockley, fought out a 1-1 friendly draw with Yugoslavia at Wembley. With his second cap, won on St Valentine's Day 1973 as England's 5-0 drubbing of the Scots at Hampden Park inflicted a nightmare start to Willie Ormond's job as new Scottish manager, Channon's first international goal arrived. It was a night on which, the forward said, 'everything clicked'. It was also a night when, as fate would have it, he was partnering Chivers up front, their twin threat giving England a spark they had been missing for some time. In subsequent games, whenever the two were paired up, it was something of a source of bemusement and amusement to television viewers how ITV match commentator Hugh Johns pronounced Channon, 'Shannon' but never called Chivers, 'Shivers'.

Over a year later, following England's short summer tour of Eastern Europe – Channon scoring in all three games – the man increasingly renowned for his whirling windmill-of-an-arm goal celebration had 19 caps to his name, and seven in his international 'goals for' column. Yet for all his confidence about Southampton's second-tier prospects, a predicted 'procession' never materialised. While Manchester United and Norwich City made immediate returns, there was to be no speedy going back to the big time for the club from the south coast.

By the time they did next grace English football's highest echelon, in 1978, Channon was no longer with them, the player seemingly contented with his first and only club having packed his suitcase and headed north to Maine Road, Manchester, to join Tony Book's ambitious City side in the close season of 1977. Before then, however, Channon had made a significant contribution to the most famous result in Southampton football club's history.

On 1 May 1976 Manchester United, the three-time winners appearing in their sixth final, their fifth post-war, were the hottest favourites to secure the FA Cup since Wolves in 1939 and Leeds in 1973 – both of whom lost. Few could foresee anything but a

Wembley triumph by two or three clear goals for the new, youthful Red Devils who, in their first season back in the top flight, had won millions of fans with their brisk, adventurous football and were on the brink of claiming third spot in the table. Their opponents at the Empire Stadium? Lawrie McMenemy's Southampton, sixth in the Second Division and appearing at Wembley for the very first time, having contested and lost the FA Cup Finals of 1900 and 1902 as a Southern League club – to Bury and Sheffield United, after a replay, respectively – at Crystal Palace.

A dismissive Tommy Docherty, United's boss, had already indicated that, whoever they faced in the final, he reckoned a win for his side was little more than a formality when, following the club's quarter-final success over Wolves, he'd said, 'This is the first time that the Cup Final will be played at Hillsborough – for what else can you call our semi-final match against Derby? The other semi-final [Southampton versus Crystal Palace] is a bit of a joke really.' Jack Charlton, on the other hand, was sceptical. 'I see gremlins, leprechauns and ghosts all over the place,' the then Boro boss wrote in a *TVTimes* match preview. 'I hear alarm bells clanging loud enough to drown the noise of the 100,000 crowd.'

The ex-Leeds centre-half had been an ITV co-commentator three years prior when his old club – 'the legendary giants' under Don Revie – were humbled by Sunderland. It was, he said, 'one of the worst days of my life' and 'I wept real tears for the teammates with whom I'd shared so much that day'. Now, as with the Wearsiders, Southampton were given little or no chance even before the kick-off. It wasn't a question of if the south-coast club would lose, the consensus was, but by how many. Yet if most regarded the story as already written, Charlton foresaw a tearing up of the script. Southampton might be wearing yellow and blue due to a colour clash but no matter: 'Second Division ghosts in red and white striped shirts,' Charlton believed, were again 'rattling their chains' as Saturday's supposedly foregone conclusion loomed.

The Saints, with wily old campaigners like captain Peter Rodrigues, Jim McCalliog, Mel Blyth and Peter Osgood, had the experience that United lacked 'and you must never, ever discount that at Wembley'. They were 'blokes with many big-time occasions under their belts'. People were saying that Docherty's youngsters would run them into the ground; Charlton didn't concur. 'Pace doesn't count that much at Wembley. Pacing yourself does. You can gallop off like a wild horse all over the park and be shattered at half-time at Wembley. Once, Wembley seemed ankle-deep in lush, stamina-sapping grass compared to the pitches at Football League grounds. Since it was relaid following the show jumping there [in 1969], it isn't nearly so spongy. It is just big, wide and swallows up players who want to run around getting nowhere.'

As Charlton predicted, Southampton's players, despite The Dell being one of the smallest grounds in the country, made Wembley work for them. They hadn't been conned by all the raving about United's invincibility. A busy side, running for each other, never allowing the opposition to relax, always chasing back, United were good, but they weren't unstoppable. A weakness was noticeable down the middle of defence, whilst their attacking game revolved almost exclusively around the penetration of Hill and Coppell. '[You] sit on them, force them inside and the much-vaunted "Red Army" begins to look like a rabble,' Charlton assessed.

On the day, Southampton did just that, negating the threat of the two lively wingmen almost from the kick-off. Far from employing a policy of containment, though, McMenemy's men, after a nervy start, took the game to their First Division opponents, Mick Channon exploiting space in United's back line, only denied when Alex Stepney came out to thwart the striker after he was through on goal. Docherty's side failed to benefit from the few chances they created and, proving far more flexible and better organised, Southampton adapted, adjusted and ultimately capitalised on United's erratic ways. Before the game, Channon, a racehorse owner, who knew a thing about betting, couldn't believe the bookies' prices: Southampton were so unfancied, they were 5/1 in a two-horse race. Yet he and his teammates made a mockery of such odds. When Bobby Stokes, just outside the penalty area, latched on to McCalliog's lofted pass in the 83rd minute to hit a low, angled left-footed drive first-time past United keeper Alex Stepney, it was the underdogs who took the decisive bite and seven minutes later had produced one of the greatest upsets of all time in English football.

Lawrie McMenemy, in a May 1980 issue of *Radio Times*, described the time remaining after Stokes's goal as 'the longest seven minutes of my life'. For the ex-Guardsman, the win was a moment to savour as the Saints fans gave him a rousing ovation. 'It's not so long ago they were throwing things at me,' he joked to reporters post-match. Vilified by many supporters for the club's struggles in the second tier, the line between hero and villain status had never been thinner than when, in the cup's third round, but for a last-minute leveller by Hugh Fisher, Southampton would have exited the competition at home at the hands of Aston Villa. Now they and their manager were revelling in a first major trophy in the club's history. It had been a well-deserved victory. 'Everybody called us homely and hospitable,' McMenemy said. 'What they forgot to say is that we are also professional, ruthless, determined and have a lot of ability.'

Two days later, Channon, Saints's leading scorer in six out of the seven seasons from 1969/70 to 1975/76, enjoyed the 'bumper testimonial match' Clough had said he would. A near-capacity crowd of 29,508 at The Dell turned up to watch a 2-2 draw with QPR, but the attendance was clearly far higher than the official one. There was a party atmosphere all night. Stokes got both the Saints goals. Prior to kick-off, the Wembley match-winner had been presented with a Ford Granada Ghia as a gift from the local car plant for his history-making strike. He hadn't even passed his driving test. It was that sort of evening.

At the time of his testimonial, despite being at a Second Division side, Channon was the one player who'd featured in every England international since Don Revie was appointed as manager. (In October 1975, it was Channon who'd registered the first goal of Revie's reign in a 3-0 Wembley win over Czechoslovakia as England opened their 1976 European Championship qualifying campaign.) By the summer of the following year, the lean, leggy striker whose dazzling runs could make defenders dizzy, *was* readying to play in the top flight – but in new colours.

In 1976/77, Southampton, whilst performing impressively in the European Cup Winners' Cup – going out 3-2 on aggregate at the quarter-finals stage to eventual finalists Anderlecht of Belgium – could only finish ninth in the Second Division. Channon had long made it clear that in no way did he feel he was losing his edge in a lower division, maintaining that First Division defences left a little more space that allowed a player to run at them. On the contrary, with players marking that more closely in the second tier, his task if anything was harder. But with Southampton failing to get even close to a promotion spot once more, Channon decided it was time for pastures new.

Other things might have influenced his thinking. Channon's England buddy Kevin Keegan, feeling it wasn't enough just to play for Liverpool and the need to motivate his career by looking outside England towards Europe, was about to embark on a fresh phase with Germany's Hamburg. Perhaps Channon thought you can have too much of a good thing. There was his international position to consider, too. Many critics had been posing the question for some time: 'Just how long can Mick Channon stay as a regular fixture in the England side?' when, in February 1977, the striker was dropped for a friendly clash against the Dutch at Wembley. If the best way to silence the doubters was to go out and prove them wrong, wasn't it easier to do so performing against the best players in the country?

Whatever the reason, the self-styled 'Squire of Hampshire' made what Brian Moore, in *Look-in*, September 1977, described as 'what will most likely be the biggest decision of his footballing career', exchanging the serene surroundings of his farm (Channon, by his own admission, 'a bit of a country bumpkin at heart', bought a £45,000 farm on four acres of land in the heart of the Hampshire countryside in 1973) and The Dell for, as Moore termed it, 'that soccer hotbed of the north, the Citadel of Manchester'.

City, runners-up to champions Liverpool in 1976/77, had a squad maturing sufficiently to make them odds-on favourites to win something big. Starved of league success since 1968, they were hungry. Shelling out £300,000 – at the time, a huge sum – on Channon was a clear statement of intent. With their new purchase in place, they began promisingly, top of the division after an 11-game unbeaten run. Channon, arguably able to now lay claim to the title of the country's most efficient goal merchant, was delivering the goods, as usual, and all looked well.

An inconsistent campaign, however, saw the Manchester club ultimately end in fourth, 12 points behind Clough's title-winning Forest, and make disappointing exits from the cup competitions. The following season, when poor form and results meant the return to Maine Road of 'the prodigal son', Malcolm Allison, the strong foundations Tony Book had built up were swiftly dismantled. A wholesale shake-up, Allison decided, was necessary. Soon after, Channon was placed on the transfer list. Although at the start of 1979/80 the striker was still at the club, he'd missed the season's opener, dropped after criticising Allison for fielding a forward, Barry Silkman, as a sweeper in pre-season. Channon was recalled briefly but the relationship with City's boss was fractured beyond repair. No sooner was September under way than Channon was sold. The fee? £200,000, a whole £100,000 less than City had paid. His destination? The Dell.

Channon appeared for his country just once as a Manchester City player, starting in attack but replaced at half-time by Gordon Hill as England struggled to a 0-0 friendly draw with the Swiss at Wembley on 7 September 1977. It was new supremo Ron Greenwood's first match in charge. He never selected Channon again. After 46 games in which he scored 21 times – his last goal coming from the penalty spot on the June afternoon in 1977 the Scots won 2-1 at Wembley and their fans took home much of the turf as souvenirs – Channon's international days were over. England's failure to qualify for three major international tournaments during Channon's career left him as the most-capped player never to have been named for a World Cup or European Championship squad.

When Channon went back to Southampton they were now in the First Division, having finally ended their four-year exile, the filling in a Bolton-Tottenham promotion sandwich at the end of 1977/78. There, during what would be another three-year stint at the south-coast club, he would soon team up with Keegan, The Dell also the somewhat surprising new dwelling for the England captain coming home from his European adventure the following summer. It was Keegan who, in the mid-70s, had once told an *On the Ball* audience he considered Channon 'the best striker in the world'.

A few months earlier, on 17 March 1979, McMenemy had guided his troops to Wembley again, Saints losing the League Cup Final 3-2 to Clough's Forest, the first club to successfully defend the trophy. Only two players that figured that afternoon remained from the 1976 FA Cup Final starting line-up – David Peach and Nick Holmes – a clear indication of how ruthlessly the Geordie 'nice guy' McMenemy had transformed the squad in an effort to revive the club's fortunes. It was the two survivors – Peach and Holmes – who were on the scoresheet in the defeat.

Channon might have missed out on that encounter with Clough, but, over the years, had numerous often notorious confrontations with him in the ITV studios, the pair performing as pundits during coverage of the 1982 and 1986 World Cup finals. It was during the latter tournament in Mexico, with Clough still holding the reins at the City Ground and Channon now retired after a short period with Southampton's sworn enemies, Portsmouth, that the duo enjoyed a humorous off-field meeting before the television cameras.

Channon had an easygoing manner, but was as opinionated about football as the best of them. Including Clough. Typically passionate in his belief that England, going forward, needed to get more bodies in the box, Channon, with his unmistakable West Country accent, insisted to Clough after the national side's inept start to the competition, 'The Irish have done it, the French do it, the West Germans do it. We don't.' To which a quick-thinking Clough, recalling the Cole Porter lyric to the old song 'Let's Do It', retorted wittily with, 'Even educated bees do it.' It might not exactly have been TV gold – Clough had mistakenly exchanged 'bees' for Porter's 'fleas' as well – but it still had host Brian Moore giggling away.

Moore once said that Channon had 'a soft burr in his voice that would not be out of place in *The Archers*'. He also had an amusing talent for mispronunciation of certain footballers' names, most notably England's Gary Lineker, variously referred to by Channon as 'Linacre' and 'Lyneacre'. During one ITV preview show for the 1986 World Cup, the tournament where Lineker was to really make his name on the international stage, Channon was in full flow about the prospects for Bobby Robson's side when Moore quipped that – never mind the football – 'I think we've got a month to get you to say Lineker properly for a start.' A running joke was born.

Channon never did get it right. He didn't even attempt to. 'Channon is a Muppet' was the message on one Scottish supporter's homemade banner the day at Wembley in 1977 the striker scored his final England goal. It wasn't intended as a compliment. Yet just like those loveable furry puppets, Channon was an entertainer with a style uniquely his own. And, whether on the grassy platform of a football pitch or under the bright lights of a TV studio, he was one, too, who usually left the bulk of those who watched him feeling all the happier for having done so.

7–13 September 1974

After Women's Lib, Player's Lib. Never before have so many footballers complained about their money and the conditions of their trade. Here, Brian Clough pinpoints the main problems and suggests a few answers …

PLAYER'S LIB? I'M ALL FOR IT

PLAYERS in revolt. Players refusing to sign new contracts. Players asking for transfers. Players picking up their cards. Far more than the game itself, these have been the issues of football – and all of this following the official report on the clash between footballers and their clubs filed by the Commission on Industrial Relations.

Let's get it straight. There is no rebellion among professional footballers. They know they have to earn their bread and butter, and the caviar, by booting a ball about.

But that's not to say there aren't a lot of problems in the game today, particularly the way players are now demanding their true worth in pounds and pence from the people who employ them.

We're getting a new breed of player coming into the game today, blokes who a few years ago, when the stakes weren't quite as high, would have gone on to university and played football in their spare time.

Players like Duncan McKenzie, my new signing from Nottingham Forest and £250,000 worth of player if ever there was. If he hadn't been coaxed into the game by the big rewards, he would be in a top job in industry with a degree behind him by now. And players like George Eastham, who ten years ago became the hero of Player's Lib by testing the conditions of a footballer's employment in the High Court, and won.

The problem is that, 15 or 20 years ago, when players still laboured under the maximum wage, the game didn't attract intelligent blokes who could make a fortune elsewhere.

Clubs took advantage of this. Players then weren't well-educated enough to stand up to a tough-talking manager, or the elderly businessman who held the club purse strings. They accepted their lot and took what they could get.

Not any more.

At Nottingham Forest 24-year-old Duncan McKenzie was chosen for England's close-season tour and promised to be a star of British football. He'd put his A-levels away for a career in football, and as a striker he knew that he only had six or seven years left in the game.

So he asked for more money. And when he didn't get it, he had the courage to walk out. I am not criticising Forest – they offered McKenzie what they believed to be a good wage – but I admire the player's strength of character in being prepared to walk out on his career over a principle.

There is no rule which says that a man cannot ask for more money. If a bloke working in one factory thinks he can get more at another he has every right to take a better-paid job. In the entertainment world, it's established practice to hold out for the highest bidder. So why not footballers?

If a lad is getting £60 a week and he thinks he's worth £200 – and I'm not saying these are the figures in McKenzie's case – who can say he's bigheaded and wrong to try to get what he can? If he says he has six or seven years to earn a few bob before his main asset – his skill with a football – is finished, then I'm right behind him.

So I bought McKenzie and I'm convinced he'll pay Leeds back every penny of that enormous transfer fee and do himself a bit of good, too. But the first thing I told him, when I met him to sign on the dotted line, was, 'If you ever attempt to walk out on me, if you ever want your cards from Leeds, don't bother trying to walk back in.'

I always challenge any player that if he can find a better manager, a better club, to look after him, to go out and find them.

Another uneasy aspect of the McKenzie transfer is that he is in dispute about whether he can claim five per cent of the transfer fee – that's about £12,500. The rule states that if a player asks for a transfer he doesn't get his cut, but if the club instigate the transfer, he does.

What a farcical state of affairs. Who is to draw a line between a player wanting to move and a player put on sale by his club? If a respected player is stuck in the reserve team, who can blame him for wanting to move? Yet if he does, he gets nothing out of his cattle-market fee. I say all players transferred should get the five per cent, and good luck to them.

But that's only a detail of the transfer system. It's the system itself which the Commission on Industrial Relations says needs an overhaul. If a player's contract expires, the Commission's report says he should have the freedom to move to any club he wants, just as anyone in employment can move freely between jobs when they're not tied by a contract. As things stand, a player is stuck with a club until he is put on the market and another club coughs up the appropriate transfer fee.

Only one man has challenged this to date, and that was George Eastham, now assistant manager at Stoke, who was in dispute with his club, Newcastle, and wanted to move. When he took his case to court he got a ruling that the present system was 'an unreasonable restraint' of trade and he joined Arsenal without any problems.

But although the League has introduced a few new rules since then, allowing a player various roads of appeal, the law has never really been tested again. We can be pretty sure that the way things stand at the moment, more players might fight the system. My view is that the present system can be changed too much, because, although a big change might free players from the feudal system now operating, football itself would be the loser.

In Holland, players can move from club to club at the end of their contracts without transfer fees. Now all the top players are cornered in a couple of big clubs – Ajax and Feyenoord.

The same thing would happen here. Within months, the rich clubs would be putting out feelers and luring the best players in with offers they can't refuse. This would weaken our leagues by making them less competitive.

Somehow we must keep the transfer system but allow players more freedom at the same time.

But the important thing to recognise is that we are only talking about a lucky few players who make the headlines in six-figure deals. Underneath the cream, there's a vast army of players who don't own boutiques or run Lamborghinis, whose main interest is getting a few quid together to pay the mortgage.

Only 12 per cent of First Division players earn more than £100 a week. At the other end of the scale, 33 per cent of Fourth Division players earn less than £35 a week, and 11 per cent under £25 a week. And these are official figures from the Professional Players' Association.

Which is why a 29-year-old lad who played for Reading last season, Percy Freeman, went into his club in the summer and picked up his cards. He was earning £29.18 a week. Now he earns £60 a week as a scaffolder.

'When I told my mates what I was earning,' said Freeman, 'they didn't believe me. They thought every footballer picked up at least £100 a week.'

It just goes to show that there's another side to the glamour life of footballers, other than the one painted in the papers every week.

Football is not yet a millionaire's playground. And like Duncan McKenzie, I don't blame any player for getting as much as he can out of it, if he's got the ability, the courage, and the brains.

14–20 September 1974

In the south of England this Saturday, Southampton take on neighbours Portsmouth, and Exeter play their Fourth Division companions Torquay. So this week Brian Clough turns away from the big guns and focuses on the twilight clubs of the south coast, including his old team Brighton ...

ALL FOOTBALL'S GHOST TOWNS NEED IS SPIRIT

THINK of football in Britain and you think of clubs like Liverpool, Leeds, Celtic, Wolves and Spurs. The power and the glory has rested with a handful of clubs who take their football seriously.

But there is a curious strip of country which for years hasn't felt the squeeze of an excited crowd on the terraces, the smell of the big match – a ribbon of seven clubs along the south coast from Brighton to Plymouth, two in the Second Division, the other five struggling to fight their way out of the bottom two divisions.

There is a different attitude to football in the south. There is more money, higher employment, more sunshine, and they don't seem to bother about football as much as the Glaswegian or Geordie. I even know of a large comprehensive school in Sussex which doesn't include football on the boys' curriculum. When I arrived at Brighton last autumn, the ground had more of an atmosphere of an old pensioners' rest home than a professional football club.

But Carlisle United have shown how a small club – given the right management and inspiration – can snap out of its daydream and find success. There is a fair smattering of youthful, go-ahead management in the south now, and this could be the season when the 'south-coast syndrome' takes a beating and these clubs awake from their sleeping sickness.

There is no better place for this to start than at Brighton. At the Goldstone Ground, with Peter Taylor and myself in charge, we cleared out most of the existing playing staff and signed 12 new players in nine months. Today the club is starting almost completely afresh, and with Peter Taylor I believe they have a better chance than most of shooting into the Second Division this season. When they beat Malcolm Allison's Crystal Palace in the opening match of the season everything pointed to a good campaign. Taylor and I were in management together for ten years, and in that time a great deal of rubbish was talked about him. People called him the devoted servant, the universal number two. In fact, Taylor was never my assistant. We were a unit; we shared the job completely. He is the best judge of a player in football today, he is as hard as nails and compassionate at the same time, and these are the essential qualities of a good football manager. I believe he will set alight that enormous area around Brighton, where there are literally millions of people dying to see a good game of football.

Further along the coast, at Bournemouth, is a good example of a south-coast club that always promised big things and never got anywhere. For 46 years Bournemouth have laboured in the Third Division. For a while, former manager John Bond looked as if he was going to work the spell, but when they finished third in the Third Division in 1972, narrowly missing promotion, it was a blow which took the sting out of their challenge. Last season they only managed a half-way place.

Further west, Torquay and Exeter meet in the Devon derby on Saturday, a match which will probably attract Torquay's biggest gate of the season. But the two clubs have always been also-rans in league football.

Last season Torquay finished 16th and Exeter tenth in the Fourth Division. I can't help thinking it would need a Guy Fawkes in the manager's chair to set these clubs alight. It is a thankless task in which the trick is not only to buy the players you need, but to also find the right mix for success when there is an overdraft in the bank and only a few thousand drift in to watch every week.

Mind you, Malcolm Musgrove, who has only been there a few months, is a young, experienced man who understands the game inside out. He could be the inspiration they need. He came to Torquay from the coaching staff at Manchester United, so I doubt that he will want to spend too long in the depths of the league.

At Plymouth, 17th in Division Three last season, Tony Waiters is another young manager who could shake the town. Last year he took the side to the brink of a Wembley final when they beat Birmingham on the way to the League Cup semi-final. Then Manchester City put them out, leaving Waiters, whose name was seriously talked about in connection with the England manager's job, in a good position, with an enormous football-hungry population to tap.

Southampton and Portsmouth, the two Second Division teams along the southern coastline, have the best chances of making it into Division One.

There was a time, 25 years ago, when the name Portsmouth would have any supporter bolting down his Saturday dinner to catch an early bus to the local ground; when they won the league championship two years running. Recently, a lot of money has been spent at Fratton Park to improve the playing staff, but for a decade they have failed to attract attention and last year they finished half-way down the Second Division.

Southampton are in a different boat. They dropped into the Second Division this season, victims of the new three-up, three-down rule which, incidentally, I think is the best league reform for years. In the close season, manager Lawrie McMenemy was bubbling with confidence, saying his team was ready and determined to bounce straight back into the First Division.

People have been saying that this season is going to be a testing time for me. I suggest it's going to be a make-or-break season for Lawrie McMenemy, because he came to Southampton last year and they went down. Unless they hit a winning streak early this season, they are in great danger of sliding into the bottom half of the table and losing all that heady momentum that kept their heads proud when they were relegated.

The most important asset at any club should be the players – but a manager is responsible for his players, for buying and selling them, and for the way he uses them on the pitch. These south 'ghost' teams need, more than anything, managerial inspiration, someone to detonate the interest of their supporters and generate effort in the players.

I *want* these teams to do well and find success, because I want names like Carlisle and Luton bursting through like a breath of fresh air into the First Division. It's good for the game because it stimulates the interest and competition on which the game thrives.

* * * *

In 1974/75 Southampton and Portsmouth were competing in the same division for the first time since 1966, when the Saints, with Martin Chivers scoring 30 of their 85 league goals, went marching in to the runners-up spot in the Second Division behind Manchester City, while Pompey languished in mid-table. Their clash on 14 September took place at the end of a turbulent few days for the Fratton Park club.

On 6 September Portsmouth had 'suspended' manager John Mortimore, offering the ex-Chelsea player the job of scouting for the club, with Ron Tindall (the man Mortimore had replaced in the spring of the previous year) taking over until a new boss was installed. Chairman John Deacon, a Southampton-based property man, who'd assumed full control of Portsmouth in May 1973 after joining the board several months earlier, had invested heavily in backing his promise that he would get the club out of the Second Division within three years. Peter Marinello – 'the new George Best' – from Arsenal, Ron Davies (Southampton), Phil Roberts (Bristol Rovers), Paul Went (Fulham) and Malcolm Manley (Leicester) were all big-money signings, with Deacon believing they'd form the foundation of a side that would, as of old, be rivalling the game's reigning giants. But the cash injection failed to bring the desired results. The big-name players flattered to deceive and, rather than a return to the glory days the chairman and the fans were hoping for, the club stagnated in the lower reaches of the second tier. To make matters worse, losses of £167,000 were revealed.

On 'suspending' Mortimore, Deacon declared, 'We feel that we must get a great manager to get a proper return for our investment. I was very depressed last season when I read phrases like "the straw man of Pompey".' The 'great manager' Deacon wanted was none other than the one-time Southampton right-back Sir Alf Ramsey. However, it proved a fruitless chase. Given the chop by England earlier in the year, Ramsey wasn't yet ready to come back into the game, he said, and couldn't be tempted. Deacon's offer got refused.

Instead, it was a Scot that took up residence in the Portsmouth hotseat. The day before the derby clash, former Liverpool forward Ian St John was announced as Mortimore's successor, Portsmouth agreeing to pay Scottish League Division One club Motherwell compensation for their manager's services. St John, after just one term in charge at Fir Park, had impressed Leeds sufficiently for the West Yorkshire club to consider him as a possible replacement for Don Revie, but even though Clough got the nod ahead of him, St John was still keen to try his luck south of the border.

It was his old Anfield chief Bill Shankly who convinced him to give it a go at Fratton Park. Lured by Deacon's promises of a substantial budget for fresh personnel and the plan to build a brand-new stadium on the edge of town (neither of which materialised), St John was excited by the challenge at the club – at least until the reality hit soon after. 'I had the worst group of players you have ever seen in your life,' St John reflected years later, and 'the worst job in football'.

As it turned out, the game at The Dell, St John's first in charge, was a fairly memorable affair – for the wrong reasons. Won 2-1 by the home side, with both goals from Peter Osgood, the encounter, watched by 19,361, was marred when a fan ran on to the pitch and pushed Welsh referee Clive Thomas. The following Monday, Thomas, the man who less than two years later would officiate at Wembley on the most famous day in Southampton's history, took out a summons alleging common assault against his aggressor.

Saturday had been an ugly day throughout the Football League both on and off the field. A trainload of Portsmouth fans were arrested at Southampton station prior to the game, whilst fighting had taken place in Birmingham (before West Brom's match with Manchester United, also in the Second Division) and at Stamford Bridge where Arsenal were the visitors in the First Division.

At Turf Moor, as Burnley got the better of Leeds 2-1 on the afternoon that the Bob Lord Stand was officially opened by then Leader of the Opposition Edward Heath, the home side's centre-forward Ray Hankin and Leeds's Scottish centre-half Gordon McQueen were both dismissed, a double sending-off a real rarity in those days of relative leniency from referees. With the score tied at 1-1 (Fletcher scoring for Burnley, Lorimer for the visitors), Hankin was impeded while jumping to head a cross and Welsh winger Leighton James converted the resulting spot kick for what would prove to be the winning goal. Soon after, Hankin, breaking through from the halfway line and heading for the Leeds goal, was halted when McQueen, 'like a page boy clutching a bride's train' according to *The Observer's* Peter Corrigan, took hold of his opponent's shirt; when Hankin spun round and swung a punch, the inevitable quickly followed – with he and McQueen having already been booked, both received their marching orders. Rather amusingly, when interviewed in a Burnley matchday programme a little later that season and asked, 'Who is the best defender you have faced?' Hankin nominated McQueen. 'He is strong, tough and difficult to get past,' the burly striker said.

Presumably bygones remained bygones, nonetheless, when the two became teammates in 1976 after Jimmy Armfield took Hankin to Elland Road for a fee of £172,000 – by some strange coincidence, Hankin putting pen to paper on the same date, 1 September, that McQueen had signed for Leeds from St Mirren four years earlier – though as McQueen was to lamp his own keeper David Harvey in an FA Cup tie versus Manchester City in January 1978, who knows?

McQueen's sending off that Saturday in September 1974 only added to Leeds's troubles. It was the first fixture for the West Yorkshire club since the sacking of Clough earlier that week, and the defeat (which, with Burnley hitting the woodwork three times, could easily have been by a wider margin) left them staying firmly in 19th place, on the edge of the relegation zone. Significantly, assistant manager Maurice Lindley, chief coach Syd Owen and suspended skipper Billy Bremner picked the squad for the match and none of the three Clough signings – McKenzie, McGovern and O'Hare – were in the party.

By the end of the campaign, under Armfield's guidance, the Leeds ship was steered into much safer waters and sailing higher seas once more. Leeds finished the season ninth in the table as well as reaching the European Cup Final. But, there in Paris, what should have been their finest hour turned into 90 minutes of total frustration on the pitch and a night of shame off it. Against Bayern Munich, the English club had by far the greater percentage of the game; they were denied a goal for a questionable 'offside' decision – sparking unrest on the terraces from the Leeds fans – and should have had two penalties for blatant offences by Beckenbauer, yet lost 2-0. 'I am even more convinced now that Bayern Munich must be the most fortunate European champions ever,' Armfield reflected shortly afterwards in *Shoot!* Still, St John must have looked on from a distance with envy, almost certainly wishing he was at the Elland Road helm, overseeing a side crammed with internationals at the Parc des Princes rather than on the south coast with what he later described as 'a skid row club', Portsmouth ending the campaign 17th in the Second Division (one place below Nottingham Forest, managed by a certain Brian Clough).

Of all the south-coast clubs, it was Lawrie McMenemy's Saints that came out best-placed in the league, Mick Channon's 19 goals helping them to 13th spot. Yet despite also reaching the final of the Texaco Cup – losing 3-1 over two legs to top-flight Newcastle – it was a poor return for a side of whom much better was expected.

Brighton, too, endured a torrid time of it, getting knocked out of the FA Cup at the third-round stage by amateurs Leatherhead, and coming closer to dropping into the Fourth Division than shooting into the Second. One of a trio of southern clubs narrowly missing the drop – along with Southend in 18th and Aldershot 20th

– Albion ended a lowly 19th, and Peter Taylor in sole charge was no nearer setting alight to the area than he had been alongside Clough.

That trio survived at the expense of Bournemouth who were relegated in 21st (the Cherries dispensing with the services of Trevor Hartley, the league's youngest manager at 27, on 2 January), while at the top end of the table, Plymouth Argyle enjoyed a much happier season, sealing promotion to the Second Division, runners-up a point behind Blackburn Rovers.

In the fourth tier, neither Exeter (ninth) nor Torquay (14th) pulled up any trees, with honours remaining even between the clubs in the two derby clashes; on 14 September, in the game at Plainmoor, they shared four goals, while the rematch at St James Park on Boxing Day was anything but a Christmas cracker, ending goalless.

So while Clough was no doubt sincere in his wish for their success, for the twilight clubs of the south coast it was still dusk and, indeed, it would be some time yet before any of them cured their sleeping sickness and awoke to a bright new dawn.

21–27 September 1974

In a season when the newspapers have been packed with tales of football hooliganism, Brian Clough turns his attention to a more pleasant aspect of watching football. The scarves, pennants and stickers that add colour to the game – the souvenir boom, which is bounding ahead …

THE POWER OF THE
NAUGHTY NIGHTIES

NOT so long ago, the football fan turned up to see his side play with a striped woollen scarf coiled around his neck (knitted by grandma on dark winter evenings), a wooden rattle in his hand (painted in the shed with some of dad's old gloss paint) and a couple of rosettes pinned to his raincoat (bought for a bob from the street seller outside the ground).

Today, football souvenirs are big business. Most league clubs have their own shops built under the stand, selling everything from tracksuits, ballpoint pens and vacuum flasks to penknives, watches and swimsuits – all embossed in the team's crest and colours. Arsenal lead the field with six shops, one open all through the week and five open inside the ground on matchdays. My shop at Leeds is doing a roaring trade, too, in football paraphernalia.

We've come a long way since my days as a young supporter, when I used to borrow my dad's season ticket to watch Middlesbrough. I think football clubs used to think they were some sort of secret service which had nothing to do with people at all. They opened the gates on Saturday afternoons and waited for the fans to file in, and if you were lucky you could buy a cardboard cup of scalding tea at half-time as the rain dripped down your collar.

Today, clubs are getting used to the idea that their supporters *belong* – that without the fans there wouldn't be any football – and these souvenir shops are a first-class link between club and fan, with the clubs getting the profits into the bargain.

Ninety per cent of the rosettes, badges, scarves, pennants, and all the rest in the supporters' supermarkets come from a firm in north London run by Arthur and Ron Coffer.

If you want ten dozen rosettes in purple and green or a couple of thousand specially minted enamel badges, the Coffers are the blokes to get on to. They have their own design department producing the latest football fads five days a week, while Arthur and Ron keep their eyes open for new ideas from abroad to adapt for the British market.

Latest additions are imitation leather-covered tankards and enamel-buckled belts, both carrying the club's crest and both inspired by American baseball souvenirs, and football identity bracelets, a popular idea in Germany.

'There's a big demand for the better quality, more expensive goods,' says Arthur Coffer. 'Like the classy covered tankards, which cost about 85p. I think in the past we have sold things too cheaply because we didn't think there would be a demand.'

You would be surprised where some of the demand comes from. The Gunners shop at Arsenal's ground, run by former Welsh international goalkeeper Jack Kelsey, does a nice line in ladies' nighties and men's underpants, all carrying the Arsenal badge. 'We started the nighties as a gimmick,' says Jack Kelsey. 'Men bought them for their wives or girlfriends as a joke. Then we found women coming into the shop to buy them for themselves.

'We run the shop here only at a small profit,' says Kelsey. 'What we are really trying to do is encourage support. A father might buy some Arsenal kit for his son, so the son starts to think red and white, and we've got a fan for life. Jimmy Hill started the idea at Coventry more than ten years ago, and the whole business has exploded since then.'

The souvenir business is a good pointer for the changing character of the football fan. Rattles, for instance, which used to be rammed inside every ten-year-old boy's Christmas stocking, are seldom seen now, and many clubs have banned them as offensive weapons – a sad commentary on the state of some of our alleged supporters these days.

But rosettes still sell like hot tea on a chilly terrace. The Coffers produce more than 100,000 a season in the colours of every league club, in their alternative colours for away games, and with a trophy pinned to the centre for cup matches.

But the rosette, like chewing gum, doesn't last. 'People tend to throw them away after a few games,' says Arthur Coffer. The sellers themselves reckon they get rid of most of their rosettes one hour before a match, but he'll be selling the winning team's colours for half an hour afterwards as well. Mind you, they don't sell any post-match souvenirs of the losing team … the sweepers-up find quite a few of them torn up on the terraces.

The Coffers' nightmare is that a club might suddenly decide to change their colours without informing them. 'I know one shop manager,' says Arthur Coffer, 'who took delivery of a new consignment of rosettes, then read in the evening paper that his team had changed their colours. He had to chuck the lot away.'

Mr Coffer had to get busy recently when he heard that Leeds United were playing in a new strip for away games – a vivid yellow with blue-and-white stripes on the sleeves. Now he's turning out some new rosettes to meet demand.

The biggest seller at the moment is the satin scarf with the name of your team printed on it; they're so smooth and sleek you could get away with one at a wedding. But continental ideas are catching on fast.

Cotton caps with the teams' colours are selling well. And metal badges are becoming the new status symbol. All over Europe boys collect these miniature enamel pin-sticker badges as if they are diamonds. When I was in Spain with Derby County last year, I had to carry a pocketful around with me to dish out everywhere I went. And in Germany, you sometimes see 60 or 70 of them stuck into a supporter's hat. 'They're going to be very big here,' says Arthur Coffer, 'and I think the klaxon will make its mark, too. In Germany, there are thousands of them in every stadium, and just as we've adopted the continental habit of whistling our disapproval instead of booing, we'll soon be sounding our klaxons instead of clapping.'

Despite the enormous range of goods, the Coffers' business makes a profit only in its dealings with popular clubs – teams like Liverpool, Leeds, Manchester United, Celtic, Everton, and the London clubs. 'Everybody is talking about a super league,' says Arthur Coffer, 'but to me it already exists. These top clubs sell more souvenirs than the rest put together.'

While the clubs fill their coffers and the Coffers fill the clubs with their gear, the street corner rosette seller still survives. Often he's somebody like a docker, whose wife stitches the rosettes together during the week on her sewing machine. And on Saturday he makes for the ground and earns himself a few bob.

It doesn't matter who makes the souvenirs, people love to *belong* to something. And, if a football club can nourish that need by selling supporters scarves and bags and mementoes, it's strengthening the link between the supporter who pays his money at the turnstiles and the players who perform on the pitch. What the club – the players and the manager – must do, is to make sure that what the supporter sees is worthy of his loyalty.

That means playing football, keeping it clean, giving 90 minutes' worth of honest effort and skill in return for the fan's support.

23–29 November 1974

Last year, as manager of Brighton, Brian Clough watched his team eclipsed 4-0 by 'unknown' amateurs Walton in the first round of the FA Cup. Other managers will perhaps suffer that agony during Saturday's first-round matches. Here, Clough looks at great cup upsets of the past and examines the anatomy of a giant-killer ...

THE CRAZY SCORELINE THAT TURNS FOOTBALL MANAGERS GREY

ON 3 May 1975, two teams, 100,000 fans and millions of television viewers will spend 90 minutes indulging in that annual carnival of football, the FA Cup Final.

The bookies are already laying odds on who the two teams might be – teams like Leeds, Liverpool, Everton and Manchester City. But the FA Cup is more than a lavishly presented showpiece at Wembley. Below the tip of the iceberg, it is a unique competition that stirs everybody's imagination.

In the Cup there can be no favourites. For every one of the 450 teams who enter – from Nuneaton Borough in the Southern League to Newcastle – glory could be just around the corner. Not a year passes without a crazy scoreline which turns the leagues topsy-turvy and a few well-known managers grey with despair.

By this Saturday, when the first-round proper gets under way, the teams will include Third and Fourth Division clubs, plus a hopeful smattering of non-league teams. But somewhere in the draw, destiny has carved a special path for a couple of struggling clubs.

Not since 1902, when Southampton, then in the Southern League, lost 2-1 in a replay against Sheffield United, has a club from outside the First and Second Divisions reached the cup final. But there have been some close shaves …

Four clubs from the Third Division have reached the semi-final stage – Millwall in 1937, Port Vale in 1954, York a year later, and Norwich in 1959. And those last two teams took their opponents to a replay before they lost the chance of a Wembley spot.

Ronnie Ashman was captain and left-back for Norwich City during their mind-boggling run in 1959. Along with Terry Bly and Bobby Brennan, his name was on the lips of every football supporter in Britain until Luton finally put paid to their chances in their semi-final replay at Hillsborough, Sheffield. Norwich beat Sheffield United, Cardiff, Tottenham and Manchester United on the way to the semi-final.

'We were a struggling side at the foot of the Third Division when the cup rounds began,' remembers Ashman. 'Then the cup caught us like a disease. We started winning and everything seemed to go right.

'Our confidence rocketed sky-high. Manager Archie Macaulay gave us precise instructions before each match. We knew all about the opposition and he told us to go out and harass and chase them everywhere, not give them a chance.'

Ashman is now manager of Third Division Grimsby, and every time the Cup comes round, he gets that burning feeling that this might be his year again.

'In the Cup it's always going to be somebody's year. It doesn't matter how brilliant the First Division teams are, there will always be freak results.'

The greatest giant-killing act since Norwich came when Colchester, bobbing around the top half of the Fourth Division, took on Leeds, then First Division leaders, in 1971. Under the shrewd and experienced management of Dick Graham, who had actually played with Leeds manager Don Revie when they were at Leicester, Colchester never regarded themselves as a lost cause.

'I never doubted that we could win,' says Graham. 'Every team, every player, even the greatest, has weaknesses, and I set out to find and exploit them.

'I decided that Leeds were vulnerable to the high, old-fashioned cross, and in the two weeks before the match I impressed this on the players. I saw that they were nicely relaxed and took them away to a Clacton hotel before the game. I can honestly say that by the time we kicked off I was confident we would get a result.'

The rest is history. Colchester scored two early goals, both as a result of high crosses, and then they took a 3-0 lead. Leeds pulled back two goals and Dick Graham describes the final five minutes as 'absolutely agony. I said a little prayer and it worked. I believe many small clubs try to beat First Division teams by putting on the rough stuff, kicking them off the park. That's not the way to do it. We beat Leeds by pure football because we believed in our own ability.

'A lot of small clubs field former First Division stars who are far from finished. We had, for instance, Ray Crawford, who played for England in the early 60s. And when these players find themselves playing against a top club again, something happens. I think it becomes a matter of pride that they turn on their best form to prove that they still have it in them. Crawford was magnificent in our game against Leeds, scoring two goals.

'In general, I think it is a greater achievement for a Third or Fourth Division club to reach the sixth round of the Cup than it is for a First Division club to make the final at Wembley.'

Dick Graham has seen the Cup from the happy side, as a winner who beat all the odds. But there are two sides to every Cup story. This time last year, as manager of Brighton, I suffered the nightmare of being drawn against a non-league side, Walton & Hersham, in the first round of the Cup. And when we slithered to a 4-0 defeat in the replay, it ranks as the worst 90 minutes I have ever spent on a touchline.

Mine was the agony of a Third Division manager watching the eclipse of his side by a bunch of part-time unknowns from the Surrey stockbroker belt.

This season every First Division manager, as he listens to the draw on the radio, will be praying that his team isn't matched up against a shoestring side, that they won't have to negotiate the famous Yeovil slope, or Colchester's narrow strip of turf. Ask any top manager if he'd rather play Barrow or Burnley, and he'll choose the devil he knows every time.

Football thrives on the fact that it is a game of upset, shock and unpredictability, that the mighty sometimes fall – and mighty hard. And nowhere is it better demonstrated than in the FA Cup.

30 November–6 December 1974

With the footballing public crying out for more goals, Brian Clough's selection of Player of the Month for November is a man who unashamedly says that his job is to find the back of the net in every match. He's bandy, bold, and brash and is never afraid to dive in where the action is thickest. Sometimes known as Supermouth, more often as Supermac, he is Newcastle's Malcolm Macdonald …

SUPERMAC – THE MAN WITH THE KILLER TOUCH

MALCOLM Macdonald is the best centre-forward in England. That's my opinion, despite Don Revie ignoring him when he selected his 24-strong squad for the England team which played Czechoslovakia last month.

If I had the opportunity to select an England side today, Macdonald, with his skill, spirit and power, would be in it, playing his heart out where it really matters – in the penalty area.

I feel Macdonald has been left out of the reckoning because of indifferent top-level performances in the past – an apparent lack of big-match temperament. But has he really been given a chance?

From his debut in a 3-0 defeat of Wales at Ninian Park, Cardiff, two years ago, he has played seven times for England. But on four of those occasions he was substitute, thrown on to the pitch in the dying minutes of a game to put some fire into the attack.

In those circumstances, I don't find it surprising that he hasn't done the job he was called up for – to score goals. It simply isn't good enough to disregard a player of Macdonald's quality on the strength of three full international performances.

Macdonald is still only 24 and despite being left out of the squad he has the temperament and character to bounce back. Moreover, Macdonald has an abundance of football's most valued commodity: goalscoring power. His philosophy is simple: goals win matches, goals attract crowds, and goals are the lifeblood of the game. And season after season he has thumped them in. A self-appointed executioner of First Division defences.

Before this season started, Macdonald had chalked up a total of 109 league goals, a very high total in this era of rock-hard defences. This season he has been banging them in with that lethal left boot at the customary rate for Newcastle.

It may not please football purists to know that Macdonald believes his job is to score goals, and that the other ten players in his team are there to help him do it. But I believe that if he can get his name on the scoresheet as often as he does, there's no argument.

This man lives, sleeps and breathes goals, and as I scored a few in my own playing days, I know there's no greater feeling than the joy of putting the ball in the net. In today's football a centre-forward is lucky to have two or three clear chances in the whole 90 minutes, but Macdonald hangs round the penalty box like a trigger-happy gunman in a western, waiting for his chance to strike. And he seldom disappoints.

His sharpness and his ability to be in the right place at the right time remind me of Jimmy Greaves at his poaching best. But Macdonald has other qualities. He has the strength of a front-row forward in rugby and he uses this force, fairly and squarely, to get into goalscoring situations. And when he sniffs goals, he lets fly.

A friendly that Newcastle played against St Johnstone a few years ago best illustrates Macdonald's hunger for goals. As the game started, he noticed that the St Johnstone goalkeeper wasn't in position, so when the ball was side-footed to him at kick-off, he belted the ball 50 yards into the net.

I believe that, nicely balanced as Don Revie's team is, he needs that extra aggression in attack which Macdonald could offer – that killer touch which makes all the difference. And it's typical of Macdonald's confidence that when he heard Revie had left him out he still blew his own trumpet. 'Not only did I expect to be in the squad,' he said, 'I thought I would play. I still think I'm the best in the country.'

Fighting talk for a lad who learned the hard way. Macdonald, a Londoner, wasn't spotted by a top scout when he was barely out of nappies. He played for non-league Barnet and then Tonbridge before Fulham noticed his ability and signed him on.

He maintains that the London club didn't explore his talents before they sold him to Luton (then in the Third Division), where he soon found his feet and caused a good number of defenders to fear him.

When, inevitably, the offers came in from First Division clubs, it was Manchester United who had first option. But managerial upheavals at Old Trafford forced United to drop out of the race, and Joe Harvey of Newcastle tore off the biggest cheque he has ever handed over in his life – for £180,000 – to buy Macdonald. I say that Joe wouldn't have been robbed if he'd paid twice that figure.

Luton boss Harry Haslam admits that selling Macdonald was forced upon him by the sheer economic circumstances within the club.

Since then Macdonald has rewarded the Tynesiders' faith with consistent displays of goalscoring which have earned him the title Supermac (a nickname he accepted without a blush!).

I believe Malcolm Macdonald's international football career is far from over, for two reasons. First, the player himself insists that he doesn't want to be just a good club player, he wants to play for England more than anything else in the game.

Second, if I know Malcolm Macdonald, being left out of the England squad is going to get his back up. He'll be out to score so many goals in the next few months that Don Revie will *have* to pick him.

* * * *

If Don Revie ever read *TVTimes*, he didn't show it: all of Clough's loud entreaties to his fellow ex-Leeds United boss for Malcolm Macdonald's selection in the national side went unheeded; after missing out against the Czechs, Macdonald was also omitted for England's next game, another European Championship qualifier, at home to Portugal on 20 November 1974. He was sorely missed. Despite dominating the match against ultra-defensive opponents, England failed to make their possession count and after a disjointed performance on a rain-heavy surface trooped off the Wembley pitch to boos from the home contingent in the 84,461 crowd following a goalless draw.

It wasn't only Clough who felt that Macdonald warranted a place spearheading the England front line; the national press were also clamouring for his inclusion. Relatively small for a conventional number nine, just 5ft 8in – as a boy Macdonald suffered curvature of the spine and legs so bandy he'd have gained height if he'd had them straightened – what the stocky Londoner lacked in stature he more than made up for in electric pace and power. Like one of the old-fashioned crash-bang-wallop forwards of former years, he would charge at defences like a battering ram and, though far more than a mere speed merchant, he certainly knew the quickest route to goal. Most importantly, when Macdonald got there, he had an abnormal hunger for hitting it.

Macdonald's explosive style had detonated defences for fun ever since his signing for Newcastle as a 21-year-old in 1971. The legend of 'Supermac' was born almost instantly. On his home debut, he'd made an immediate impact, bagging a hat-trick against Liverpool, before limping off, his head bleeding and missing four front teeth after being clattered by Ray Clemence, with the St James' Park crowd rising to applaud him and the terraces ringing with the chant of 'Supermac, superstar, how many goals have you scored so far?'

He'd had his doubters; in a game obsessed with tactical sophistication and the versatility of players, Macdonald's glaring weaknesses – he was one-footed, he couldn't head, he was too greedy, his critics said – would be shown up against the tight-marking well-drilled defences of the First Division. But, like Clough before him, the brash Macdonald held an unflinching self-belief in his own ability and was quite unafraid to lay his reputation on the line. Telling the press that his target in his first season on Tyneside was 30 goals, he was also tagged as 'Supermouth'. But it was a target that he hit. If, in subsequent years, occasionally failing to deliver on his own promises laid the striker open to widespread mockery – most notably following the 1974 FA Cup Final – his shoulders were broad enough to bear it.

Macdonald worked on a theory of percentages; if he was going to be a 30-goals-a-season forward, he had, he reflected years later, 'sense enough to realise that I had to miss a number of times for every goal I scored'. That didn't stop him worrying 'like mad' if he wasted any opportunity. 'If I come off the field having scored one and missed one, I feel sick,' he once confessed during his playing days. 'If the team wins and I haven't scored, I still feel sick.' Not everything he touched turned to gold – or goals. Macdonald readily admitted that 'if there had been a league table for the men who missed the highest number of chances, I'd have been at the top!' More often than not, though, the theory worked well.

A deadly finisher with foot (predominantly the left) or head and from all angles and distances, Macdonald, as the *Shoot!* annual of 1981 put it, usually 'scored goals in the grand manner'. It wasn't his style to nick them from one or two yards out. So clinical was Macdonald from even the longest range that, according to the writer, 'Goalkeepers twitched in nervous anticipation of a thunderbolt when he was within 30 yards of their netting.'

By March 1975, he'd got 27 in all competitions that season, including two in a game with Liverpool on a chilly Wednesday night the month before when Newcastle gained a measure of revenge for their cup final mauling, steamrollering the Reds on the way to a 4-1 victory at St James' Park (though the Geordies were again the victims of another Liverpool-inflicted slaughter not long after, losing 4-0 at Anfield in the reverse league fixture the following month). With England due to face West Germany in a friendly on 12 March, even Revie found it impossible to ignore Macdonald's claims for another chance on the international stage, the striker finally getting the call for what was the 100th full international at Wembley.

But if Revie had at last bowed to journalistic pressure, he made sure Macdonald knew he'd done so reluctantly. According to Macdonald, when he arrived at the team hotel, the first thing Revie said to him was that the Newcastle player was only there because the press were demanding it. Macdonald was informed that if he didn't score he would never be picked again. It was, Macdonald considered, 'a really outrageous thing' for Revie to do, but, wisely, that 'Supermouth' remained tight-lipped and he kept it to himself.

On the night, he did score, adding a second on 66 minutes to Colin Bell's first-half strike as England beat the world champions 2-0. But Revie's words to him had stung Macdonald. When Revie repeated them before England's next clash, another European Championship qualifier at home to Cyprus, Macdonald was determined to ram them down the manager's throat. 'I thought: "How dare you, you bastard." I told Alan Ball, and he said: "You just leave it with me." On the day of the game we had a team meeting. At the end, as everybody was leaving, Alan got hold of Mick Channon, Alan Hudson and myself. He quickly related the tale to the other two. He said he had a plan. "Do you know what England's goalscoring record is?" he asked. We all shook our heads. He said: "Willie Hall scored five against Northern Ireland in 1938. Tonight," pointing to me, "this man's going to score six and," pointing to himself and the other two, "we are going to make it happen. Now, are you up for it?"'

They almost did it, as well. After getting his first as early as the second minute when he headed in Hudson's free kick, by the end of the 90 minutes Macdonald had five goals to his name – four with his head and one with that lethal left foot – and an indisputable claim on the match ball. But he'd also had one disallowed for offside and hit the post before the final whistle, too. 'To be honest,' Macdonald admitted post-match, 'I should have had eight goals. I managed to miss three fairly easy chances. But I suppose I can't complain!'

In typical bulldog manner, he'd risen to the occasion and his one-man spectacular was the perfect retort to his critic, the England manager. As he told *The Guardian* in 2010, as the electronic scoreboard above the tunnel at Wembley flashed up: 'Congratulations – Supermac 5 Cyprus 0', the striker's focus turned to Revie. 'There he was in his trenchcoat, head hunched down, hands in his pockets, heading back to the tunnel,' Macdonald said. 'I knew he couldn't hear me, but I pointed at the scoreboard and shouted at him: "Read that and weep, you bastard. Read that and weep."'

Macdonald's strikes against the Germans then Cyprus made him the only player to score six successive England goals. His five-goal feat has not been duplicated since by any English footballer. Although three pre-war players, Howard Vaughton (on his debut), Steve Bloomer and Willie Hall, had previously scored five for England, Macdonald was the first, and remains the only, player to do so in a competitive international against a non-British country, and at the Empire Stadium, too. Yet they proved to be his last-ever goals for his country. And he never played for England at Wembley again.

After featuring in the return match with Cyprus in Limassol (Revie's side mustering a 1-0 victory), the goalless Home Internationals clash at Windsor Park with Northern Ireland, a 2-1 friendly win in Basle (when Macdonald came on as sub), then the 2-1 away defeat in late October 1975 to Czechoslovakia in a crucial European Championship qualifier (England losing for a first time under Revie), Macdonald played his 14th and last international before 60,000 in Lisbon's Stadio José Alvalade as England drew 1-1 against Portugal on 19 November 1975, and their European qualification hopes were put to bed. On 76 minutes, the 25-year-old was replaced by Allan Clarke.

The following summer, after five years in black and white and 257 appearances that saw him score 30, 24, 28, 32, then 24 times (an incredible return of 138 goals in total), Macdonald flew the Magpies's nest, becoming new Arsenal boss Terry Neill's first signing, the Londoners handing over a slightly bizarre-looking £333,333 for his services. Joe Harvey, the man who took Macdonald to the North East, reckoned the striker's mere presence in the Newcastle side added a few thousand to every home gate. But big gates and goal returns weren't enough for Gordon Lee, who took over from Harvey in the summer of 1975. Big egos were a definite no-no for the notoriously no-nonsense manager. Lee and Macdonald were soon on a collision course, with the striker, despite doing his utmost to keep his nose clean and perform for the team (even when played out of position), sensing that Lee 'was absolutely anti-me in every conceivable way' and wanted rid of him.

Unsurprisingly, Lee's controversial decision to sell Macdonald wasn't well received among the majority of the Toon Army for whom the buccaneering frontman had become the undisputed King of Tyneside. But their loss was the Gooners's gain. After finishing 17th the previous season, their lowest position for more than 50 years, Arsenal were looking for a considerable improvement under their new management. As expected, Macdonald prophesised that he was the one to make it happen. 'I am the man who will fire the bullets for the Gunners,' was how the striker greeted the Highbury fans after his switch. He was true to his word. His 25 league goals (29 in all competitions), including a hat-trick in Arsenal's 5-3 win over Newcastle United, meant that Macdonald was the joint winner of England's Golden Boot with Villa's Andy Gray.

All the same, Arsenal could still only manage a disappointing eighth spot in the division. At one stage in the season, after the turn of the year, they lost seven league games on the bounce. And the course of Macdonald's career with the Gunners, too, was never to run that smoothly either. Niggled by injuries, he also endured an uneasy relationship with the man who took him to Highbury. In July 1977, during a three-week end-of-season tour of the Far East and Australia, Macdonald and Alan Hudson were sent home over a drinking incident in Sydney. There were even suggestions that the two England internationals – who together cost more than £500,000 – would be put up for sale. Just two of the Arsenal team who'd clashed with Neill during the Northern Irishman's first year in charge – Jimmy Rimmer, Liam Brady, George Armstrong and Trevor Ross had all asked to leave – Macdonald and Hudson stayed put, the latter for the time being at least.

The following May, both were in the north London club's starting line-up that came up against Bobby Robson's Ipswich

Town in the FA Cup Final. It was Robson, then in charge of Fulham, who, ten years earlier, had signed Macdonald as a full-back from Southern League Tonbridge for £1,000 before selling him on to Luton after only 13 league appearances. Red-hot favourites to win, on the day Arsenal's city slickers were instead totally outplayed by Ipswich's country cousins, and Macdonald, after two losing cup final appearances for Newcastle, against Liverpool in the FA Cup and Manchester City in the League Cup (at the end of which he'd knelt on the Wembley turf and wept), made it a hat-trick as the Suffolk club, beaten 6-1 by Aston Villa in the league a week previously, claimed a 1-0 triumph.

'Punch on the nose number three,' was how Macdonald later described it. When Bournemouth referee Derek Nippard, officiating his last-ever fixture, signalled the end of the match, it had left the forward feeling 'numb', he said, and 'nobody knows how much it hurt'.

The place almost seemed jinxed for him. Supremely optimistic, as was his nature, Macdonald had talked a good game beforehand but once he stepped out on to the pitch, as one reporter put it, 'his legs filled with mercury rather than blood and his shooting left foot fell into a deep sleep'. The resultant *Superflop!* headlines were somewhat inevitable.

The previous month, as well as bagging a brace in an FA Cup semi-final for the second time in his career (after two majestic strikes versus Burnley in 1974, this time against Orient at Stamford Bridge with a couple of deflected goals in the space of three first-half minutes in a comprehensive 3-0 victory), Macdonald was in the right place to poach a pair as Arsenal registered a third consecutive 3-1 home win over Manchester United. They were the very last goals Macdonald would score at Highbury. On 29 August 1978, a week after pouncing to score the 240th goal of his club career in a 1-1 draw at Manchester City, disaster struck for Macdonald in the South Yorkshire rain, as the Gunners tumbled out of the League Cup in the second round at Third Division Rotherham. Macdonald tore a cartilage towards the end of the game but was inexplicably left on to hobble through the last 15 minutes with a locked knee before being carried off at full time by physio Fred Street and coach Don Howe.

After a summer operation on his right knee following the cup final defeat, Macdonald now required another procedure; a second in three months, to have the remaining cartilage removed from his other knee. It was surgery from which he never fully recovered. On 14 May 1979, 48 hours after Macdonald's cup finals misery had been completed – not fully match fit, he'd missed out on Arsenal's last-gasp 3-2 Wembley triumph against Dave Sexton's Manchester United – the curtain was brought down on the league season and the injury-ravaged striker played what proved to be his last game for the Gunners.

Typically, he scored in a 1-1 draw with rock bottom, soon-to-be-relegated Chelsea at Stamford Bridge, a far-post header from a David O'Leary cross. Later that year, before the start of the 1979/80 season, Macdonald retired from the English game. He was only 29 years old.

Stan Bowles, speaking in 1976, was rather dismissive of Macdonald's talents. 'He's fast, and he's a big strong boy, but if he played on the continent, he'd be third-rate,' Bowles told interviewer Roger Hutchinson, 'defences would just nullify him; they'd be too clever for him. Out there, you've got to do something unexpected, which he can't do. Over here, everybody knows what he's going to do, but he gets away with it simply because he's so fast.'

Macdonald himself, despite the swagger, was under no illusions about his limitations. 'I know my faults better than anyone and the list's as long as my arm,' he'd said in 1972. 'My good points are few but I have two that are vital – I can run like the wind and I can put the ball in the back of the net. These days that commodity is as precious as gold, and I'm hoping it can sustain me at the top for another ten years.'

Scoring goals was meat and drink to him. His appetite was seemingly insatiable. At Arsenal he managed an impressive 57 in 108 appearances. A year before he quit, Macdonald reasoned, 'Only when I am forced to retire will I judge whether I have been a winner in my football career. And even then I will stand up and point to the fact that I have scored goals consistently for my clubs and helped Arsenal and Newcastle to reach those cup finals.'

Supermac didn't quite make ten years, but in the time he did grace the game, his 'good points' served him very well indeed. Those who didn't see him play in his prime and at the peak of his fast-running, free-scoring powers missed something special. The ones who did regarded themselves as enormously fortunate. Was he a 'winner'? Even if he had any doubts himself, the jury surely wasn't still out. Not, at any rate, when its foreman was another one-time forward forced into premature retirement through injury while still in his 20s; one who, like Macdonald, also possessed a mouth to match his sizeable football talent.

Bibliography

Baldwin, Bob (Editor); Fay, Peter (Editor). *The Official Football League Year Book 1972/73* (St Nicolas Press Ltd, 1972)

Bale, Bernard. *Bremner! The Legend of Billy Bremner* (Andre Deutsch Ltd, 1999)

Butler, Bryon. *The Football League 1888-1988: The Official Illustrated History* (Queen Anne Press, 1987)

Clough, Brian. *Cloughie: Walking on Water* (Headline, 2002)

Glanville, Brian. *Football Memories: 50 Years of the Beautiful Game* (Robson Books, 2004)

Hermiston, Roger. *Clough and Revie: The Rivals Who Changed the Face of English Football* (Mainstream Publishing, 2011)

McIlvanney, Hugh. *McIlvanney on Football* (Mainstream Publishing, 1994)

Miller, David. *Cup Magic* (Sidgwick & Jackson, 1981)

Moore, Brian. *Big Match: Brian Moore's World of Soccer* (Artus, 1976)

Nawrat, Chris (Editor); Hutchings, Steve (Editor). *The Sunday Times Illustrated History of Football* (Hamlyn, 1994)

Nicklin, Frank (Editor). *The Sun Soccer Annual 1972* (World Distributors Publishers, 1971)

Saffer, David. *Sniffer: The Life and Times of Allan Clarke* (Tempus, 2001)

Soar, Phil; Tyler, Martin. *Encyclopaedia of British Football* (Marshall Cavendish, 1979)

Tomas, Jason. *Malcolm Macdonald: An Autobiography* (Arthur Barker Ltd, 1983)

Taylor, Peter. *With Clough By Taylor* (Sidgwick & Jackson, 1980)

No Stated Author. *Shoot! Annual 1981* (IPC Magazines Fleetway, 1980)

No Stated Author. *Shoot! Annual 1982* (IPC Magazines Fleetway, 1981)

No Stated Author. *The Sun Soccer Annual 1981* (Ring, 1980)

Websites

https://genome.ch.bbc.co.uk

www.11v11.com

www.citytilidie.com

www.comicus.co.uk

www.englandfootballonline.com

www.lfchistory.net

www.mightyleeds.co.uk

www.ozwhitelufc.net.au

www.rsssf.com

www.thecelticwiki.com

www.wsc.co.uk

Newspapers

The Newcastle Chronicle

The Stoke Sentinel

The Guardian (*16 April 1975: England's Malcolm Macdonald scores five against Cyprus* by Malcolm Macdonald, 17 April 2010)

The Scotsman (Interview: *Bruce Rioch on why he shouldn't have played against Peru* by Aidan Smith, 26 May 2018)

Other sources

Additional David Miller quotes taken from 'The Official Documentation of the Organising Committee for the 1974 World Cup Football Tournament'

Bibliography

Stan Bowles quotes taken from 'Stan the Man: A Footballer in Limbo', Roger Hutchinson, first appeared in No.17 (Volume 1) of 'Street Life', 12–23 June 1976

Don Watson quoted from 'Psycho Mike and the Phantom Ice Rink' (from *My Favourite Year: A Collection of New Football Writing*, edited by Nick Hornby, Gollancz/Witherby, 1993)

Graham Denton is the author of the highly acclaimed Pitch Publishing book, *The Odd Man Out: The Fascinating Story of Ron Saunders' Reign at Aston Villa*. He first fell in love with football in the early 1970s and has retained a particular passion for writing about the game and its characters during that decade ever since.